❧ RENAISSANCE WOMAN ❧

renaissance Woman

❧ **GAIA SERVADIO** ☙

I.B. TAURIS

LONDON · NEW YORK

Published in 2005 by I.B. Tauris & Co Ltd
6 Salem Road, London W2 4BU
175 Fifth Avenue, New York NY 10010
www.ibtauris.com

In the United States of America and Canada
distributed by Palgrave Macmillan a division of St Martin's Press
175 Fifth Avenue, New York NY 10010

ISBN 1 85043 421 2
EAN 978 1 85043 421 4

A full CIP record for this book is available from the British Library
A full CIP record is available from the Library of Congress

Library of Congress Catalog Card Number: available

Typeset in Garamond by JCS Publishing Services
Printed and bound in Great Britain by MPG Books Ltd, Bodmin

Ne reprenez, Dames, si j'ay aymé:
Si j'ay senti mile torches ardentes,
Mile travaus, mile douleurs mordantes:
Si en pleurant j'ay mon tems consumé,

Las que mon nom n'en soit par vous blamé;
Si j'ay faille, les peines sont presentes,
N'aigressez point leurs pointes violentes:
Mais estimez qu'Amour, à point nommé.

Sans votre ardeur d'un Vulcan excuser,
Sans la beauté d'Adonis accuser,
Pourra, s'il veut, plus vous render amoureuses:

Et ayant moins que moy d'occasion,
Et plus d'estrange et forte passion.
Et gardez vous d'estre plus malheueuses.

Louise Labé

Poetry is more philosophical and more weighty than history, for poetry
speaks rather of the universal, history of the particular. By the universal I
mean that such a kind of man will say or do such and such things from
probability or necessity; that is the aim of poetry, adding proper names to
the characters.

Aristotle, Politics

❧ ❧

TO J. KENT

❧ ❧

Contents

List of illustrations

❧ CHAPTER ONE ❧

*t*rends

The Renaissance created a new vision of womanhood; it also created the modern woman. She rose from the foam of the waves of the Renaissance just like the Venus painted by Botticelli, naked and innocent, ready to awake to a world that so far had bypassed her.

Why the birth or, rather, this awakening took place at that time, is the subject of this book. By enlisting some specific characters and by telling their stories entwined with contemporary historical events – all important to the shaping of the consciousness of a generation, of a culture, of religions – I want to demonstrate that women caused the Renaissance to mature and advance, I want to suggest that without the active presence of women, the Renaissance would have not flourished as indeed the absence of women from the Islamic world pinpointed the end of their Renaissance. I will also argue that the movement of the Renaissance developed from the minds of those women who had achieved learning and sophistication because of their historical, geographic and social circumstances.

Impossible as it is to put a date on the beginning of a movement, the Renaissance is generally given a date of birth of 1492, that's what we study at school and it is certainly a very tempting date, but it is a masculine date. In that year Lorenzo de' Medici died and Rodrigo Borgia was elected pope, taking the name of Alexander VI. It is also the date of the discovery of America. The edict against the Jews and the Moors was signed in Granada in 1492, impoverishing Spain of intellect and trade, and giving power to the Inquisition; the great thinker Erasmus of Rotterdam (1469–1536) was ordained a priest. But as I want to date the birth of the Renaissance with women in mind, I would ascribe it to Gutenberg's invention of the printing press because it was the availability of education to women that made them equal to men. Books, hence knowledge, spread.

Johannes Gutenberg's invention of the printing press in 1456 changed the world and it reflected not only the need for the individual to know more, but also the efforts of enquiring minds, of explorers, of scientists. Women began to make intellectual efforts. Communication was all-important to that new spirit, and only by learning did women stand a chance of becoming individuals – individuality being a prime concept of the Renaissance. Besides the Old Testament, a text that is still alien to the Roman Church, but basic to the Reformation, there are many themes of the Renaissance: rebellion and the individual confronting and interpreting a great text. The Old Testament is also a book where women play a positive role and are allowed initiative. Italian art, especially in the north (further from the rule of the Church), "discovered" the themes of Judith, Jael, Ruth, Esther.

The printing press travelled with greater speed than most new discoveries, in spite of patents which hampered its spread. It reached Italy in 1465, Paris in 1470, London in 1477, Stockholm in 1483, and Madrid in 1499. By the end of the sixteenth century, about 9 million printed books were in circulation, compared to approximately 40,000 manuscripts which, until then, had been the only source of knowledge and literature.

The Renaissance also started when women became more masculine and men more feminine; by becoming more learned, women were able to argue, to give their opinion, to rule. Men had more time for leisure and dedicated themselves to pleasure, the very theme of the Renaissance. It could even be argued that the Renaissance, a "feminine" movement, sprang from the new status of women.

It flared up in Tuscany in the middle of the fifteenth century, and spread to most of Italy; it lost momentum and breadth just over a century later when the dark hand of the Counter-Reformation repressed not only women's position in Italian society, but also scientific curiosity and appetite for life. So it moved to France, towards 1530, and then, fifty years or so later, on to England, Holland and the Low Countries where the new status of the working woman created a healthy middle class.

But, before developing my argument on women, it must be understood that the Renaissance was not just a trend or a concept; it was a revolutionary movement that enveloped society, and those who lived it were well aware that they experienced an exceptional moment. "Without doubt, this is a golden age", declared the writer and philosopher Marsilio Ficino (1433–99) and Erasmus, in 1517, added that the century was "a golden age".

The Renaissance was characterized by observation, study, analysis, and an unwillingness to accept attitudes inherited from the past. Indeed the key factor about the Renaissance was the new compulsion to research, to seek the root of everything. In 1543, when Copernicus published his account of the earth rotating on its axis and circling the sun, he stated that his discovery was no hypothesis, but was based on original research. Meanwhile, Leonardo da Vinci (1452–1519) was advising his fellow artists to study mathematics so as to be able to achieve visual perspective and understand physiology.

The human mind had been allowed to think for itself, breaking through previous conventions. And one of the previous dogmas was about the intellectual inferiority of the woman. So, it was scientifically argued, if women were made of the same stuff as men, why should they be regarded as different? Why should they be treated as inferior?

Plato and Aristotle became the two most popular philosophers, as we can see from Raphael's *The School of Athens* in the Vatican, since their enquiry was based

on reason; the revived philosophy of Neo-Platonism which stressed the importance of the intellect and of the soul over the body became a kind of religion; the
Academy founded by Lorenzo de' Medici was Neo-Platonic in contrast with Aris-
totelian philosophy which was based on scientific enquiry. The idealized woman,
the perfect woman, was the object of Neo-Platonic reverence and aspired to being
loved platonically, not for her ability to make children or to extinguish a masculine need, but for her intellectual gifts. Indeed, due to the unearthing of classical
aesthetics, woman became a symbol, a Muse, she was depicted as a positive figure
in the guise of Spring, Venice, Faith, Knowledge, Justice. Apart from this kind of
representation there was a switch in her physical shape. The Renaissance created a
vision of womanhood which contrasted with the amply formed mother-figure of
the past. The new woman that appears on the frescos and paintings of the Renaissance, whether in the guise of a Virgin Mary or of a goddess, was slender, almost
androgynous. Botticelli and Raphael, Piero della Francesca and Donatello
depicted her as the embodiment of Neo-Platonism.

Youth and beauty were cultivated. Make-up, creams and beautifying liquids
were used as copiously as today. Some women kept recipes for ointments to beau-
tify their hair and keep their skin pale – a white skin was the image of money, it
showed that the woman need not expose her face to the sun, that she was no
peasant. Ultimately, fashion in beauty is always a question of economics.

In spite of the fact that preachers and poets made fun of heavy make-up, they
were ignored even by respectable matrons. False hair made of silk was used to
recapture the abundance of youth. Scents were used in profusion and clothes were
designed to enhance the beauty of the body. Fashions changed from city to city, as
the mother of Lorenzo de' Medici remarked when visiting her future daughter-in-
law in Rome. These girls, she wrote, wore such thick veils that one could hardly
see what they looked like, even at home; and they also covered their bust.
Besides, she lamented, aristocratic Roman girls had dark hair and their necks did
not have the wonderful long line of the Florentines. Girls from Florence were so
graceful! Married to Marco Vespucci and many times portrayed by Botticelli,
Simonetta embodied the Neo-Platonic idea of beauty with her languid innocence
and the illusion of eternal youth. The mistress of Giuliano de' Medici, her death
at the age of twenty-three inspired Lorenzo il Magnifico, Giuliano's brother, to
write two sonnets.

In Ted Hughes' beautiful translation:

> ... *now you cry in the everlasting.*
>   *Happy Spring to bitter Winter suddenly*
> *Turned back* ......
> .... *Now I know love.*

And

1. *The Birth of Venus* by Sandro Botticelli

Although married to Marco Vespucci, Simonetta was openly the mistress of
Giuliano de' Medici and the object of love of his brother Lorenzo. E. H. Gombrich in *Symbols and Images* contends that she may have been the model for Venus
in this painting.

Maybe those splendid eyes that stole from us
Cruel death, too much presume
That now you may, with your great flame,
Take the marvellous chariot from Phoebus.

This or maybe you are a new star
Whose unfamiliar dazzle giddies heaven.

Rich women loaded themselves with ornament to demonstrate their power. The young Beatrice d'Este (born in 1475), who married the Duke of Milan, spent an enormous amount of money on jewels and she hired Leonardo da Vinci, so that he could design her hairstyle; which is how Leonardo came to live in Milan in 1482. Lucrezia Borgia's striped dress which she wore on her arrival as Duchess of Spoleto – fish scales of woven gold – was valued at 5,000 ducats. Following the example of Elizabeth Tudor, the English court made costume into a fantastic game of colours, velvets, and silks. Women wore ruffs, skirts grew wider and fuller, and were supported by petticoats stiffened with whalebone. More jewels were worn in the hair, and hung from the belt and the waist. Poor and rich did not wear underpants, hence the amazement of one of our characters later on in this book at his discovery that Spanish women did – *calzone*s. Because other women did not, when menstruating they stayed at home, but there was no mention of them being "impure" during their time of bleeding unlike in Hebrew and Islamic societies. At night they all wore a bedcap to shelter their hair from lice and during the day a headdress or an elaborate veil was desirable. But middle-class women followed fashion with an eye on their purse and another on the necessity to keep their movements free, hence no headdress when they were working. Shoes were the subject of great attention. The rich wore embroidered slippers to show that their feet never touched the muddy and dirty ground: indeed, when they went out they were carried or they rode on a mule or a horse; those who had to walk, like courtesans, wore very high heels, in fact kinds of pedestals, to avoid soiling the rim of their skirts. It became so fashionable to be taller, and therefore to be noticed, that these pedestals grew to a disproportionate height.

The Renaissance was also a time, a short span of time, during which people wanted to enjoy themselves. "The Renaissance bears witness to a sociology, a psychology of joy. Rarely in history did people feel so powerfully that they were living in fortunate times. The *Memento Mori* of the Middle Ages was replaced by a *memento vivere*", writes Fernand Braudel. There was almost a haste to have a good time. Poliziano, Lorenzo de' Medici and the balladeers exhorted girls to live their youth to the full: "How beautiful is youth which, even as you live it, slips away: seize it if you want to be happy: there is no certitude in the future."

The Renaissance's sense of aesthetics was also novel: the pleasure of the table, of music, of literature. Necessity was no longer the driving force; people now had spare time and that allowed them to long for entertainment. In Italian courts,

2. *Cecilia Gallerani*, drawing by Leonardo da Vinci

Cecilia Gallerani was born around 1473. Very beautiful and famously portrayed by Leonardo in *Lady with an Ermine*, Cecilia kept a literary salon and wrote Latin verse. She was a true daughter of the Renaissance and became prominent at the court of her lover Ludovico Sforza, called "Il Moro". In 1491 however, Ludovico married the very young Beatrice d'Este, the sister of Isabella Gonzaga. In the same year Cecilia gave birth to Ludovico's son. She died in 1536.

3. *Primavera* by Botticelli

In this painting Botticelli, who was born in Florence in 1445 the youngest son of a simple tanner, followed Ovid's description of the arrival of Spring. The poet Poliziano, Lorenzo's teacher, and Marsilio Ficino who was the voice of Medicean Renaissance, gave him instructions on the position of each character. "One cannot describe how more easily the spirit of Beauty inspires love than words", wrote Ficino in a letter to both Lorenzo and Bernado Bembo.

especially in Ferrara, Mantua and Florence, women wore beautiful clothes to enhance the beauty of their slender bodies and also their status, their cultural level. Architecture in the Renaissance took gentler shapes and moved away from the Gothic, which Raphael defined as "barbarian, Germanic". The movement invented the country house, no longer a defensive castle but the venue for leisure – as well as a place in which to escape the cities infested by deadly epidemics. There is no trace, for example, of castellation in Careggi, the Medicean country house frescoed by Pontormo, or in Palladio's country villas in the Veneto. Leon Battista Alberti, one of the "fathers" of Renaissance form, designed lay basilicas, no longer celebrations of God but of man, like the Tempio Malatestiano at Rimini. Like Michelangelo, Donatello and Botticelli, Alberti was homosexual, a man of feminine sensitivity. He gave a lot of thought to life shared between man and woman. "Each room should have its own door. Off the wife's bedroom should be a dressing room and off the husband's a library". A friend of Piero della Francesca and Mantegna, Alberti was at the centre of a group who wrote on architecture and discussed what the new city should look like, with open roads and large piazzas. *The Ideal City* was depicted in three predellas by Piero della Francesca(?), and in Raphael's *Wedding of the Virgin*, as well as in paintings by Signorelli and Mantegna, but not in earlier paintings and frescos by Giotto, Carpaccio or Masaccio, where the city is still a wonderful medieval mish mash of narrow streets.

How did women live during the Renaissance? Broadly speaking, they were cast into categories: the ideal romantic woman, the brave virago, the courtesan, and the wife. The aristocracy married early in life, the poor late. But the wife was not the vehicle of ideals and ideas, conversation or sexual recreation, and men, then as now, depicted wives as a tiresome duty they owed to society.

For the Catholics, marriage was a sacrament, for the Protestants a contract. But in both northern and southern Europe, conventions which applied to the middle-class married woman were restrictive: they should not leave their houses alone, should not dress too sumptuously; husbands should not bring their male friends home in order to tempt either their wives or their friends. A good wife should not drink wine. In short, a good woman, wrote Robert Burton, should go out of her house three times in her life: for her baptism, her marriage, and her funeral.

Women's sexual life was almost public in houses where the corridor had not been invented, and privacy – a luxury unnecessary to men – must have been desired by women. Marriages were planned by relatives, and the high death rate meant that people often remarried several times.

"The whole business of childbirth was dangerous", writes Alison Weir in *Elizabeth the Queen*, "and mortality rates were high". Jane Seymour, Catherine Parr and Elizabeth of York died of puerperal fever and the Duchess of Norfolk "could marry, conceive, give birth and die within the space of a year". Wealthy women

4. *The Ideal City* by Leon Battista Alberti or Piero della Francesca

With the Renaissance, city architecture was revolutionized by a circle which included Bramante, Brunelleschi, Donatello, Mantegna, Piero della Francesca and Laurana. But the person who intellectualized it was the formidable Alberti who, studying Vitruvius, preached quality of life and harmony.

turned their babies over to wet nurses and later to be educated in some great household. This at times happened very early, as we shall see from one of our case histories, even when the children were three or four: women learnt to grow up quickly, to be adults earlier than today. "The education given to women in the upper classes was essentially the same as that given to men," wrote Jacob Burckhardt, the great historian of the Italian Renaissance. But, in religious circles, woman was still considered a matrix, the symbol of sin, who could be redeemed only by procreation.

Prostitution was thought to be a necessity, even by the Church. Rome and Venice were famous for their courtesans; in Venice travellers could buy a guide, which gave the name, address and cost of each prostitute – a kind of *Guide Michelin*. But there was a great difference between a prostitute and a courtesan; the latter was a kind of geisha who held a salon, she could play musical instruments and had a lovely voice. The difference was also in price. More prosaically, in Paris and Nuremberg prostitutes were required to stay in state-licensed brothels.

In this era, women's sexuality became a fact to be dealt with and Erasmus mentioned lesbianism as a matter of fact; in Holland young women were even encouraged to have sex before marriage because, with children and a husband to look after, there would be no time to enjoy physical love later; but as the mood of the times was ripe for a certain liberation, freedom in sex soon came to a halt because of the scourge of the age: syphilis. Marin Sanuto, the Venetian writer, described the purulent sores, and the threat of such a contagious disease which "many say came from the French, as they have had it for a long time, but they [the French] call it Italian disease." Syphilis – the AIDS of antiquity – killed in the end, but first covered the face and body with horrible, putrid blotches; many people thought that, like the Black Death, it had been sent by God to punish their sins. A courtesan describes the end of her career, of her life:

> Io era pulchra e piena d'ogni odore
> hor piena son di puzza e di vil fezza
> e ció pensando si me creppa il core.
>
> Ove son hora le mie bionde drezza
> ove la faccia mia tanto bianchissima
> ove il mio canto pieno di dolcezza …
>
> Ove gli canti e soni e bel danzare
> ove gli amici c'ho a visitarmi
> soglion venir e mie compagne care …
>
> Hor su mia lingua piú non puol parlare
> la morte é gionta el suo fiero arco scocca
> tutti vi lasso ch'l spirito sento mancare
> con gran velocità esce di bocca.

I was beautiful and scented;
now I am stinky and horrible
and thinking of this, my heart cries out.

Where are they gone my fair braids
where is my glowing skin
and my voice full of sweetness?

Where are my songs and my fine dancing
where are my friends who used to come and visit me
and my dear women companions …?

Now that my tongue cannot talk,
death has come and its fierce bow trembles.
I leave you all, that I feel my spirit fail
and depart from my mouth with great speed.

As, towards the end of the sixteenth century, syphilis spread its deadly wings, and the shadow of the Counter-Reformation darkened the age, the courtesans were the first to pay. Their riches were confiscated, and the Church tried to humiliate them in every way; papal bull after papal bull attacked their very existence. By 1560, they could not receive married men; they had to live in a ghetto, and were forbidden to appear in public. From enjoying the total approval of society, they had become outcasts. Indeed, the Renaissance movement for the liberation of women was suppressed by using the courtesan as a bad example, the liberated woman forcibly became either a heretic or a courtesan, or both. On the other hand, women "can taunt men for lack of chastity more freely than men can sting them", Baldassarre Castiglione wrote in his famous book *The Courtier*, "and this is because we ourselves have made a law, according to which a dissolute life is not a fault of degradation in us, whereas in women it is an utter disgrace and shame …".

The Courtier was a bestseller; it was a "feminist" book, not only on the side of women but it also confirmed, through education, the important role of women in society. As education spread amongst the middle classes we find non-aristocrats coming to prominence. Isotta Nogarola (1418–66) and her sister Ginevra (1417–61) came from Verona; with her knowledge of Greek and Latin, Isotta was on the fringes of the humanists, who never quite accepted her, but considered Isotta as erudite as a man and a fine writer. While her sister Ginevra married, Isotta dedicated herself to knowledge. In one of her *Dialoghi* (it was the custom to write books based on the concept of the Platonic dialogues), she is seen to debate with Ludovico Contarini, a Venetian nobleman: "… only because [Eve] had been first deceived by the serpent's evil persuasion, did she indulge in the delights of paradise; but she would have harmed only herself and in no way endangered human posterity if the consent of the first-born man had not been offered. Therefore Eve was no danger to posterity but merely to herself …". She goes on debating the point that Eve's sin is not as grave as Adam's while Ludovico is trying to prove

the opposite. "Eve sinned out of ignorance and inconstancy, and hence you con-
tend that she sinned more gravely", she writes, "but Eve's ignorance was
implanted by nature of which nature God himself is the author and founder.
Many think that he who knows less sins less; like a boy who sins less than an old
man or a peasant less than a noble."

Cassandra Fedele (1465–1558) came from a high-brow but middle-class family, she was taught Latin and Greek privately and was such a good orator that she
was paid by the Venetian Republic to talk publicly. This was something very rare
in a woman's case; so much so that Cassandra was looked upon as an oddity, and
people came, not only to hear her, but also to have a look at this anomaly. Even
somebody as highly placed as Angelo Poliziano wrote to her (1491): "I begin to
revere you, Cassandra". After living in great poverty, she was "rediscovered" at
the age of ninety-one when she gave a speech in honour of the Queen of Poland's
visit. The quotation below comes from a speech she gave in honour of a Paduan
relative:–

> ... I've chosen as the subject of my praise the threefold tradition of Cicero, Plato, and
> the Peripatetics who believed that man derived true honour from the goods of the soul,
> the goods of the body and from those goods that some prominent philosophers ascribed
> to fortune. Therefore, I beseech you, illustrious gentlemen, to pay close attention,
> although I know that you expect no profound insights from me. ...

And then, of course, she goes on with fireworks of amazing scholarly quotations.
Pausing to consider her own lucky status, she adds, "Happy, therefore, are you,
Cassandra, that happened to be born into these times! Happy this age and this
excellent city of Padua, full of so many scholarly people ...".

Literacy made it difficult to accept the traditional view of the papacy and the
clergy. Francesco Guicciardini, who worked for the pope, confessed to himself (his
Ricordi were published posthumously),

> I don't know anyone to whom the ambition, avarice and corruption of the clergy is
> more distasteful than to myself ... Nonetheless, the status which I have enjoyed with
> several popes has made it necessary for me to pursue, for my own return, their great-
> ness; and if it had not been like this, I would have loved Martino Luther [sic] as
> myself: not in order to free myself from the Christian law in the sense that it is inter-
> preted and understood commonly, but to see this mass of corrupt priests [scelerati]
> reduced to order – that is, that they should be either without vice, or without
> authority.

The Church had exploited superstition in men and women all over Europe. But
the invention of the printing press meant that the clergy no longer held the
monopoly of learning – and knowledge was the lever which brought about the
movement of reform. The Reformation meant more than adjusting religion to
enlightened needs: the temporal power and greed of the Church pervaded most
aspects of life. By then, the Roman Catholic Church was devoid of that mysticism

which had surfaced earlier with Francis of Assisi. St Francis's Protestantism *ante litteram* had already worried the Roman Church. The idea of a spiritual life, of direct contact with God, attracted many cultivated women all over Europe who tried to reform the Church from within; others gave up the fight and became Calvinist. All of them had read the works of Erasmus, the enquiring approach to religion. While, in general, women were more spiritually attracted to a change of mores in the Church, most men had a more political purpose in desiring a reform of the papacy. For example, Niccoló Machiavelli (*I Discorsi*, I, XII, 1513) saw in the pontifical estate an entity whose historical function had ended. The papal territories had been expanded by Alexander VI and then by Pope Julius II. In achieving such territorial strength, the papacy had divided and ruined Italy.

Having infested Italy with foreign armies, the Church transformed it into a battlefield. Cries of protest rose against the corruption, nepotism and political scheming of the popes – like the sermons of the monk Girolamo Savonarola (1452–98) who, like most "puritans" was a misogynist, finding it easy to think of women as a source of sin and temptation. Preachers like Savonarola became fashionable; for women of all social levels it was the thing to do, to go and listen to the sermons of the most famous amongst them and they would turn up dressed in those fine clothes that the preachers were about to condemn. Savonarola was one of the first; most of these mystics worked outside the Church and became popular in the mid-sixteenth century when the Renaissance was fading into tragedy.

Illiteracy, in spite of what I have just said, was still widespread especially amongst women and was a main cause for the popularity of such preachers because, unable to read, women were after entertainment. The southern piazzas were the natural places for these gatherings, not the church, because preachers were often controversial.

Florence, Naples and Ferrara became focal points of the Reformation; this last city for a time was ruled by a French Protestant duchess who was sheltering those who, being Protestants, were escaping the long arms of the Inquisition. When we travel to Ferrara, the first city that we shall visit, John Calvin was living there.

Savonarola, who was indeed born in Ferrara, was the first of the popular preachers – apparently popular only up to a point since he ended up at the stake in Florence, where he had moved. A gloomy, ascetic Dominican friar given to composing melancholic verses, Savonarola's sermons became so popular that they had to be delivered in the Cathedral of Florence. He never spoke to women but they doted on him because he was convinced that: "It is not I who preach but God who speaks through me." He "saw" the grim future that awaited the Church; it had to go through total destruction in order to rise again. Only a return to the simplicity of the early Christian Church could save it. Aristotle and Plato were to be discarded, sensual pleasures destroyed and the Medici family reformed. For the sake of the Florentines' souls, carnivals, palio races, fine clothes and scent were to be abolished: women should cover their faces, their bodies, their souls. Savonarola's sermons and the sermons of those who followed his example, echo the gospel of the Talibans and of those who, every so often in history, see themselves as the voice of an angry and dictatorial God – and know that they are the truth. In a way, Calvin in his later years, John Knox, and even Trotsky at times, repeat Savonarola's words. After Lorenzo de' Medici's death, Savonarola warned of disasters to come and spoke of the "Sword of the Lord" hanging over Florence, of plague and wars. People listened in fear. "A Dominican friar has so terrified all the Florentines …" the Mantua envoy wrote to Isabella Gonzaga, "all the girls and many of the wives have taken refuge in convents so that only men and youths and old women are now to be seen in the streets."

I ignore women in Spain, although the presence of Spanish intolerant power towers in this book. I do this because the Renaissance did not touch the Iberian Peninsula. I cannot see fifteenth- and sixteenth-century Spain but as a force of destruction, a culture which tended to erase, unable to absorb, eager to destroy. Even the "mother" of Spain, Isabel the Catholic (1451–1504) – one of the most influential persons in Europe but no Renaissance woman – while unifying her country was a carrier of intolerance. She instituted the Inquisition, in the process destroying the ethnic groups of the Moors and Jews, a source of culture, wealth and trade. Only the Netherlands survived the Spanish occupation by their fierce rebellion against it.

I could have elaborated on German women of the Renaissance, there are many; I could have gone into the role of Luther's wife, who had the courage to leave her nunnery and would marry no one but her hero. Or look into the life of Marie Dentière who, by publishing the truth about women's mistreatment by Catholics and Calvinists alike, was quickly silenced. But not only do we have few documents on their lives, but their roles were not as entwined with great historical events as the women whose stories are told here.

The spread of written texts amongst women was suspect; the Church could not allow the rediscovery of the original word of Christ which stated that human beings forged their own destinies and that women were equal to men. And indeed the end of European religious unity came when Martin Luther, having preached against the corruption of the Roman Church, declared that faith alone could save mankind and condemned most sacraments. The territorial and spiritual power of the Church, precariously guaranteed by the Emperor, was not to be questioned but intellectual voices threatened this balance and those voices tended to belong to women, the ones who were to lose by the change. Prominent aristocratic and deeply religious women were seen by the Church of Rome as a real threat. The Church was supported by the concept of the empire; the emperor could be anointed by the pope alone, and the pope represented God. Only with this divine support would the over-extended empire look up to the elected emperor. The rite of the coronation, invented by Charlemagne, imitated the imperial ritual of the Romans. In order to give authority to his otherwise

questionable heritage, Charlemagne needed God and it was he who really estab-
lished the otherwise wobbly and practically unrecognized papacy. But during the
Renaissance, the new spirit defied divinity or, rather, divinity as understood in the
Middle Ages.

Education had became the liberating factor and it allowed women to write letters not only to each other but to their men. They could communicate and also
write verse and stories. The abundance of this written material makes my task
easier in the sense that I can read not only official papers but also those confidential letters that women wrote in which they expressed their doubts and
difficulties. This was a time when women, who had just found this new liberty of
expression, wrote long letters that, thanks to the improved communication system (cf. Braudel), seemed to arrive promptly. They exchanged sonnets and
madrigals; they wrote diaries. In spite of the fact that so much has disappeared –

5. *The Ancient Basilica of St Peter* by Marten van Heemskerch, Albertina, Vienna
St John in Lateran was the main residence of the popes until St Peter was rebuilt;
the various designs were by Sangallo, Bernini, and famously by Michelangelo (for
the revolutionary cupola).

the Inquisition was responsible for burning private papers and literature that was not seen as viable – a vast amount has survived. And writing was considered a nobler form than painting. Painters were communicators, regarded as we would journalists today, on the other hand, those who could write were welcomed everywhere. And even an "upstart" like Pietro Aretino, a pamphleteer and a friend of Titian, who portrayed him several times, was revered and feared by the most powerful men of his time, from the King of France to that of Spain. Another scourge of the mighty was the broken-up statue, Il Pasquino, which can still be seen in Rome, near piazza Navona and to which people still attach their written protests – possibly in verse (these days the eroded marble of Il Pasquino is almost covered with anti-Berlusconi verse). To this statue Renaissance people attached greater importance than today though, because it was one of the rare weapons of social satire. Between its stone fingers, or at its feet, the literate wrote protests, attacking and criticizing, often in the shape of anonymous couplets. It was something like Peking's wall, where the Chinese used to write what they couldn't say.

The new type of Renaissance woman produced few children; hence she had the time to cultivate herself. Like her Greek and Latin "foremothers", she knew something about birth control and practised it without giving much thought to the dictates of the Church. In spite of the fact that it was punishable by death, abortion was common. Otherwise, women used internal douches, generally made with vinegar, which killed sperm, and other herbs. From the second century BC, women had known about "abstention from coitus at times which we have indicated" (Soranus of Ephestus), and about a form of coil, a foreign body placed inside the uterus, although, since hygiene did not exist as a concept, this device led to internal infections. Postponement of marriage, abstinence, infanticide, but, most of all, infant mortality were other "methods" of birth control. To rid themselves of unwanted offspring, poor women left their babies in baskets, near convents and hospitals. This was such a common practice that the Medici built the famous Hospital of the Innocents with its harmonious portico. The Sienese called them instead *gettatelli* and built a most wonderful *spedale* to house them. While they grew up, the city would educate the *gettatelli* and later find them employment, for the *gettatelle* the earnings of washer-women or cleaners would go towards a dowry. In a series of frescos in the Spedale alla Scala we can observe how the girls would be looked after, given dresses and wooden shoes and married; many would work as wet nurses for the newcomers or for the nobility. Of course the Sienese Republic wanted to present a democratic and generous image of itself, but still the story told in this cycle of frescos is very impressive.

Many families unburdened themselves of surplus daughters by sending them to convents of the closed orders: these were nests of ignorance and reaction. Unlike monasteries, they enjoyed neither the pleasures of nature nor those of sacred texts and music. That so many young women were sent to convents probably partly accounts for the fact that women were scarcer than men.

As the means of communication spread, so did commerce, and a European middle class was thus created. Especially in the north of Europe, wives of travelling traders looked after their businesses at home. But, in the countryside, towards the second part of the Renaissance, poverty, sickness and destitution levelled life to a low common denominator. The Renaissance was an era of great advances, but it was also a dreadfully precarious age: soldiers and bandits roamed the countryside, looting and raping; violence was the norm; life was cheap. Ignorance, and hence superstition, flourished.

Elsewhere, this period witnessed the shaping of national unities. In the fifteenth century people had no sense of allegiance to the "nation". It was difficult for most Europeans to feel the unity of the Holy Roman Empire, which Voltaire, two centuries later, said was not holy, Roman, or an empire. Many rebellions within the empire were motivated by religious and economic causes. But the shedding of blood for a common cause often achieved a sense of nationalism, as was the case in Holland, where the Reformation gave purpose and moral integrity to a divided people; France was unified by a strong family – the Valois – while Italy remained divided under powerful occupiers but the longing for unity was voiced as early as in Dante's and Petrach's poetry. This era saw the birth of a more efficient political communion than the feudal order. Heads of state claimed the loyalty of many Europeans to one or other nation and were more significant figures than in the past. Their courts became richer, more important and more uniform. Spain, which at the beginning of the fifteenth century was no nation at all, achieved national unity by rallying the people against common enemies, the Moors and the Jews, and those glittering civilizations were replaced by a repressive and fanatical Christian rule. The English achieved nationalism not only through the ability of Henry VII, who established himself as a powerful monarch, but by the long war against France, another common foe. At the same time, a strong monarchy and a hostile empire surrounding France united that territorially diverse kingdom.

The Church made it impossible for one single state to lead and it cut the Italian Renaissance short: it could not have been otherwise. Political unity would have threatened the Church's territorial power while knowledge, science and individual freedom of expression were more dangerous than the plague. Counter-Reformation returned women to the position they had occupied before the Renaissance, they once again became the main source of sin; for the reasons stated by Machiavelli, Italy did not develop into a nation. In short, the Italian Renaissance was smothered by the Inquisition, the Counter-Reformation, the Church's territorial aspirations, and protracted use of foreign armies. The Spaniards and the French, with their Swiss and German mercenaries, roamed Italy, burning and destroying. The ultimately victorious Spaniards brought into Italy that seed of destruction which followed their conquests everywhere they went, from the Old World to the New. But, in refusing to reform the abuses of the Roman Church, Italy and Spain lagged behind northern Europe.

The discovery of new territories also weakened the focal point of the Renaissance, shifting the centre of economic and inventive power to the more strategic north and west of Europe. The clergy was a society of men. The new religious order, the Society of Jesus, created by a Spaniard to fight heresy, argued that cultivated women were dangerous. Although useful to society, prostitutes, like Jews, were demonized and had to be shamed publicly, the former wearing a yellow veil and the latter a yellow sign – not the star of David. It's odd that yellow, the colour of the sun, should have been turned into the colour of shame. Fashion and art followed the dictates of a set of rules, which were drawn at Trent by a specially appointed council to counterbalance the spread of the Reformation. But, although pagan paintings gave way to altarpieces, to vast canvases depicting miracles and elaborately clothed women, the female body was still revealed – and admired – under hypocritical covers: Roman charities, virtues, symbols of cities, the faith. But it changed, it became more abundant, it reverted to a fertile body, a source of babies rather than a source of Neo-Platonic thinking.

Renaissance women lived through the two aspects of the age, the beautiful and the ugly, but were more often the victims of the latter than its active participants. Part of the reality of the Renaissance was violence while, at the same time, refinement of language, eloquence and aesthetics were basic to times of peace. The Renaissance woman was the passive spectator of violence. Corpses hung from the city walls, and at Castel Sant'Angelo in Rome there was always the odd rotten body hanging from the ramparts. Young girls would be taken to the spectacle of people being publicly quartered, when pieces of flesh drenched the ground with sticky red, or to watch somebody burn at the stake, inhaling the stench of burnt flesh.

Fratricide and uxoricide do not seem to have stirred family unity. The great composer, Gesualdo, Duke of Venosa, was badly received at the Este court not because he had killed his adulterous wife and her lover, but because he had commissioned the murder from an underling. It was the letter from Isabella Gonzaga to her brother, Duke Alfonso d'Este, brought at the last minute by her messenger that saved her two younger brothers from execution. Her plea was accepted by Alfonso, who then locked the two unfortunate princes in the Este Castle's prison – two horrible hovels lit only by a multi-barred hole at the level of the putrid moat, which often overflowed. Upstairs Alfonso received his guests and listened to songs and poetry with his wife, Lucrezia Borgia, while his brothers rotted away below.

There was another kind of woman who was well accepted in Renaissance times and who possibly was the heiress of the ancient Sybil. Each village, each hamlet even, had a woman, often eccentric, who served a social need. Women went to see her to confess their loves and hatreds, purchase herbs and magic liquids. Indeed, the figure of the witch is still present in some parts of Europe. The witch was often an outcast, a non-conformist, perhaps because of poverty or deformity or even of epilepsy, a disease that was widespread and not recognized as a nervous ailment. Suddenly many of these women who had been welcomed by society were accused of sorcery, for example, Gentile Budrioli, the wife of a surgeon, who was burnt alive in 1498 in the main square of Bologna. She was described by a chronicler as "a great witch who gave her soul away to the Devil".

In 1484, Pope Innocent published a bull against witches, although most aristocrats believed in their magic powers. Even Eleonora Concini, a favourite of the queen of France, Catherine de' Medici, was burnt at the stake as a witch. Hated by many, Catherine herself was reputed to have dealings with the devil; her son Henri III was called *"le fils aîné du Diable"*, but many women were denounced as witches as a convenient way of getting rid of them, often by public burning. If they were old, illiterate or poor, they had no defence, and many died in this way. And if they were rich or well-off, better still: since the wealth of the condemned was then distributed between the Inquisiton and the accusers. But there is no record of these women's lives.

On the other hand, the lives of the illiterate slaves, peasants, nuns and victims of the Inquisition followed the same pattern as that of victims before – and after – the Renaissance. The life of a destitute woman in, say, India is outside history: it is the same kind of life as it was 2,000 years before her time, because the printing press has not reached her. The Italian woman who lives in the southern countryside has not yet been through the Renaissance either: Christ stopped at Eboli; most of Italy remained in the Dark Ages, in the dark. So it can be argued that the Renaissance, like all great moments, was absorbed by some, lived by an elite. The lives of women who, whether courtesans, painters, poets, mystics, or *grandes dames*, were part of the elite throw more light on the Renaissance than would the dramatic record of the life of a poor woman, of a slave, of a nun, even if such an archive existed.

The renaissance of womanhood was the main contribution to the quality of contemporary life because it was the woman who introduced a degree of comfort to her habitat, who sought for the poetic vein in the books she read, looking for information and perhaps unconsciously lifted the level, not so much of thought, but of aesthetics. Aesthetics also meant respect for one's body; it meant giving importance to other people, to their gardens and houses. The dining table became a feast for the eye and banquets were accompanied by music. This is true of the privileged, of course; amongst the poor, there was no music and hardly any food on the table. But that is also true today.

In choosing case histories to illustrate women's lives during the Renaissance, to develop those great themes of individuality, freedom achieved through knowledge, the cult of beauty, mysticism, reform and reformation, I am well aware that I can be accused of cheating. The majority of women had no access to learning: they did not write and so they have left no records of their lives. This is so even in the case of many aristocratic women, or ladies of great power. Would we know that Isotta Malatesta ever existed if it were not for the wonderful temple in Rimini that her husband dedicated to her? Isotta could not write, so we know very little about her.

There was little sense of charity, and the lot of poor women did not concern the most fortunate. And yet, how interesting it would be to know what happened to a slave in the Renaissance, how other women treated her. There were plenty of slaves in Europe, imported at moments of shortage of labour. Women slaves often ended up as domestic workers: some, like Simonetta da Collavecchio, a black slave, bore important children, such as Alessandro de' Medici, Duke of Tuscany.

In the course of this story we shall get acquainted with women who had little in common but whose lives often merged. This was so because they lived during the same era and also because educated Europe was small; these women often followed similar paths and their way was one of questioning. Learning liberated women – those women, that is, who had access to it. If she were able to write gracefully a woman acquired a status unique to her condition – whether a tart or an aristocrat. When she married and left Ferrara for Mantua, for example, Isabella Gonzaga arranged for a fine scholar, Niccolo Panizeato, to live in Mantua and tutor her in classics (for three ducats a month).

In the Renaissance, women began to emerge politically: Margaret of Austria (1480–1530), Regent of the Low Countries; her namesake, Margaret of Parma, the bastard daughter of Charles V (1522–86); another royal Margaret (1492–1549), married to the Duke of Alençon and, in 1527, to Henry d'Albret titular King of Navarre (1492–1545), writer and mother of Jeanne d'Albret. Catherine de' Medici (1519–89), Queen of France and Isabella Gonzaga, who was an Este by birth (1474–1539), were politically forceful – often more so than their husbands.

During the second half of the sixteenth century Renaissance Europe was plagued by religious wars. Broadly speaking, women did not participate directly in these but Jeanne d'Albret, Queen of Navarre, the mother of Henry Bourbon – who was to unify France under the same religious banner – led her Protestant armies, shouting anti-papist slogans. She put into words her resentment against priests and men:–

> *Those who say that it is not up to women*
> *To read the Sacred Texts*
> *Are nasty, infamous men*
> *seductors and anti-Christ.*
> *Be aware, my ladies,*
> *Do not allow your poor souls*
> *To be governed*
> *By such great demons.*

She was an amazingly forceful woman, three times married, who owed a lot to the fine education that her mother Marguerite had given her. Both mother and daughter were Reformists and they both battled on the front of literature and in the field of arms. Earlier Caterina Sforza, "la prima donna d'Italia", the first of Italian women, was admired for being a virago, the word virago, then, implied praise alone – being as daring as the best of men, from the Latin *vir*, man. "The most beautiful woman of the century" Caterina, bravely defended her city of Forlí against Cesare Borgia in 1499. But finally the son of the pope captured the woman and the city. Borgia kept Caterina, by then three times a widow, in chains at Castel Sant'Angelo and abused her for sixteen long months, after which she was liberated through French intervention. It must have been more than bitter for a woman of Caterina's character, fiercely independent and brave, to languish in the foul prison of the same castle that once had been ruled by her when she was sixteen and newly married. Finally free, she died in 1509, aged forty-six, still beautiful. Her only son Giovanni, whom she had from the man she had passionately loved, was to become the head of the Medicean dynasty. She was mourned by her military staff: Caterina had been a great soldier.

Surely the presence of women in active life gave tremendous impetus to the Renaissance. If nothing else, emancipated women were able to give a good education to their children, thus preparing a future generation. Women's impact on the development of civilization is all too clear from the role they played in Holland and the Low Countries and, indeed, in the contrast between the north of Italy, and Spain and the Italian south, which did not accept their intrusion. In the course of this tale we shall travel to some Italian states, on to France, Lyons and Paris, and then to England and Holland. But we shall travel with women in mind; each city offering a different vision of the Renaissance woman.

CHAPTER TWO

Women at Ferrara

We start our journey in Ferrara and meet some of our protagonists, women in the middle of their lives who are in this city, the seat of the Este family, for different reasons. A vassal of the papacy but often in conflict with it, Ferrara was philosophically open to new ideas, to science. Its school of painting, with Cossa, Tura and Roberti, was eccentric, new. The Duke Ercole's aunt, Isabella Gonzaga, Marchioness of Mantua, was a typical product of such a world. The Ferrara ducal family, the Este, had a long tradition of honouring *les belles lettres*; Matteo Maria Boiardo had written *Orlando Innamorato* there, and Ariosto had given lustre to the court.

In spite of the fact that the Este family had killed and imprisoned each other like barbarians, their city of Ferrara was modern, with straight, wide streets, the seat of a great university. It was one of Europe's larger cities, with 41,000 inhabitants, according to a census taken in 1520. (Milan numbered 100,000 in 1510; Lucca 32,000 in 1527; but Rome, after the sack of 1527, had lost a third of its population and was reduced to 30,000 inhabitants.)

The duke's lands stretched to the Paduan valley, controlling the river Pó, an important link for trade because it was navigable. He owned the cities of Modena and Piacenza and his domain extended to the other side of the peninsula; it was also a buffer between the papal territories and the Republic of Venice, *La Serenissima* – the prime enemy of the papacy, too rich and independent a Republic, and a friend of the "infidels".

Since Ferrara's lands were agriculturally rich, the Duke of Este was wealthy. Like all the lords, he derived his income from an assortment of taxes on goods such as food staples, duties on exports and imports, taxes on mills, salt and on every contract exchanged in his territory (nothing is new under the sun – these were the forerunners of VAT). On the other hand, there was a great deal of money to be spent on wars, and buying cardinalships. Marriages were expensive too and state visits even more so; the purchase of titles and legitimacy was also a drain on resources.

Most of the Este dukes were or had been *condottieri*, like the Sforzas, Montefeltros, Gonzagas, the Colonnas and the d'Avalos. Whenever expenditure exceeded revenue – which was often – the lords had to seek military commissions (*condotte*). The boys of the nobility were therefore trained in swordsmanship and martial combat, horsemanship and hunting; luxurious displays of arms were part of the life of a young nobleman, and the dignity of a prince was often combined with the stipend of a *condottiere*. Young boys would be sent away from home to train with a "free-lance" *condottiere*. Switching sides was not considered dishonourable, and soldiers of fortune generally played a "civilized" war, trying to lose as few men and horses as possible; besides, live prisoners meant good ransoms.

One of the protagonists of this tale is Vittoria Colonna, whom we find in Ferrara, a city that had become a nest of the Reform. A true daughter of the Renaissance, Vittoria's liberation coincided with her need for spiritual reform within society and within the Church. When, on 8 April 1537, she arrived in Ferrara, "that pleasant place of all festivities", Vittoria Colonna, Marchioness of Pescara, was a celebrated poet at the peak of her fame. Some of her sonnets had been published the year before, and all the major poets of her time had paid homage to the mastery of her art, to the high degree of her inspiration.

6. *The Gonzaga Family and Court* by Andrea Mantegna

The Gonzagas became powerful through political and matrimonial alliances; they ruled Mantua (Virgil's birthplace) and made this northern city into an important centre. They were *condottieri*, captains-at-arms, although Francesco, Isabella's husband, was given the title of marques (by the pope) and his son duke (by Charles V). In this fresco, Ercole, Francesco's younger brother, is coming home after being created cardinal (1527). He studied at Bologna and inherited his mother's brilliance.

7. *Vittoria Colonna* (?) by Sebastiano del Piombo

The daughter of one of the most ancient families in Italy, Vittoria was married when she was nineteen to Fernando d'Avalos, the son of the Marquess of Pescara and dedicated poems to him, but her love for him was unrequited. She was celebrated all over Italy for her literary gifts and also for her virtue.

Vittoria's work was so well known because she herself encouraged the public to copy down her sonnets in manuscript form and people knew her poems by heart. Not only was she a celebrity but she belonged to one of Italy's noblest and oldest families. She had lost some of her good looks by then – she was forty-seven and in poor health. She dressed sombrely, no longer with the jewels and silks of her youth, but in dark velvets, a chaste veil over her greying hair. This style of dress was in huge contrast to the ever festive court of Ferrara, a centre of fashion,

8. *Lucrezia Borgia* by Pinturicchio
The daughter of Pope Alexander VI and sister of Cesare Borgia, Lucrezia was married three times. Her third husband was Alfonso d'Este, brother of Isabella and Beatrice. She was beautiful and unhappy; among her lovers was the writer Bembo and her brother-in-law Francesco Gonzaga.

culture and arts, where Duke Ercole II entertained a sophisticated crowd of courtiers, poets, doctors, and musicians.

In 1523, thirty-five years before Vittoria's arrival, her father Fabrizio Colonna had been a prisoner at the court of Ferrara. He had been captured in battle and sent to Ferrara, hardly a prison for a dashing *condottiere* like Fabrizio. In fact, he had fallen in love with Nicola Trotti and had been a great success; he had heard that the Ferrarese ladies wore knickers under their skirts, in the Spanish fashion and, among giggles, tried to check the unusual garment for himself. He was the centre of many banquets which his "hostess", Lucrezia Borgia, then the Duchess of Este, gave in his honour.

To be a prisoner at Ferrara was, for Fabrizio Colonna, like being a guest in a friendly home or, we should say, in the luxurious and sophisticated palace decorated with rugs from Persia and silks from Damascus which Lucrezia had brought with her as dowry. The daughter of the pope, Lucrezia, sister of Cesare Borgia, already had two husbands and several lovers, including cardinal Pietro Bembo, with whom she exchanged beautiful love letters. She also fell in love with her new brother-in-law, the Marquess of Gonzaga.

But on 6 June 1508, the poet, Ercole Strozzi, a leading courtier, was found stabbed twenty-two times. Lucrezia's husband, Alfonso, had had him murdered because he had defiantly assisted Lucrezia's *affaire* with Francesco Gonzaga, his sister Isabella's husband. But Lucrezia was rich, and her wealth gave her licence to act as she chose.

Her bridal journey from Rome to Ferrara in January 1502 at the head of a cortège of 700 courtiers and servants (financed by the papacy) was famous for its display of wealth. Rugs and silks were only a small part of her dowry because the bulk consisted of 100,000 ducats paid to Alfonso, as much again in land pilfered from the diocese of Bologna, 75,000 ducats in jewels, plate, cloths, linen, tapestry and – even more important – a reduction from 4,000 to 100 ducats in the annual tribute due from the vassal duchy of Ferrara to the papacy.

It is difficult to compare the buying power of the ducat (or scudo, approximately the same value) with today's currencies, although some sources give it at £150. It is useful to compare Renaissance dowries and payments: Vittoria's 14,000 ducats, for example, to Lucrezia Borgia's 100,000 ducats; or the three ducats Isabella Gonzaga paid monthly to her tutor in classics, which was considered a good wage. Or the 100,000 ducats – an enormous amount of money – spent by Vittoria's grandfather, Federigo da Montefeltro, to build his fairytale castle at Urbino. Maybe I should again quote Braudel on the value of money, always a difficult but central item in history.

> In 1517 the ducat ceased to be a unit of real money represented by the gold piece and became a money of account at the henceforward invariable rate of 6 lire 4 soldi. The ducat, since it was an actual coin, simply passed into the same category, which is now headed, as the soldo and the lira, also moneys

of account. The sequin, which was a real coin, was in 1517 worth 6 lire 10 scudi (6 soldi more than the ducat); ten years later, in 1526, it was worth 7 lire 10 soldi.

Blonde and unconforming, Lucrezia Borgia had brought with her an exotic aura and was disliked by her husband's people. Surrounded by her Spanish and Roman ladies-in-waiting, she was lonely in the huge Este castle. Her many pregnancies, her many miscarriages, her weak health and the flat landscape of Ferrara depressed her. When her father the pope died and her brother fell from power, she could easily have been dismissed by her husband – and she knew it. But Alfonso did not divorce her, and she gave him five children. At times, depressed and lonely, she withdrew into a convent; at others she entertained extravagantly and, when Prospero Colonna, Vittoria's cousin, came to visit Ferrara, she offered him wonderful meals and rare Muscat wine; sturgeon, frogs' legs and eels were displayed on massive silver dishes.

But, by 1537 when Vittoria Colonna arrived in Ferrara, Lucrezia was dead and her eldest son, Ercole, was duke. From his mother he had inherited a certain flamboyance and love of poetry: in fact he was delighted to give hospitality to Vittoria Colonna, not only because their families had been friends for generations, but because she was a famous literary figure. The aristocratic lady, dressed in severe colours, had rented a small palazzetto which was not far from the grand Este castle where the court resided and where Ercole gave brilliant banquets and entertained with music composed for each occasion.

From the pope's point of view – this was the time of the Farnese Paul III – the lay court of Ferrara was rotten. The summer before Vittoria's visit, John Calvin had sought refuge with the Duchess. At the age of twenty-six, Calvin had just published his first book, *The Institutes of the Christian Religion*, which started the great movement of reform in France, French Switzerland and Italy; it had far more influence in southern Europe than Luther's work and was the first text to explain the doctrines of the Reformation.

Calvin's presence was not the only reason for the pope's suspicion of the court of Ferrara: at the age of twenty, the duke, son of that celebrated sinner – but what a beautiful sinner! – Lucrezia Borgia, had married Renée of Valois, guaranteeing France's protection. Renée was the youngest daughter of Louis XII of France, and the sister-in-law of Francis I, the new French king, quite a catch for the lord of a small vassal state. But she was ugly. And her subjects, accustomed to the beauty of the duchesses (from Leonora d'Aragon, mother of Isabella Gonzaga and Beatrice d'Este, themselves famous beauties, to Lucrezia Borgia) called her "the monster". Moreover Renée had been educated by Bishop Briçonnet, a Protestant and a close friend of another powerful woman, Margaret, Queen of Navarre. Margaret was a writer of note and the declared enemy of the Church of Rome.

The Duke and Duchess of Ferrara did not love each other. Ercole, who delighted in beauty and pleasure, almost fainted when he first saw his wife in

1528. Renée of France was miserable; to her friend and relative, Margaret of Navarre, she described her husband's treatment of her: "He said such rude and strange words to me that you would have been amazed to hear them."

In the middle of her husband's court, Renée had formed quite a different entourage, a group of heretics in the eyes of the popes. One of them was Clement Marot, a French poet who, in 1528, had written a poem in honour of Renée's marriage. Marot, whom we shall meet again in Lyons, was a follower of Calvin. At the age of forty-one, famous and admired all over Europe, Marot fled to Ferrara from France. To Margaret of Navarre, in a letter sent from Venice on his way back to France, Marot described Renée's difficulties:—

> Ha, Marguerite, escoute la souffrance
> Du noble coeur de Renée de France
> Puis comme soeur plus fort que d'espérance,
>   Console-la!

> *Ah, Margaret, listen to the suffering*
> *Of the noble heart of Renée of France*
> *Then, as a sister, stronger than hope,*
>   *Console her!*

Of Renée, with whom he shared a lifelong friendship, as well as a strong sympathy for John Calvin, Marot said, "She is a flower among thorns."

Inside the mighty ducal castle, frescoed with pagan images, where Lucrezia Borgia had adorned her own apartments in gold, Renée had a small chapel built for her prayers. This room consisted of a severe space decorated only with precious marbles. Not one image! Not a painting, not a fresco! In fact, it looks more like a Mogul mosque than a Christian chapel, and there Renée, alone, would pray to her Calvinist God.

The modern age may find some difficulty in understanding why Europe seemed to be split by such an issue as the Reformation, why people had to live in exile or die for their beliefs. To sympathize with the reform was the equivalent of being "left-wing" today. Indeed, most intellectuals were drawn to a more spiritual and less pagan brand of faith than that of the established Church. Besides, the papacy and the clergy made a squalid spectacle of themselves in their greed for money and worldly pleasures, which is why some monastic orders split and others, like the Franciscans, were reformed from within to achieve the mysticism that the reformers wished to revive. But such movements encountered bitter opposition: to recognize the new orders implied that something was wrong with the existing clergy. The reason for which Vittoria had come to Ferrara concerned exactly this, the recognition of a new order and the sheltering of a preacher who was almost regarded as a heretic by the holy see.

Besides fleeing from Rome, Vittoria's principal aim in Ferrara was to help a monk, Bernardo Ochino to open a monastery. This monk was no ordinary preacher: his passionate words, the way in which he condemned the abuses of the Roman Church, the corruption of the rich, the lack of chastity in contemporary women, would move his hearers to tears. When he preached, people crowded around him, listening to his fervent rhetoric, admiring the strength of his conviction. To listen to Ochino had become the fashionable thing to do. Even courtesans would go to the square, the street corners, or to the church where Ochino was to give one of his sermons, and respectable matrons would take their daughters. Some women burst into tears, others wanted to follow the preacher's words to the letter, some just went there to show off their new clothes. But Ochino's following was not only mostly feminine, it was vast.

Times were ripe for this; after the first joyful explosion of the Renaissance, there had been calamities, so that preachers promising damnation started to roam the squares and churches of Italy gathering faithful and followers. The fact that Savonarola had been burnt at the stake prompted an even stronger stream of advocates of doom. Like Savonarola, Bernardo Ochino was a reformist, a Protestant *ante litteram*. Everybody knew that Ochino was a protégé of many a powerful woman, not only of Renée and of Vittoria Colonna, but of Giulia Gonzaga, who was the beautiful cousin of Vittoria and was herself Lady of Fondi, and even of Caterina Cybo, the niece of a previous pope.

Ochino belonged to the Reformed Franciscan order (later to be called the Capuchins) and was a follower of Juan Valdés, a Spanish friar. In fact, his speeches were not so different from Savonarola's. But Vittoria Colonna was surprised when the monk was accused of having "dangerous tendencies towards Lutheran theories". Nor did she see herself as a heretic, even though she had criticized the state of the Church and the papacy in her sonnets.

As soon as she arrived at Ferrara, Vittoria began to prepare the way for Ochino: she wrote feverishly, a great many letters, from which it is clear that Ochino and his reformed order were encountering opposition. Amongst her correspondents was Eleonora Gonzaga della Rovere, Duchess of Urbino, one of the most outstanding wits of her time. Vittoria told her of Ochino and of "this poor Reform persecuted by all men of the world" (27 June 1536). She also wrote to Cardinal Agostino Trivulzio (3 October 1536): "They've closed the doors when these friars wanted to enter, hoping to reduce this reform to nothing and wanting to reform them!" To Giulia Gonzaga, widow of Vespasiano Colonna (3 December), she wrote: "I have heard that Your Ladyship sent me *L'Esposizione sopra San Paolo* which was most desired by me and which I needed; I thank you and I shall thank you more when, God willing, I shall see you."

This book, written by Juan Valdés, was considered dangerous and heretical; not a copy is extant since it was put on the Index and every single copy burnt. After receiving it from her cousin, Vittoria Colonna read it and kept it with her at all times. With her force of influence, Vittoria succeeded in persuading the duke to force a Ferrarese nobleman to give up his house and property on the bank of the river Pó, which became a monastery for Ochino and for the order he was about to form. And then, on 18 August, Ochino, accompanied by several monks his followers, arrived in Ferrara. There is no doubt that Vittoria had let herself be excessively influenced by the demanding Ochino. But, since her husband's death, she had been unconsciously seeking outlets for her energy. Her years of marriage which, in retrospect, she coloured with happiness, had mostly been spent in solitude or with women: only in maturity did she choose close friendships with men, for many of whom she developed a strong infatuation. Like other women of strong character, she liked to be with the famous who, in turn, could not but be flattered by the company of the *Diva*, the Divine, as the whole of Italy now called Vittoria Colonna, Marchioness of Pescara.

While she was in Ferrara, the relationship between the duke and the duchess eased a little, and this was probably due to Vittoria's presence: she attracted the duke with her art and noble conversation, the duchess with her mysticism. In turn Ferrara seemed to animate Vittoria, who was to shed her sombre clothes: "This morning the lady Marchioness of Pescara came to visit the lady duchess wearing a very vulgar dress", says a letter addressed to Isabella Gonzaga (8 June 1537). "They spent a great deal of time together and then the marchioness dined with them." This happened a few days before the birth of the new princess, who was christened Eleonora on 19 June. Vittoria was her godmother and the child was to be another celebrated lady, the friend of Torquato Tasso, Gesualdo de Venosa, and of the arts.

While leading a rather withdrawn life, writing her interminable letters, sponsoring Ochino, listening to him and following him around, Vittoria participated in the court's festivities whenever there was a musical or literary gathering, at which she would recite her own poems. And when Gian Matteo Giberti, Bishop of Verona sent his envoy to Ferrara to ask her to visit him, she was reluctant to leave, in spite of her affection for the bishop. Giberti's envoy wrote back to Verona saying that in trying to get Vittoria away from Ferrara he stood between two dangers: to be exiled by the duke or to be stoned by the population for robbing the city of "such a beautiful ornament". She was also corresponding with Pietro Aretino, letters that that opportunist poet was later to publish in order to glorify himself: to correspond with Vittoria Colonna was a great honour or, as Ludovico Ariosto had written, guaranteed eternal fame. Pietro Aretino (1492–1556), nicknamed "the scourge of the princes", was the recipient of a letter from Vittoria dated 25 September 1537. She wrote "al magnifico Messer Pietro Aretino". She thanked him for sending her a "beautiful and valuable work" and also for "your liberality in presenting me with the balance of 30 scudi, for which, as well as those paid over, I became a debtor through other people's fault". At that time, Vittoria was in financial difficulties, as she had already been in the past. She then goes on to tell Aretino about herself. "I stayed some time at Lucca, but not at Pisa, as your letter states. I passed from there; and being unable to go to

Jerusalem, I remained here: but I am compelled to go back to Rome by His Holiness, instigated by your friend and mine, the Marchese del Vasto, as it seems to him that His Holiness is offended by my Christian humility." Two months later, she answered another letter of Aretino's, somewhat more briskly. "Molto magnifico signor. I know not whether I ought to praise or censure you for the book you sent me: to praise you for the style, because you truly deserve it; or to censure you, because you employ your great talents on other subjects than those of religion, thus proving yourself less grateful to God and less useful to the world." If only Vittoria had known Aretino's erotic verses! And she ends her letter in a hasty, most "modern" way: "I have no time to reply to that youth belonging to you who sent me the book. Pray excuse me." She signed very formally and a bit distantly, "La Marchesana di Pescara".

Another woman who is going to be one of my main characters was in Ferrara at the same time as Vittoria. Tullia d'Aragona, also a poet, could have not been more different from Vittoria and, unlike Vittoria, derived her celebrity from the oldest trade in the world.

Thin, rather tall, sumptuously dressed, Tullia used to hide among the Ferrarese crowds to hear Ochino's sermons. She was the most famous courtesan of her times and Aretino resented her intellectual pretensions, saying that he liked only straightforward prostitutes. And he added that (6 June 1537), "Tullia has accumulated so much treasure that no matter how much she may spend she will never exhaust it! And her immodesty does so much to her credit that she can be envied by those women who are chaste and most fortunate."

Tullia had settled down and kept a rich salon in Ferrara; she was famous for the fine jewels and sumptuous clothes she wore and probably had never set foot in the Este castle, although that was certainly her ambition: to be invited at court. At precisely that time Tullia addressed a poem to Ochino, in which she challenged the monk's condemnation of music, of dance, of pretty clothes:–

> Bernardo, ben potea bastarvi avere
> co'l dolce dir, ch'a voi natura infonde,
> qui dove'l re dei fiumi ha piú chiare onde,
> acceso i cuori a le sante opere eterne.
>
> Che se pur sono in voi pure l'interne
> voglie, e la vita al vestir corrisponde
> non uom di frale carne ed ossa immonde,
> ma siete in voi le schiere superne.
>
> Or le finte apparenze, e'l ballo e il suono
> chiesti dal tempo e dall'antica usanza
> a che cosí da voi vietati sono?
>
> Non fora santitá, fora arroganza
> torre il libero arbitrio, il maggior dono
> che Dio ne dié nella primiera stanza.

Bernardo, you should have been fulfilled
to have fired all hearts to the holy eternal pursuits
with your sweet words inspired by your nature,
here [at Ferrara] where the king of the rivers [the Pó] has cleaner waves.

Even if your inner desires are pure
and your way of life corresponds to your dress
you are nevertheless only a man of mere flesh and bones
and still within you is the holy host.

Now why do you have to censor
the luxuries and the dancing and the music
required by convention and by old customs?

It is not holiness, it is arrogance
to forbid the liberty of choice, the greatest gift
which God gave us from the very beginning.

This poem endeared Tullia, who was herself a skilled musician, to the Este court. Tullia and Vittoria saw each other often at Ochino's sermons, and one day, after one such meeting, a small crowd stopped outside the church where Ochino had been preaching, talking, standing in groups on the stairs of the church. The Ferrarese intellectuals such as Girolamo Muzio, the outstanding poet of the court, were there, and they gathered around the two famous women, forming two distinctive groups, one around Vittoria, the famous poet, the daughter of one of Europe's noblest families, and the other around Tullia, the courtesan and poet. As they all knew each other, the two groups merged, chroniclers recount, and the two ladies curtsied and talked to each other "very cordially". Vittoria would have been graceful towards the lesser person out of good breeding and kindness; Tullia would have tried to please the aristocratic woman who at the moment was in disgrace, not in Ferrara but in Rome. Like her, Tullia too had fled from Rome — where her reputation had been badly stained — and very hastily too.

In setting herself up in luxury, displaying her erudition, Tullia became another Ferrarese attraction. Girolamo Muzio, aged forty, fell in love with her. The beautiful poems which he dedicated to Tullia ("Le Amorose", "Belladonna") were the best advertisement for her at the court of the Estes. Indeed, Muzio's descriptions of Tullia so inflamed the curiosity of the duke that he sent Muzio away in order to be free to sample Tullia's body and see for himself.

Tullia's progress was described to Isabella Gonzaga, the duke's aunt, who was kept informed of the gossip at Ferrara by a man who wrote to her under the pseudonym Apollo. Isabella wanted to know what happened in her native city, week by week. "Apollo", whose real name was Battista Stabellino, using language proper for Isabella, a noble lady, described Tullia as a Roman courtesan. She was

most delightful, discreet and intelligent, also gifted with excellent and goddess-like manners, she can sing at sight any motet or song. In conversation her voice has unique charm and she carries herself in such a manner that there is not a man or a woman in these parts who is her equal, even though that most excellent and illustrious lady, the Marchioness of Pescara, is here, as Your Excellency knows. Her house is always full of interesting people and at any time one can visit her, and she is rich with money and jewels, necklaces, rings and other things of note; not least she is well suited to all this.

The two women were quite different on the surface: Vittoria was older than Tullia (whose date of birth is variously given as 1505, 1508 or 1510) and had always shown disdain, if not stern contempt, for women who sold their bodies. Anything overtly sexual horrified her: to a poet who had addressed a Latin elegy to a courtesan, she said that he was "whitewashing crows" and "painting doves black". Unlike Vittoria, Tullia used men to promote her fame as a poet, and she was right to use them: men had used her so.

But like Vittoria, Tullia liked men with whom she had a common intellectual bond and both had struggled to be individuals in their own right – Vittoria to be more than the wife of a leading *condottiere*; Tullia, more than a successful courtesan. In fact, Tullia's life had been a nest of thorns. She had been followed by envy and calumny everywhere she had gone; people like Pietro Aretino were only appeased when they saw her old and destitute.

Yet it is not so odd to compare the two: a contemporary poet did so, saying, "Vittoria is the moon, but Tullia is the sun."

At Ferrara, Tullia found a young nobleman who wanted to marry her. Isabella Gonzaga's social informer, "Apollo", delighted in every detail of the amusing and scandalous story in a long letter to his lady in Mantua; but he did not mention the young man's name, since he belonged to the Ferrarese nobility, which Isabella knew well.

The young man in question "was burning with the flames of love and took courage from his intimacy with Tullia". After giving her many jewels, he told her that "anybody of her choice being present as a witness, he wanted to take her as his wife". But Tullia, dismissing him, answered that she had no intention of getting married: she wanted to dedicate herself entirely to poetry. After a while, the young aristocrat decided to try again; he wrote to Tullia saying that his sister and another relative would like to dine with her: they wanted to meet her because they had heard of how delightful Tullia's company was. Tullia answered that she would be pleased to receive them, and, on the day, the young man sent his cook and a great many delicacies to Tullia's house. In the evening she waited and waited, in vain.

Late at night, the young man arrived, accompanied by a man friend, and apologized for his relatives, who had been unable to dine with her: their husbands had forbidden them to go out at night. The three of them dined alone, but when the clock struck two in the morning, Tullia remarked that it was late. "It is time, gentle youth, for you to go back to your house." By that time, it was dangerous for him to be out in the streets, he told Tullia, and after giving her a jewel of pearls worth 100 scudi and two rings "of good value" which he took from his own fingers, he repeated: "Call whoever you want to be present here and I shall marry you!" Tullia refused again, and the friend of the young man departed, leaving the aristocrat white and silent "like a marble statue". But then, recovering his wits, he extracted a dagger and, very operatically, tried to kill himself under Tullia's cool eyes. She observed that he had only wounded himself, but called for help, and for some friends of hers to spend the night at her house, in order to avoid a scandal (as if people did not know that she was likely to sleep with a man more often than not). In the morning, the young man returned to his house: he had lost so much blood that he nearly died.

It might seem strange that Tullia d'Aragona – whose mother, incidentally, also came from Ferrara and that is probably why we find her in the city of the Este – did not take this opportunity to get married: marriage could have given her respectability. But she may have feared a bigger scandal had she accepted: the Ferrarese nobility would never allow one of their breed to marry a notorious courtesan. Besides, Tullia probably thought, the young man would have taken all the money that she had so strenuously accumulated and money was all she cared about at that moment.

Vittoria must have heard of the "Tullia scandal"; the duke would make jokes about it, but not his chaste wife Renée, the daughter of Louis XII of France and Anne de Bretagne (1510–75). But what Vittoria must have resented was the sonnet that Tullia had written, a reproach, almost an attack against Ochino, the saintly man Vittoria protected.

CHAPTER THREE

Women in Rome

Rome was the symbol of the rediscovery of antiquity. Filippo Brunelleschi (1377–1446) and Donatello (1386–1466) had together excavated and examined buried capitals and statues: the two great friends were nicknamed "the treasure seekers". Previously every pagan statue had been destroyed apart from the monument to Marcus Aurelius, now on the Capitol hill, which had been saved from the iconoclasts because it was believed to portray the Emperor Constantine. But now, with the new taste, every time a classical statue was uncovered, it was hailed by the Romans, sometimes even covered with garlands.

But Rome was also a dangerous, unsafe place, much more so than Venice or Ferrara. Pilgrims knew the saying "Rome is holy but its population is wicked". Riddled with little alleys, no one was safe in Rome at night, or sometimes even in daytime. Mugging was as popular then as it is now. Many districts belonged to noble families, often at war with each other – or against the papacy. In "wartime", these districts turned into fortresses; from over 300 towers, stones and incendiary material were thrown across the streets. Palaces and grand houses had tiny doors, to make forced entrance difficult; at times, they did not even have internal stairs. Circulation in the streets was hampered by mobs of ferocious destitutes, of begging monks, or poor women – the ground was littered with broken-down walls, ruins, refuse, filthy water, open sewers. People of wealth never walked, but rode mules.

Martin Luther, who had visited Rome in his youth, had been horrified by the devastation, the ruins which served as nests of bandits, and at seeing that the monument to the woman-pope, the English Papessa Giovanna – Pope Joan – was still standing. He had gone to Rome to confess his sins and kiss its ground, but in the clergy he found "very ignorant men". Had he not seen Rome, Luther wrote, he would never have believed that such nastiness could exist. "In fact", he added, "Bembo, a learned man, after having well observed Rome, said that it was the sewer of all the world." And Il Pasquino decreed, "You who want to live a holy life leave Rome. Here everything is allowed, but for honesty."

Before 1490, out of a population of 100,000, there were 6,800 registered prostitutes in Rome. Towards 1520, the authorities tried to "clean up" the city, but gave up because they found that they would have had to expel over 25,000 people. Around the courtesans there grew crowds of pimps, and pimps were often used as spies. Courtesans also assumed this role, whether willingly or not; at the top of their profession, they received the powerful, even kings (like Veronica Franco who, in Venice, entertained Henri III of France but, since Henri was homosexual, they might have limited themselves to talk about poetry).

The reason for which Tullia d'Aragona had had to flee from Rome was typical of her time and of her status. At the peak of her fame as the most important courtesan in Rome, Tullia had made the mistake of agreeing to sleep with a German, thus debasing herself and, in turn, her customary clients, who were polished noblemen. It had been her mother's fault. Not accustomed to a profession whose nuances had changed, Giulia Campana, thought that Tullia, her daughter, with her salon where people chatted about Petrarch's poetry, wasted time – and money. Giulia therefore negotiated terms with the rich German.

As we said, Giulia had come to Rome from Ferrara to try her fortunes in the most ancient of all professions: she was only one of many. Pretty young women with no money flocked to Rome from all over Italy, and also from Spain, Holland, Germany and France. Rome was a city of rich bachelors: priests and cardinals (the latter were not necessarily ordained; in fact, they seldom were), travellers and diplomats, tourists and pilgrims. The "eternal city" was actually known as *terra di donne*, but the truth was the opposite; it was a land of men looking for sex. Although this was beginning to be less true in Renaissance times, the married woman had been given an essentially maternal role, young girls and widows were often forced to withdraw to nunneries. And in Rome young unmarried women do not seem to have appeared in public as they did in Florence or Ferrara. So there were few women who, besides offering sex, could share a pleasant conversation or entertain men with their presence and the most intelligent courtesans took the place in Roman society that was left empty.

In order to find a succession of men who could keep her, possibly in splendour, the Renaissance courtesan had to attract the Renaissance man. To do so, and in the middle of fierce competition, she had to offer beauty, knowledge and marvellous manners, which Baldassarre Castiglione described in *The Courtier*, his "bestseller". *Cortegiana*, the feminine form of the word which expressed all the qualities of a gentlewoman, indicated the status of a geisha – an articulate geisha. Thomas Coryat, an Englishman who visited Venice, described how the word derived from "courtesy" and that the courtesan was rather like the Greek *hetera*, a "social woman". When entering their palaces, one had the impression of seeing Venus's paradise, he wrote, embellished with sumptuous tapestries and leather, and the portrait of the courtesan, generally painted by a well-known artist. Coryat was horrified by the amount of cosmetics courtesans used; their hairstyle was typical of their trade: fair braids building up a kind of double horn over their foreheads. Their clothes were incredibly rich, made from damasks and gold, and they wore jewels in their ears, and diamonds and chains of gold; their silk stockings were flesh-coloured, their breath and all over their bodies were scented.

Contemporary censuses show that courtesans were officially called *meretrices honestae* (honest prostitutes); these were followed by the *cortesane de minor sorte* (courtesans of a minor kind), and by those of *la candela* (candle) or *da lume* (light), probably because, not having any servants, they had to carry the lights themselves. These censuses give details of others who, besides having a day job like that of a washerwoman or street-vendor, "professed" at night. All details of sexual specializations are coolly given beside the fee.

Among the merits of successful courtesans was that of introducing elegant manners and ingredients to the table like "sumptuous dishes, and the objects for the very delicate ingredients spread out on tablecloths and rich rugs". The *meretrices* mixed in society freely; some lived in clusters, in the same district; others mixed with different trades and people. Until the end of the reign of Leo X (1475–1521; his papacy lasted from 1513 to 1521), Rome was very liberal. In a census which was probably taken around 1518, we find that courtesans lived in the same buildings as noble families. In fact, the social strata were truly mixed: at a house in Santo Stefano in Piscinula we find the noble Madonna Vannozza Borgia (mother of Cesare and Lucrezia); a washerwoman on the ground floor; a Florentine carpenter in the "upper habitations". Next to a very old and poor Spanish woman was Mastro Jacopo Antonio, a blacksmith, with a courtesan *de la candela* living underneath. In another building at Campo Marzio, there was a school for children (*di putti*), a bishop and also Donna Speranza and Donna Vasca, *cortesane*.

Pilgrims who went around Rome, the only apostolic city left to Christendom, were accompanied by an armed escort and came for business or piety. Courtesans like Giulia, Tullia's mother, did well because travellers had some fixed points of interest in Rome – the antiquities, the courtesans and Il Pasquino, the mutilated statue that had been unearthed in 1501. To go back to Tullia's recent misadventures, it must be said that even Il Pasquino had spread the story of how Tullia had made a deal with a "repulsive" German to sleep with him for a week; she was to receive the astonishing fee of 100 scudi a night. This gives one an idea of the popularity of both Tullia and of the truncated statue that not even the popes dared to pull down.

Il Pasquino, became the symbol of satirical comments, of lampoons, of "pasquinades". (Cf. Dryden: "The precious wits, who Satire first began / Were pleasant Pasquins on the life of man.") Anonymous authors wrote lampoons and Pasquin became the imaginary personage to which they were ascribed. Il Pasquino (whose name capriciously came from a barber who lived nearby) gave advice to travellers:–

> *Most useful advice given by the Excellent*
> *Doctor, Mastro Pasquino, to all gentlemen,*
> *officials, procurators, notaries, artists*
> *and bravacci* [criminals]*, lately come to*

9. Courtesans

Because the top courtesans were close to affairs of state, ambassadors reported on their movements: where they went, how many servants followed them, how many pieces of luggage they carried when they entered a city with their caval-cades of liveried gentlemen, how much money they had.

Rome; translated from the Greek into
Latin and from Latin into Italian:
Leave the courtesans alone
if you don't want to lose all you have,
they're prostitutes, like the rest,
but at a higher price they sell their fruit.

Pietro Aretino was one of the anonymous contributors to Il Pasquino, his sharp comments and revelations struck home. Il Pasquino commented on how popes had bought the papacy, how they promoted corrupt nephews and sons, how vast riches were accumulated in a short span of time: it was the *Private Eye* of Renaissance times.

In the midst of violence, the courtesans represented a haven. At their salons people discussed literature. The elegance of the language was strictly observed: stylistically, the sentences had to be flawless. Courtesans knew Petrarch by heart – Petrarch, who had heralded a period of rediscovery of the past, stimulated those who, in daytime, poisoned and schemed against each other into reading and learning.

One evening at Tullia's house, a learned group was debating on to what extent Petrarch had drawn from ancient poetry – an episode which is related to us by a contemporary poet and printer, Ludovico Domenichini. They were talking and talking, everybody showing off his and, in Tullia's case, her knowledge, when Umore Da Bologna, a latecomer known for his jokes, arrived at Tullia's salon, bringing some fresh air into the conversation. He said that Petrarch was both clever and ingenious; he had composed his verses basing them on classic authors and made them his own by adding some ornaments; like the Spaniards who, at night-time, steal cloaks and then change their ornaments so that nobody will recognize them on the morrow. Unknown to Umore, among the distinguished crowd there was a Spaniard who had not quite followed what was being said by the Italian. "*Que dizis vos, segnor, de los Espagnoles?*" (sic) he asked. Luckily, Umore Da Bologna turned everything into a joke rather than explain what he had said, thus avoiding a duel. Asking the servant to bring back his cloak, he seized it quickly and departed, as if to save it from the hands of the Spaniard. No one explained the joke to the unfortunate Spaniard, who went on wondering why the company, and Tullia herself, were roaring with laughter.

A courtesan like Tullia was like a movie star and, when she went out, either in a carriage or riding an ornate mule, people left their houses and hovels in order to watch the elegant woman, her rich clothes and jewels. She was always followed by a retinue, servants and friends, who escorted her, also for safety: those jewels attracted thieves. Many gathered to pay homage, cardinals and bishops came to chat, showing publicly that they did not disdain a courtesan's society. Since churches were important social meeting points, the courtesans were assiduous frequenters of such holy places (where, anyway, people went to gossip, to eye one another, to flirt and to show off their clothes). Inside the church the courtesans stood near the altar, next to the great ladies of the nobility. To a severe matron who looked annoyed by such proximity, a quick-tongued courtesan whispered, "Don't fear, milady, my sin is not contagious, unless you desire it."

Courtesans' houses were not open to everyone; in fact, it was difficult to be received by somebody like Tullia. All sorts of introductions were needed – that is why the episode of the "repulsive" German to whom she had sold herself had offended so many and had instigated so much ridicule. Tullia, who danced so well *la pavana*, *la rosina*, the *brando*, who sang so beautifully! About whom one of her most fervent admirers (Zilioli) had written, "She talked with such a grace and rare eloquence when joking or when she was debating serious subjects so that she drew and conquered the soul of her listeners, like another Cleopatra." How could she debase herself in this way?

Although Tullia was the daughter of a prostitute, on her father's side she had royal blood. After her arrival in Rome, Giulia had soon become the mistress of Ludovico d'Aragona who was descended from the royal house of Naples and who had been married to a Cybo princess – from the papal family; when Ludovico d'Aragona became a widower, Alexander VI made him a cardinal. He was a culti-vated man, the best protector Giulia could ever have aspired to. Moreover, he loved and kept her for a long time: when Tullia was born, he allowed her to carry his name. Tullia's detractors – and there were many – doubted her claim of being an Aragona. Very vulgarly, a friend of l'Aretino commented, "His Eminence's mule might have relieved itself from time to time in the courtyard of the house where Tullia was born." And also:-

> In nome regio invan s'usurpa e piglia
> la mal vissuta vecchia e l'empia figlia.
>
> *In vain the royal name is usurped*
> *by the evil-living old woman and her impious daughter.*

But there is no doubt that Tullia was the intelligent daughter of the cardinal who doted on her and looked after her education. Cardinal Ludovico spent time and money on both his mistress and his daughter: as a child Tullia could already read and speak Latin perfectly; she learnt singing and classical languages, and she showed a marked talent for music. But when Ludovico had to flee from Rome, fearing – like so many before and after him – the Borgias' poison, the two women were short of money. They moved to Siena where Tullia polished her accent – the *Senese* was, and is, considered the best Italian. And in Siena she grew up into a beautiful girl, though just how beautiful it is difficult to tell. Some contemporary commentators tell us that she was too tall, had thin lips, too large a mouth and – what was really the most offensive of her features – a vast nose. But she looks very attractive in the portrait that Alessandro Bonvicino (il Moretto) painted of her when she was twenty. Her eyes are finely cut and beautifully apart, and a fetching mixture of intelligence and innocence lights up Tullia's face; her body is harmonious. Her left arm carries the sceptre of poetry: she was already known for her verses. Later, and probably in order to make the portrait fit for Counter-Reformation times, another hand painted an inscription on the marble pedestal on which Tullia's arm is resting. This inscription turns Tullia into a Salome, but there is no doubt that this is Tullia and those are the eyes which Muzio extolled:–

> ... *beautiful eyes*
> *graceful eyes, loving and dear eyes*
> *more beautiful than the stars and the sun.*

Giulia then took her, by then "ripe", daughter from Siena back to Rome and started her off on the only possible path from which she could have earned a living for herself, and for her mother. How else could a woman, even as well brought-up as Tullia, but not a noble, hope to lead a decent, wealthy life? She could have chosen to marry, but not into the aristocracy; that would have been impossible because her mother was a prostitute. As the wife of a worker, Tullia would have been unable to keep servants who could carry water home from Rome's fountains, and take away pots of urine and shit. She could not have bought the expensive scents which would confuse and evaporate nasty smells, she would have been unable to fight the fleas, the insects which pestered most people's houses.

When Giulia was still one of the top courtesans of her time, the real star was Imperia, whose beauty was legendary. She was a close friend of Raphael, who painted her often when he came to Rome (1508). Like all courtesans of her time, Imperia would spend long boring hours standing by the window, beautifully attired, looking at what happened below in the street and, more important, being eyed by possible clients.

Imperia was probably born in 1485 and by the age of seventeen she was already the mother of a daughter called Lucrezia, whose paternity was either attributable to the distinguished Giacomo Sadoleto, friend of Vittoria Colonna, or more likely to the very rich and urbane Florentine banker, Agostino Chigi. A man of average height, blue-eyed, aquiline nose, Chigi had become the richest banker in the world. Rome, then as now a city that spent a lot and produced nothing, was a Mecca for bankers. Chigi was so famous that he was known at the court of the sultan as *magnus mercator christianus*, the great Christian trader, and the sultan sent him as a personal gift a number of very rare hunting dogs and a splendid horse.

Chigi was a banker, but a man of the Renaissance: he had the beautiful Imperia as his mistress; Raphael, Sebastiano del Piombo and Sodoma to decorate his house by the Tiber; his own printing press which published the very first Greek book to be printed in Rome – Pindar's poems – and he possessed about a hundred ships which sailed under his flag; he employed 20,000 people. He set Imperia up

10. *Imperia*, drawing by Raphael

Imperia's beauty was legendary. Raphael painted her as a Muse, as Galatea at the
Farnesina, as a Sybil in Santa Maria della Pace.

in a house, the luxury of which astonished the friar Matteo Bandello. He described it: every room was

so magnificently furnished that in them one saw nothing but velvet and brocade, and on the floor there were the finest carpets. In the cabinet where she withdrew when she received some great personage the walls were covered with hangings of embroidered cloth of gold, falling in rich folds. Above the hangings there was a cornice decorated with gold and ultramarine. On the cornice stood wondrous vases of various precious marbles – alabaster, porphyry, serpentine, and a thousand other kinds. Many chests and coffers were displayed around the room, all richly carved and inlaid, and all of value. In the centre of the room there was a small table, the most beautiful in the world, covered with green velvet. And on the table there was a lute and a viola da braccio and books in Latin and Italian, all richly bound. Imperia delighted in Italian poetry and ... she had already made such progress as to have composed some pleasing sonnets and madrigals.

It is needless for me to comment that Matteo Bandello, being a man of the clergy, should not have known what Imperia's house looked like. Bandello goes on telling a story of how one day the Spanish ambassador came to visit Imperia, because "he had heard so much about her and wished to see her". Imperia greeted the ambassador at the door, as etiquette required, and the Spaniard was so taken by the luxury of her house and the beauty of the woman who inhabited it that, feeling like spitting, he called for a servant and spat on his face. "Don't be hurt," he told him, "but I don't see here anything ugly but for your face." Imperia thanked the ambassador for such a convoluted "compliment" but begged him to use a rug she showed him and which was there for that very purpose. In fact, the Spanish ambassador went back to visit Imperia for a more intimate goal and, the Ferrarese ambassador relates, only left twenty-five ducats as a "tip": almost an insult for somebody like Imperia!

Imperia's real name was Lucrezia and she surrounded herself with powerful men; Agostino Chigi was not her only lover and he knew it. One of her protectors was Sadoleto, one of the golden group around Chigi, also depicted by Raphael in the loggia of Chigi's new villa, Le Delizie – the Delights – which Baldassare Peruzzi designed for the great banker. A garden of fountains and orderly alleys, of scented laurel trees, the peace of a Muslim house, well-sheltered by high walls, an arched veranda frescoed with architectural capriccios and the gods of Olympus: Le Delizie, which is now known as La Farnesina, is one of the greatest architectural achievements, the summit of the Renaissance spirit.

Each fresco, whether by Sebastiano del Piombo, by Raphael, by Sodoma, is of supreme quality, for Agostino Chigi they all gave their best. That enlightened sponsor inspired architects and painters, gardeners and friends. On the upper floor of Le Delizie, Sodoma painted his masterpiece by frescoing Chigi's bedroom with the scene of Alexander the Great, a formidably handsome youth, approaching the fair and shy Roxane, his newly-wedded wife, modestly sitting by her bed, a halo of blonde, curly hair, her small straight nose, an Etruscan smile, her sexy young body robed by the veils which cover her, with a cloud of naughty cupids, playing maliciously and sweetly smiling. Three maids, one of whom is a negress, are ready to leave the scene, but they knowingly eye Alexander and the timid but expectant Roxane. Never had a more attractive scene, more pregnant with a magic sexual anticipation been painted. In this room Sodoma (whose nickname means "the Bugger" – and that is a Renaissance touch: in which other period was there such a freedom of mores?) gave in this fresco the best of his pictorial life. In this room we also find two faces – and bodies – directly inspired by Imperia's looks.

In 1511 Imperia poisoned herself and left behind a legendary aura – old age did not stain her. Besides her beauty, which had no vulgarity, she clearly possessed wit and intelligence. She was rich: she had a palazzo and a *vigna*, a place in the countryside, near Rome; she had what every courtesan dreamt of. The company she kept was select, as pleasant as any woman could wish. Bandello wrote:–

> I think many of us were in Rome at the time, when you all knew Imperia, the Roman courtesan, personally or by repute; how beautiful she was and how many great and rich men were in love with her. But, among the rest, the man whom she loved above all was Signor Angelo del Bufalo, a man of real personal worth, human, noble and rich. He kept her for many years and was loved by her passionately, as was shown by her end.

When del Bufalo didn't love her any more, Imperia forgot that she was a courtesan, forgot that she had a daughter to look after, that she was young and rich. Chigi, who by then was a man of forty-five, sent her the best doctors in Rome. She just had time to make a will in which her powerful friend Chigi was her chief executor; she also begged him to look after her daughter, Lucrezia, who was fourteen at the time, and to see that she would be married suitably and soon. Imperia died on 15 August, on a night when the summer sirocco exploded in frightening thunder and lightning; in this the Romans saw the anger of Jupiter for such an untimely death; others said that Zeus had descended to earth to take Imperia away with him to Olympus. And in a typical Renaissance contrast to these pagan images and Imperia's profession and sinful death, she died with papal absolution and benediction.

The distraught (but not for long) Agostino Chigi honoured her with a funeral at which all Rome was present; her death created a sensation; she was buried at one of Rome's most elegant churches, San Gregorio al Celio. On her tombstone, by order of Chigi, was inscribed:–

> Imperia, cortesana romana cuae digna tanto
> nomine rarae inter homines formae specimen
> dedit.

Imperia, Roman courtesan, who, worthy of
such a great name, gave the example of a
beauty rare among humans.

The inscription on that monument, for which Chigi paid 500 ducats, disappeared; to extol such a great sinner, in the atrium of a church, was not acceptable for the times which followed. The fine monument, beautifully sculpted, is still there, but not Imperia's body (her place was usurped by a seventeenth-century canon).

Imperia fell in love, something that Tullia was careful to avoid. Incontrovertibly beautiful, unlike Tullia, Imperia did not suffer historical disasters like the sack of Rome. Indeed, when she encountered her first rejection, she was not strong enough to take it; she was not accustomed to being denied. Imperia was truly the symbol of the earliest part of the Renaissance, an age that idolized youth and beauty, the era before the sack of Rome when courtesans graced the social life of many cities and many men.

Imperia was portrayed by Raphael as a Muse in the Vatican rooms, with her golden hair arranged in classic curls, revealing a slender neck turned towards an admiring audience; as a Sybil in Santa Maria della Pace; as Galatea, the goddess of the sea, riding a dolphin on the walls of Chigi's Le Delizie. The image of the ideal woman, of the Muse, and of the courtesan merged. Tullia d'Aragona whose poems guarantee her eternity, strove to be a Muse forever but age cheated her. Age in the sense that, while Imperia committed suicide when young, Tullia lived on pretending to be younger and younger like one of those movie stars whose face is stiffened by the surgeon's knife but whose age filters through the too many operations. But Tullia was resilient and overcame the upheavals of politics and the changes that had occurred. She tried to ignore the watershed of the Renaissance that was the sack of Rome, a catastrophe which lasted over two years and which gave way to the Counter-Reformation, to guilt, to the depth of sin.

Tullia belonged to a later age than Imperia, when time became harder for a woman alone and when society repented of having given her the liberty of thinking for herself. And a courtesan, in spite of the fact that she was surrounded by men, was always alone.

CHAPTER FOUR

Vittoria Colonna's life leading to the Sack of Rome

Vittoria Colonna was the first of Fabrizio's children. Her mother, Agnes Montefeltro, was eighteen when Vittoria was born at Marino. Of the other children, Federico, Ferdinando, Camillo, Sciarra and Ascanio, only Ascanio survived adolescence. Vittoria's was an old and important Roman family, which can be traced to Latin times. In the fourteenth century, it had been praised by Petrarch, Vittoria's literary hero:–

> Gloriosa Colonna in cui s'appoggia
> nostra speranza e il grande nom latino.

> *Glorious Column on which lean*
> *our hope and the great Latin name.*

Fabrizio Colonna was Duke of Paliano and Prince of Tagliacozzo. He inhabited the fortress of Marino, about twelve miles from Rome, in the Alban hills, which barred the way south from Rome. Famous for its vineyards and undulating hills, its lakes and its mild climate, it was also a strategic area that had been carved up between the powerful houses of the "ever-turbulent" Colonnas, Orsini and Savellis; it controlled the gates to Rome and its harbour, and for these reasons it has suffered throughout the centuries. It is laced with vineyards and volcanic lakes, woods and palaces which once belonged to mighty cardinals and are now littered with filmstars.

Fabrizio was a *condottiere*, ready to sell his military talents: fighting was his profession and he would join any cause. A scholar and a poet, he was also a man of his times: when victorious, his army was free to loot and destroy. In this way the Colonnas built up their power; and their fall began with the expansion of the territorial power of the Church, which coincided with the end of the role of the *condottiere*.

It is important to follow the continuously changing political scene in order to understand the pressures that motivated our leading characters. For example, Vittoria Colonna's early life was intertwined with politics; both her father and her husband were involved in the events that led up to the sack of Rome in 1527.

Thus, in following her life, we shall come to understand an event, which led to the defection of so many from the Roman Church – and which ended the early part of the Renaissance, the years when the hedonistic side of life was extolled. The sack of Rome: the great divide, the age of self-questioning, of crisis was now going to confront the individual, women first. Before the horror of the destruction by the imperial army there had been an earlier calamity, as if in preparation for it and that was when Charles VIII, the King of France desended on Italy. Italy, being so rich in works of art, culture and beauty, attracted the north, and many came to it to rape the country, the cities and the villages.

The many Italian states had been considered enviably stable by the rest of Europe until, in 1494, Charles VIII of France entered Italy at the head of a 30,000-strong army, of which over half were horsemen. Some of his mercenaries came from Switzerland, others from Germany and the Balkans; some were also French. Charles was claiming the crown of Naples, which he inherited from the Angevins. The Colonnas, allies of the French at this time, seized Ostia, thus threatening Rome with famine by cutting off food supplies. The Borgia pope, Alexander VI, sent his mistress, Giulia Farnese, into hiding, and himself thought of fleeing to Venice. Fabrizio and Prospero Colonna were excommunicated and all Colonna properties in Rome confiscated.

The huge army of Charles VIII entered Rome from the gate of the piazza del Popolo on 31 December 1494, preceded four days earlier by an advance guard of 1,500 French soldiers. With the king, about 20,000 soldiers, with thirty-six cannons, culverins and heavy siege-guns, entered Rome. The contemporary writer Michelet described the spectacle, which started at three in the morning and ended in torchlight at five in the evening, with "Barbarian Swiss and multi-coloured Germans" marching "to the rhythm of the drums, and the men from Gascony, the best marchers in Europe". Charles thus entered Rome as an enemy.

The occupation became a sack when the pope refused to sign a treaty: every Jew was strangled; on 3 January 1495 the first gallows were erected at Campo dei Fiori. On 6 January, the pope took refuge at Castel Sant'Angelo and a bank was robbed. The house of Pope Borgia's most famous mistress, Vannozza Cattaneo, was looted and destroyed. On 15 January, a general looting took place. Four days later, when the sack ceased, many works of art – not for the first or last time – were on their way to Paris. Finally, the pope signed a peace treaty. Supported by Cardinal della Rovere and the Colonna family, Charles Valois was free to claim – or rather to conquer – the crown of Naples.

A month had passed since his violent entry into Rome when the French king and his army left for Naples, taking with them Cesare Borgia as hostage: the Valois king wanted a guarantee that the papal army would not attack him from the rear. As Charles was marching unopposed down Italy, Alfonso of Aragon, the reigning King of Naples, abdicated in favour of his son, who fled to Ischia.

Everything seemed in favour of French rule for Naples, when the French realized that they were actually trapped. Syphilis decimated Charles's army. While
the ill-treated Neapolitan nobility and the over-taxed population showed discontent, the great powers allied themselves in a holy league: Ferdinand the Catholic
of Spain, the pope, the Doge of Venice, and the Duke of Milan signed an alliance.
Fabrizio Colonna changed sides, from the Valois camp he moved to join the
league and, in order to secure him to their cause, the Aragonese persuaded him to
betroth his tiny daughter Vittoria to Ferrante, son of the late Alfonso d'Avalos,
Marquess of Pescara, a Spaniard related to the House of Aragona.

Pressed on all sides, Charles left Naples and was beaten by the army of the
league near Fornovo. Alexander VI wanted Maximilian, the Holy Roman
Emperor, to join the struggle but Maximilian instead came to Milan and, with
Ferdinand the Catholic, arranged the marriage of his son Philip to the Infanta of
Castile. After marrying two of his children to Habsburgs, Ferdinand promised his
second daughter, Catherine of Aragon to the King of England, who had joined
the league against the French in 1496. By sheer diplomacy and political marriages, Ferdinand was encircling France and the Hapsburgs were flooding the
thrones of Europe.

When Fabrizio changed sides and his daughter was betrothed to the orphan
Ferrante d'Avalos, the children were both five years old. They were sent to be
educated together by Ferrante's aunt, Costanza, Duchess of Francavilla, a formidable and enlightened lady; the duchess had the official title of the châtelaine of
Ischia and Vittoria became a kind of hostage of her. Ischia, a Phoenician and Myc-
enean centre, was one of the most attractive places in the Mediterranean, a
volcanic island set at the mouth of the Bay of Naples, in a strategic – and heavenly – position. Covered with scented pine woods, Ischia was a paradise. The blue
sea surrounded the Aragonese castle, which stood on an isolated rock, guarding
Ischia's small harbour; it still does. The island's natural hot springs were known
to be beneficial, and from the castle the ladies could walk by the turquoise sea,
ride the steep mountains, explore the wild woods: in short, Vittoria's prison was
heaven; her gaoler, a Pallas Athena.

Costanza was a patron of learning, and her court a literary centre. She engaged
a very good tutor for the young Ferrante and Vittoria: Giovan Battista Musefilo,
a renowned man of letters, a classicist and philosopher. From Costanza, Vittoria
learnt "manners", and the arts of speaking, dressing, behaving; that was the best
"finishing" school that any aristocratic girl could have wished for. Apart from military tuition, she received exactly the same education as a boy, as was the custom
amongst the people of her class, but while Ferrante learnt, Vittoria sucked in
every notion that the excellent tutors and Costanza herself imparted.

When Vittoria was thirteen, her father and his cousin escaped from the French
and took shelter at Ischia, where they spent a few months. It is, however, unlikely
that father and daughter saw much of each other, even when living under the

same Aragonese roof; quite a roof – the castle is immense. Fabrizio was urbane, adventurous and gallant: he was to inspire Machiavelli, who used his character to illustrate the noble figure of a *condottiere* – but he was not an ideal father. He probably loved his daughter, his only one, but had hardly seen her, he certainly did not know her, and Vittoria's character was similar to her mother Agnes's, rather shy and withdrawn. The Duchess Costanza became instead Vittoria's real parent: Costanza was Vittoria's source of authority, culture and friendship. In fact, in her letters, the duchess called Vittoria "*figlia*", daughter, in spite of the fact that letter-writing was very formal, and brothers and sisters, parents and children, addressed each other by their titles.

Costanza's life had been lonely, her father had been murdered and her brothers killed in wars, leaving her to be the head of the house of d'Avalos. She studied Italian and Latin and wrote a book on *The Misfortune and Difficulties of the World*, a sombre theme, more Spanish in tone than early Italian Renaissance. The sister-in-law of the former King of Naples, she managed the office of perpetual châtelaine of Ischia and the affairs of her family wisely, a true Renaissance woman, respected as an individual and as a wit. Great poets like Jacopo Sannazzaro, Paolo Giovio and Bernardo Tasso came to stay with her at Ischia, and Costanza gave hospitality to many nobles who fled from a Naples torn by war, political upheavals and disease. Vittoria took advantage of mixing with so many interesting people. As did Ferrante, "*un garzone avvenente*", a handsome youth, although one would not judge him so by looking at his portraits, his nose being long, thin and curved in a rapacious way, his red hair giving him a wild aura. Ferrante always preferred dressing in the Spanish fashion and, although he was born in Naples, tended to speak Spanish, rather than Italian or Latin.

In 1506, Costanza sailed to Naples together with both Ferrante and Vittoria, who were then sixteen, hence grown-up by the standard of the day and ready for matrimony. Naples was getting ready for the visit of the Spanish king, Ferdinand of Aragon, who had usurped the Neapolitan throne in 1503. The king's wife, Isabella of Castile, had died two years earlier; her throne of Castile was inherited not by her husband, but by their daughter, Joanna, wife of the emperor's son, Philip of Habsburg. In 1506, Philip had died and Joanna was declared insane: Ferdinand became regent of Castile for his grandchild, Charles of Ghent, the future Emperor Charles V, who at the time was six years old.

The visit of the king in Naples was the social event of the year: a gold tent had been erected on the pier to welcome the royal ship, there were many entertainments and Laurana, possibly the greatest of the early Renaissance sculptors, had designed the triumphal arch that still graces the entrance of the Maschio Angioino Castle. King Ferdinand was thrilled by the fact that the Neapolitan noblewomen kissed his hand; he also noticed the bright young Ferrante d'Avalos, who danced beautifully; "He's a boy of promise", the king remarked.

From Naples, Vittoria went on to Marino to be separated from Ferrante until their matrimonial contracts were signed and exchanged the following year. On that day, the King of Naples had given Fabrizio Colonna the estate of Pesco Costanzo and, on 6 June 1507, at the castle of Marino, Vittoria *illustria domicella Romana*, who lived *more magnatum*, consented to marry Ferrante d'Avalos, Marquess of Pescara. On 13 June, Ferrante's contract was signed in Naples, underwritten by Fabrizio Colonna, the Duchess of Francavilla and Prospero Colonna, Duke of Traetto. The marriage took place two years later, in great pomp, at Ischia, when Vittoria was nineteen. From Marino, she arrived escorted by Roman aristocrats, bringing rich presents for the groom. Ferrante's presents were valued at 4,666 ducats. Vittoria brought 14,000 ducats as her dowry, including objects worth 2,000, but no territory.

Ferrante and Vittoria's wedding was a social occasion. The Colonnas and the d'Avalos were among the most important European families, and many guests travelled from great distances and crossed the bay in spite of the fact that the wedding was celebrated at the end of December. Ferrante was described handsome but Vittoria was clearly considered more "interesting" than beautiful, at the time. When poets praised her they mostly referred to her "head of gold", her "uncommonly luminous hair" although she looks beautiful in Raphael's *Parnassus*. Filonico Alicarnasseo, her first contemporary biographer, described her looks frankly: "... As she was engaged by matrimonial contract to such a man, she sought to increase the gifts of her soul, because she did not possess great looks ... and to conquer a beauty which does not decrease like the beauty of other women, and does not wane with the passing of time, which all things devours and kills."

On the other hand, Paolo Giovio, who knew Vittoria well, having stayed at Ischia with Costanza Francavilla and remaining a friend of Vittoria's all his life, describes her when she was forty (15 July 1530) and clearly still attractive. He loved Vittoria with "celestial, saintly and very platonic love", and admired "her round breasts as they softly and prettily move at the rhythm of her breathing" which "like doves, inflate at sweet intervals". At the time of her wedding, she was shy and pale but already proud of her education and lineage.

We know that Vittoria was portrayed by Michelangelo in his *Last Judgement*, as the Virgin Mary and St Anne, the head immediately above St Lawrence (both faces contain her features according to contemporaries). Because of Michelangelo's feelings for Vittoria (see Chapter Seven), we are convinced that she was the model for the former but, in either case, the idealized face of Vittoria is fine, with soft, round features and large eyes.

We also know that Vittoria was portrayed by Sebastiano del Piombo. The *Portrait of a Lady* in the Barcelona Museum may be that of Vittoria; in fact it is known that Vittoria's niece took to Spain a portrait of her famous aunt. The Barcelona painting is damaged and the writing on the book, to which the sitter is pointing, is no longer readable.

Vittoria's were more Colonna than Montefeltro features: an oval face, small, full lips, brown, serene eyes, long, strong hands. She had no overwhelmingly feminine looks. Vittoria attracted "platonic", "pure" love, rather than waves of sensual desire. One attribute which made Vittoria attractive was that her skin was not pock-marked like so many of the day. But although not beautiful like Lucrezia Borgia or Imperia, or pretty like Isabella Gonzaga or Tullia d'Aragona, Vittoria had the attraction of intelligence, the attribute which lights up faces and whose absence erases beauty. "She was a more withdrawn than a vain woman, more devout than sensual, and more contemplative than full of herself", wrote Alicarnasseo, her contemporary.

In 1511, the Viceroy of Naples, Don Ramon Cardona, Ferrante's uncle, was appointed to lead the papal army, and finally the impatient Ferrante was called to arms. When Ferrante marched with his troops through the north of Italy, Isabella of Mantua, surrounded by her ladies – famous for their beauty and fashionable clothes – rushed in three carts to watch him. Ferrante and his officers had some fine horses prepared for the ladies, but they preferred to ride in their heavy carts, which they did *"con molta festa e gloria"*, with much feasting and honour. Then the pretty ladies brought three mules loaded with delicious food which they gave to the captains. This glimpse of Isabella Gonzaga, riding with her damsels, meeting Ferrante for the first time, exchanging jokes and food, throws an unexpected light on warfare in the Renaissance. Both Fabrizio and Ferrante were fighting against France and its ally, the Duke of Ferrara, Isabella's brother. They were boisterous soldiers, not politicians, they did not care for the cause they fought for, they loved being on the front line, wearing their brilliant colours. Political thought was left to a more feminine mind, to women and, in some cases, to priests.

Vittoria and Ferrante spent the first three years of their marriage at the Villa Petralba – a subsequently demolished property of the d'Avalos – years which, in Vittoria's memory, were blissful, centred on her "sun" and the "sweet and youthful smile" of her husband, he who was "the brightest light that adorned and enriched an age". Their villa was built on the Sant'Ermo hill, then adorned by gardens that descended downhill towards Pizzofalcone. Vittoria was with the man she loved, facing a breathtaking panorama (hard to believe now, when Naples is suffocated by cement and fumes): the glittering gulf was framed by Vesuvius and, on the horizon, the islands of Capri, Procida and Ischia. Theirs soon became open house for the literary wits who lived in or came to Naples: the poet Jacopo Sannazzaro who had a house nearby at Mergellina, came often and he had a great influence on Vittoria's poetry; there was Benedetto Cariteo, also a poet, Bernardo Tasso and Antonio Minturno. The young Marchioness of Pescara acted as hostess; her parents visited her often; Fabrizio Colonna had been appointed High Constable of Naples and resided in the city. Vittoria came to know her two surviving brothers, Federico whom she loved best, and Ascanio, somewhat weak and greedy. But her husband, the twenty-year-old Ferrante, was interested in war and impatient with family life; he was ambitious, he wanted to be recognized and admired, like his father-in-law.

Finally, in 1503, the scandalous Pope Borgia died. The Marquess of Gonzaga wrote to his wife, Isabella: "His funeral was such a miserable thing that the wife of the lame dwarf of Mantua had a more honourable burial than this Pope." In 1498 Isabella Gonzaga wrote to Cecilia Gallerani, the Milanese beauty who had been the mistress of her sister's husband, Ludovico il Moro, Duke Sforza. Cecilia had been one of the great beauties of her age, she kept a literary "salon" and she had been painted by Leonardo da Vinci (*The Lady with the Ermine*, now in Cracow) in which we can admire her oval face and haughty and intelligent eyes. "Remembering that Leonardo had painted your portrait, we ask you if you would be good enough to send us your portrait by this messenger so that we may be able not only to compare the works of the two artists [Bellini and Leonardo] but also to have the pleasure to seeing your face again." Cecilia hesitated because Isabella was famously short of money and might have sold her portrait rather than return it to her. In fact Cecilia never sent it to Isabella.

The pope's children, Cesare and Lucrezia Borgia, fell from power overnight. The popes were soon to learn that they had to protect themselves by marrying their relatives off into mighty families, even royal houses. Pius III succeeded Borgia for a few months and then Alexander's arch-enemy, Cardinal della Rovere was elected Pope Julius II (1503–13). While the Borgias had conquered for themselves, Julius, the stern opponent of their regime, bestowed everything he won on the Church. But in spite of his motto "Away with the barbarians!" he, more than anybody, contributed to the turning of Italy into a Spanish province. It is possible that, as Cardinal della Rovere at Avignon, he had come to know the French too well and fear their expansionist policy: the greedy Valois wanted Naples and Milan and, if victorious, would have encircled the Church in French-held territory. But the otherwise perceptive, despotic pope misunderstood Spain. The old ally of France became its enemy and war was declared against Louis XII, the King of France, who claimed the duchy of Milan as his own inheritance.

So Vittoria Colonna's famous father left Naples to lead an army of papal troops and Swiss mercenaries. Fabrizio was in charge of 400 horsemen but, by fighting for the survival of the territorial power of the Church, the Colonnas were going against their Ghibelline grain, the Ghibellines being on the side of the empire.

The French and their Ferrarese ally were led by the dashing Gaston de Foix, Duke of Nemours. When, on the morning of 11 April, the two forces came face to face on the low plain near Ravenna, the battle continued for eleven hours. It ended in carnage: the French won overwhelmingly but lost their valiant commander. Vittoria Colonna's husband and father were taken prisoner – Ferrante had been wounded twice.

Vittoria remembered that day as one of her saddest. It was a rainy Easter day and she was at Ischia – she had been married only three years. She felt a strange premonition of disaster, so much so that she had talked about it to Costanza of Francavilla, who told her not to fret: the league's army was powerful. But when a messenger arrived with the news, Vittoria wrote a letter to her husband in the form of a poem – it is her first, or at least the first of her poems which has been recorded:–

> *You live cheerful, having no care;*
> *and in thinking of your newly-acquired fame,*
> *you don't grieve for depriving me of your love.*
> *While I, with angry and sad countenance,*
> *rest on your abandoned and solitary bed,*
> *feeding with hope my confused feelings,*
> *your joy only tempering my grief.*

She complained about the sadness of women's fortunes – waiting anxiously at home while their husbands were in peril. Her vision of conjugal life was unity, harmony – but it was frustrated unity, she wrote. And, in the first of her many laments, Vittoria talked with the voice of womanhood.

She was a woman tormented by love, who no longer loved Ischia – "the whole atmosphere appeared like a thick cloud, like a cavern of black fog, and the vegetation seemed stagnant, the sea looked like ink" – who reminded her husband that if he wanted victory (Vittoria) "in leaving me, lost her". She reproached him for deserting her and took the side of all women condemned to wait. She reminded him of her empty bed: was it not where he should be as her husband? Hers was a strong statement for a young woman to address to a husband who, she felt, was escaping her.

Both Fabrizio Colonna and Ferrante d'Avalos were taken as prisoners to Ferrara, where they were treated more like friendly princes than enemy prisoners. We have already seen how Fabrizio Colonna spent his time there and Ferrante too fell in love with a Ferrarese noblewoman; Vittoria's dashing husband began to be openly unfaithful to her. Ferrante's wounds, especially those on his face, began to heal and when Isabella Aragona Sforza, who was the guest of Lucrezia Borgia, saw him, she beagn to flirt with him. She told him, "I would like to be a man, my lord, merely in order to receive wounds on my face, like yours, to see whether the scar would suit my face as much as it suits yours." Having courted her in vain, Ferrante told Isabella that she was right to turn him down. He was a good captain, she answered, but he should concentrate on breaking city walls rather than bothering to break the hearts of mere women. "I want to be a cowardly soldier, milady," he answered, "if I am unable to conquer this place of yours by siege, because I would not try to destroy it." "What would the Lord Marquess say if I were to tell all this to his wife?" answered the duchess. "She would esteem me a good soldier", he answered back. Presumably the coquettish lady was captured and, after a while, Ferrante was ceded from Ferrara to the French who were asking 8,000 ducats for his ransom. So he was moved to French-occupied Milan, a great sophisticated city.

During his enforced idleness – being wounded he could not take any exercise – the Marquess of Pescara had to rest and answered his wife's letter with a long poem called "A Dialogue of Love". This was a rare occupation for Ferrante who was much more interested in arms than in literature; on the other hand it is not impossible that he should have commissioned the poem from a professional poet as was often the case. In the poem, which is now lost, he expressed his love for his young wife, his childhood companion. Happy to have received these reassuring words, Vittoria wrote back to him from Ischia sending him a present of an object representing Cupid entwined with a snake, made by herself.

But in Milan, Ferrante started another love affair with Delia, a lady-in-waiting to Duchess Isabella Sforza. Vittoria probably did not know about her husband's infidelities and would have not wanted to know. She was saddened, if not made desperate, by the fact that she seemed to be barren and yet she wanted an heir for the d'Avalos and a son for Ferrante and herself.

Negotiations for the ransom of the distinguished prisoner who, in Milan, was having a wonderful time, went on. By this stage a smaller sum was being asked, perhaps 4,000 ducats and Vittoria was short of money. She wrote to Federico Gonzaga reminding him of the 4,000 ducats that he owed her husband (8 May 1523): "I write to you and I beg you, send the payment; I have managed with great difficulty to delay the sale of a castle for 20 days." Vittoria finally found the money for her husband's ransom.

But Ferrante did not go back to Vittoria as soon as he was freed; he was having fun in the north, in the midst of the political scene. Although Vittoria did not discuss her private life either at this stage or later, she was not content to wait at home for her husband like other women, although she tried to be patient. The fact was that, although she loved Ferrante, he was not in love with her; he was fond of her, they had grown up together but he found her too serious, maybe not worldly enough, demure and introspective. Whenever "her husband was engaged in the Italian wars and upheavals, she was in Ischia and resided in Naples when he, and not rarely Alfonso del Vasto, was there" Alicarnasso related.

Alfonso del Vasto was Ferrante's young nephew and was living with Vittoria. His father, Inigo, Marquess of Vasto (Ferrante's eldest brother), had been murdered in 1503 and although the boy was obstinate and wild, Ferrante and Vittoria adopted him. Vittoria educated the child and, little by little, changed him; her influence on him was remarkable. She was to say that, in spite of the fact that she never had children, she generated Alfonso from her intellect – "... *sendo nato dal mio intelletto, costui*".

Although Vittoria felt less lonely with Alfonso, she was pining for the return of her husband and finally Ferrante came back. "My beloved returns home!" wrote Vittoria, "to make the day brilliant!" But he behaved atrociously, stealing a necklace from Vittoria and giving it to yet another beautiful Isabella, wife of the viceroy. Thinking that in "a century of gold, gold would dazzle everyone, while courting and talking to her lovingly", unseen by others, he let a jewel of pearls and other precious stones fall into Donna Isabella's lap. She said nothing to Ferrante but sent the precious object back to Vittoria, warning her that she should guard herself from domestic thieves. When Vittoria reproached her husband, saying, "I could well bear that you give away our belongings to satisfy your heart as long as your soul does not desert me", he laughed it off; he had become convinced that her studies had made her totally uninterested in precious objects, he told her. Ferrante went on courting Isabella and kissed her *ingannevolmente* – treacherously. At a dance he addressed a sonnet to her, in Spanish:–

> Mas fé y menor ventura
> La memoria es mi enemiga
> Ma solo en la memoria
> Quedará mi gloria.

> *More hope and less chance,*
> *Remembrance is my enemy*
> *But only the recollection*
> *Will fulfil all my glory.*

Once again the other Isabella, the Duchess of Milan, Isabella Aragona Sforza, possibly annoyed by the haste with which Ferrante switched sexual allegiances, noticed that a note had been handed by the marquess to the wife of the viceroy, and broke the object on which Ferrante had written the amorous rhymes. By then the wife of the viceroy had been conquered by Ferrante. A grieving Vittoria wrote of the "fraudulent and empty caresses of a magician Circe, of a witch Medea, of an enchantress Hecate". Besides, people had gossiped about another woman, a *dama*, who had been made pregnant by Ferrante and now Vittoria began to hear about his other infidelities.

The scene of all action was suddenly the north of Italy and Ferrante was soon back in Milan, on 7 October 1512. The following year Pope Julius died and Cardinal de' Medici succeeded him as Leo X; Isabella Gonzaga nicknamed him "Il Moccicone" – the sniveller.

In 1514, while Ferrante was away from Naples, the famous Isabella Gonzaga – forty and still handsome – came to Naples from Rome, where she had visited her son, who was a hostage of the pope, guaranteeing Mantua's support against the French. From Naples, in one of her many letters Isabella sent her son maternal kisses and cuddles. Although she was full of debts, Isabella bought many antiquities with borrowed money. The celebrated Isabella had just bought an "early case of art forgery", as Mary McCarthy puts it (in *The Stones of Florence*). The young Michelangelo had in fact sculpted a sleeping Cupid in the ancient manner and – on the advice of a dealer – had stained it with mud to make it appear an archaeo-

11. *Isabella d'Este* by Leonardo da Vinci

Isabella d'Este Gonzaga (1474–1539) was a typical product of the Ferrara ducal family Este. Her mother was the beautiful Leonora d'Aragona, of the Neapolitan royal family. When she married and left Ferrara for Mantua, Isabella arranged for a fine scholar to tutor her in classics (for three ducats a month). She brought the arts to Mantua, just as her sister Beatrice brought them to Milan.

logical find. The cardinal who bought it became aware of the fraud and sold it to Isabella "the greediest collector of her day". In Naples, Isabella Gonzaga was received with great splendour and met "everybody", including Vittoria Colonna: it was their first encounter. Vittoria was younger than the famous marchioness, and she was shy. Isabella was extrovert, bossy, sure of herself, Vittoria was an introvert, already a writer, but not yet famous while Isabella Gonzaga was a real star whose conversation is echoed by her entertaining and witty letters. Isabella had gone to Rome without her husband's consent: relations between the two were strained. But every cardinal in turn gave dinners, dances, and entertainments for her: Isabella was welcomed like a queen and she often found excuses to postpone her departure. In November, a play by Cardinal Bibbiena, *La Calandria*, was staged in her honour, and Isabella was rather taken aback at watching an immoral play in such surroundings. Because she was an efficient woman, she tried to talk politically to Leo, but she found the pope "selfish and unforthcoming".

There were talks of matrimonial prospects between the daughter of Isabella Aragona Sforza, Bona, who was in Naples, and Isabella Gonzaga's son, Federico, who was then only fourteen and, as we can see in Raphael's fresco in the Vatican, extremely good-looking. The Mantuan envoy had already warned Isabella Gonzaga that Bona was "a mature and ugly woman", in spite of the fact that she tried "every art to better her looks"; and Mantua's heir was spoiled by Isabella's damsels, who sent him sweet messages, kissing his "upper lip" or his "lower lip", and his "left hand" and his "right hand", and even more private parts.

When Ferrante d'Avalos returned to Naples in 1515, the political scene was once again in turmoil. In that year, Louis XII of France had died, Francis I, his successor, anxious to reverse the defeat of France dashed into Lombardy and conquered Milan. Leo X, the first of the Medici popes, came to an agreement with the new King Francis Valois. In that same year, Ferdinand the Catholic also died and his unloved grandchild, Charles of Ghent, inherited the crown of Aragon, with Sicily and Naples, as well as the regency of Castile and its American conquests: his "insane" mother, Joanna, was his nominal co-ruler. The union of Ferdinand and Isabella became thus embodied in one man, creating a single realm, although Castile and Aragon were formally united only in the eighteenth century. Charles was very young and nobody knew his character; the viceroy of Naples, judging the situation to be dangerous, kept the news of Ferdinand's death secret for five days and used Fabrizio Colonna and Ferrante d'Avalos to test the feelings of the Neapolitan aristocracy. After the two men reported back, Joanna was proclaimed queen and Charles, who was to become Charles I of Spain, became Charles IV of Naples, and – four years later – Charles V, the Holy Roman Emperor, her successor.

And now Ferrante was called to fight again, this time against a relative of his or, better, a relative of his wife Vittoria. Trying to secure a duchy, that of Urbino, for his nephew Lorenzo de' Medici, Leo X unleashed a new war against Francesco

Maria della Rovere who was Vittoria's nephew. Urbino was a vassal state of the Church and belonged to the son of Giovanna da Montefeltro, Agnes Colonna's sister. In 1517, after a peace treaty had been signed by Francis and Charles, the latter tried to pacify the Neapolitan aristocracy that had been dispossessed by the Spaniards: their confiscated properties were to be returned. This, the viceroy thought, would create havoc; so he sent Ferrante as his ambassador to Brussels to confer with the young new king. Vittoria was delighted: such an important diplomatic mission would give prestige to Ferrante and, at the same time, distract him from his Neapolitan infidelities. Ferrante was well received by Charles, who listened and agreed; his mission accomplished, Ferrante was in no hurry to leave the north of Europe, where he spent five months. Power was shifting away from the Italian states and Ferrante thought that he stood a good chance of advancement by staying close to the powerful new king to whom he hoped he might become indispensable. He hadn't understood the steely determination of Charles to rule independently, to keep away from papal intrigues and from Rome. Moreover Ferrante, being short of money, was hoping for a fief; Vittoria had brought no land, no castle. Her dowry had been a sum of money, her patrician name and also her intelligence.

While her husband was in Brussels, Vittoria once again waited at Ischia and, in February 1519, she organized the wedding of Costanza del Vasto, Alfonso's sister. She was married to Alfonso Piccolomini, Duke of Amalfi, who was as cruel as his wife was attractive and wise. The marriage took place at Ischia and the bride being an orphan, like her brother, the festivities were paid for by Vittoria who herself was always in the red. But Vittoria loved young Costanza who seemed to resemble her in spirit and who, besides the freshness of youth, was a real beauty. Later the new Duchess of Amalfi became a follower of the Reformation, and was called a heretic; her name and reputation were soiled. The echo of this might have reached England when John Webster chose *The Duchess of Malfi* for his bloody and magnificent tragedy, where women are the victims of men's brutality.

There was another wedding later that year: on 6 December, Vittoria had to be in Naples because the ugly but rich Bona Sforza, who had been turned down by Isabella Gonzaga for her son, was to be married to Sigismund, King of Poland, a widower. Bona did not want to leave the south of Italy, and her future letters from Poland describe her unhappiness in such a cold land. Eventually she returned home only to be buried in a magnificent mausoleum in Bari. Her wedding ceremony was sumptuous – after all, her Aragonese blood demanded a royal wedding.

"La Signora Vittoria, Marchesa di Pescara," a chronicler wrote, "arrived at Castel Capuano accompanied by six ladies-in-waiting dressed in azure damask, and attended by six grooms with cloaks in yellow satin. She mounted a black and white horse draped in crimson velvet trimmed in gold." On this occasion, for the first and last time, we see Vittoria in her role as one of the leaders of the

Neapolitan court, a striking woman to be admired. She herself wore a robe of brocaded crimson velvet with beaten gold on it, a crimson satin cap with a head-dress of wrought gold above it and, around her waist, a girdle also of beaten gold. After the religious ceremony was over, at six in the afternoon, she and the other guests sat down to dinner: the food and entertainment were lavish; the banquet was not over until five in the morning. A second and third day of banquets and musical entertainments followed: Naples was one of the most creative musical cities at the time. While the guests ate, the bride's trousseau was brought round the tables, article by article, to show off Bona's wealth – linen, dresses, caskets of gold and trays. Ferrante arrived on the third and last day of the celebrations; he did not even have the time to change and rode straight to Castel Capuano wearing his martial clothes, and was received by Bona's mother, Isabella of Aragon Sforza, that same woman he had courted in Milan, and who had reproached him for his scandalous infidelities. On the following day, he rode beside Bona, now Queen of Poland, to Manfredonia where, welcomed by the representatives of her husband, she set off towards Central Europe.

What the guests ate at this royal banquet is not related, but there are many details of how the Renaissance nobility entertained, what kind of music was played at their incredibly long and lavish banquets when ladies wore make-up (very white faces, red lips and cheeks, their eyebrows thinned down in the shape of a delicate arch, darkened with kohl, like their lashes) and their hair would have been elaborately dressed with jewels; throughout the banquet, their maids would have helped them to adjust their hair and complexions.

The wedding over, Vittoria's husband gone, a new group of people seem to have gathered around Vittoria who was presiding over her salon where poetry, Plato and spirituality were discussed. One of the guests who came more often and seemed to have been more than welcomed, was a nobleman, Galeazzo di Tarsi. Tarsi admired Sannazzaro, who by then lived a rather reclusive life but was to be seen in Vittoria's company. Vittoria, known for her intellect, sought after for her fine style of writing, inflamed the younger poet, who was thin and tall, delicate, possibly effeminate. All we know about this love is from Galeazzo's sonnets. Those who wrote about Vittoria Colonna in the seventeenth and nineteenth centuries refused to believe that she reciprocated his love. Her contemporaries just refer to Galeazzo's name but, from a modern viewpoint, it seems likely that Vittoria returned his love. She was a woman of the Renaissance, when adultery was common especially amongst the upper classes, and Galeazzo was a man with whom she could communicate and reason, with whom she had much in common and who admired her. Galeazzo was younger than she and this must have appealed to her frustrated maternal instincts. But he was not alone in his infatuation for Vittoria. Girolamo Britonio, a soldier in Ferrante's train, was also fascinated by Vittoria, and dedicated poems to her. He even dared to write to her (1519) praising her gifts.

12. *Scenes from the Life of Pope Sixtus, Silvio Piccolomini* by Pinturicchio
Emperor Frederick III married Eleanor of the Neapolitan Aragonese also
famously portrayed by Laurana. In this scene Pinturicchio paid attention to the
new fashion, rich damask shawls, tight waists and ethereal beauty.

Later that spring of 1519, maybe fearing that too much attention was directed to his wife, Ferrante took Vittoria to Rome, for a social trip. Of course the aristocratic couple was immediately invited to the court of the pope. Leo X, who squandered more money than can be imagined, and about whom Sannazzaro wrote the following epigram:—

Sacra sub extrema
si parte requiritis hora
cum Leo non potuit sumere:
vendiverat.

Would you, by chance, like to know
why Leo could not take
the sacraments in his last hour?
he had sold them.

Everybody wrote poetry, every cardinal was the patron of an "academy" of chosen people in whose society the fine authors of the past were much discussed. Vittoria took part in several such *accademie, cenacoli*; there were banquets dedicated to the discussion of Plato, where people like Giovio, Bembo and Michelangelo Buonarroti could be encountered. All this pleased Vittoria who, on the other hand, could not but observe the display of money, the absurd luxuries of the Roman courts and the lack of principles within the Church, where she would have expected to find most spirituality. She may have sulked inwardly but she had to appear by her husband's side, promoting his career and pleasing cardinals and princes.

↭ CHAPTER FIVE ↭

a Woman in a time of political turmoil

In Rome, Vittoria met prominent men whose friendship was to last throughout her life, men like Pietro Bembo and Jacopo Sadoleto (the former had been Lucrezia Borgia's lover; the latter had loved Imperia), both brilliant writers. She met the writer Baldassarre Castiglione who had worked for her uncle at Urbino; Gian Matteo Giberti, the young secretary of Cardinal de' Medici; fleetingly (on this occasion), Michelangelo and Ludovico Ariosto, the chief of contemporary poets.

She developed such a friendship with Castiglione that the eminent man asked Vittoria to advise him on the book he was writing. Actually, Castiglione had finished the book but was full of doubts and wanted Vittoria's enlightened opinion. Only a woman like her, a true intellect, the example of what the Renaissance man or woman should aspire, could give him an opinion on the text he had written, he thought. His book dealt with the Renaissance person, what he should be, how he should act, speak, conduct himself in his life avoiding vulgarity, being discreet and well read. Indeed, his *The Courtier* was going to be the most popular book written in the sixteenth century.

Encouraged by her, Castiglione sent Vittoria his manuscript, but after several months it was still in her hands. He wrote reminding her that he was leaving for Spain and would like his manuscript back. She answered that she wished to keep it a little longer:–

Excellent lord – I have not forgotten my promise to you. Indeed, I wish I had not remembered it so well, because my enjoyment of this beautiful book has been spoilt by the constant thought that I must return it without reading it through as often as I could have wished, in order to impress the contents upon my memory. You have done me ill service by asking for the return of your book, but as I am already in the middle of my second reading, I beg Your Excellency will allow me to finish it, and promise to return the manuscript to you directly I hear from your letter that you are leaving Rome ...

As I promised to give you my opinion, and do not care to tell you in complimentary language which you know better than I do, I will simply say the plain truth. I affirm with an oath that will prove its efficacy ... I have never seen, and never expect to see, another work in prose that is superior, or even equal to this. Besides, the new and

beautiful nature of the subject, the excellence of the style is such that, with rare sweet-
ness it leads up a pleasant and beautiful hillside, ever climbing, without making us
feel that we are no longer on the plains from which we started ... let us pass over the
marvellous subtleties, the profound thoughts that glitter like jewels set in a slender a
frame of gold as needs be to hold them together, without taking away the least part of
their lustre ... And what can I say about the perfection of the language, which truly
shows the advantage of not being restricted to the Tuscan way, but of being free to use
other words? ... But what pleases and gratifies me most of all are the praises – per-
haps deserved – which you give to the purity and virtues of women ... But your new
Italian has so rare a majesty that it does not yield in charm to any Latin prose.

20 September 1524

She admired Castiglione's use of the 'vulgaris', Italian, the dialect that everybody
was using in letters and speech. But we catch Vittoria misbehaving because, in
fact, she had transcribed parts of *The Courtier*, one of the most important books
written in the Renaissance, still in print today, and still read with great enjoyment.

Castiglione wrote again to Vittoria:-

Lately I have heard from a Neapolitan gentleman who is still in Spain, that several
chapters of the Cortegiano have been seen in Naples in the hands of persons who
boasted that they had received them from Your Excellency. This, I confess, annoyed me
considerably at the time.

So he decided to speed up the printing of his masterpiece and, although Castiglione loved Vittoria, he made her mishap public by printing a dedicatory "letter"
addressed to a Don Miguel as preface to his book:-

Since I came to Spain I have heard from Italy that the lady Vittoria Colonna,
marchesa di Pescara, to whom I had lent a copy of the book, had, contrary to her
promise, caused a considerable portion of its contents to be transcribed. This naturally
annoyed me, knowing that inconveniences often arise in such cases; but I trusted that
the wisdom and prudence of this lady, whose divine virtues I have always revered,
would suffice to avert any evil consequences that might result from my obedience to her
commands. But lately I have heard that certain fragments of the Cortegiano have
been seen in the hands of readers in Naples, and since people are always greedy for
any new thing, there seemed some danger that these portions of the book might be
printed. Filled with alarm at this danger, I determined to revise the manuscript in
the rare moments at my disposal and publish the book as soon as possible, counting it
a lesser evil for the work to appear with too few corrections from my pen than to be
badly mutilated by the hand of others.

Vittoria's uncharacteristic bad behaviour had a good outcome – that Castiglione, meticulous as he was, finally had to publish the manuscript which he had
kept, correcting and rewriting, for years. Castiglione's book was a watershed
because it demonstrated how many were eager to learn; *The Courtier* is not only
about behaviours and good manners, it's not just a how-to book, a genre that was

to flourish (to the present time). It is a manual which teaches that real pleasures come from the soul. In Italian *anima*, the word for soul, derives from the Latin *anemos* (wind). Castiglione and Vittoria followed Aristotle in believing that the soul is life to the body and to the *psyche* (breath, in Greek).

But Rome was beginning to lose that elegance of the spirit that had marked the first phase of the Renaissance and the Church, which had once given Rome prominence, was plunging the city into universal contempt. The cardinal's hat to which everybody – not only the d'Avalos – aspired in order to enrich a family, to build a seat of power, of clients, was badly misused. Cardinals, then numbered around thirty, did not necessarily take holy orders; in public ceremonials they ranked with dukes and were preceded only by the pope and kings. Most of them had one or more episcopal courts of law under their jurisdiction, and the richest held feudal estates. They lived in princely fashion: their money deriving from their episcopal courts (to which they paid scant visits, unless they were in disgrace), and from simony. The cardinals' entourages of "familiars" usually numbered about 300 – armed gentlemen, secretaries, cooks, and stable boys. The richest cardinals also kept personal musicians, buffoons, poets, painters and dwarfs, just as dukes and princes did, or even more so. The secretary of Isabella Gonzaga was so struck by the luxury into which cardinals had sunk that he wrote to the marquess, her husband: "Cardinal Riario gave us a dinner so extraordinarily sumptuous that it might well have sufficed for all the queens in the world." And the Venetian ambassador describing Cardinal Cornaro's banquet said that sixty-five courses had been served:–

> *Scarcely had we finished one delicacy than a fresh plate was set before us, and yet everything was served on the finest of silver of which his eminence has an abundant supply. At the end of the meal we rose from the table not only gorged with rich food but deafened by the continual concert carried on inside and outside the hall and proceeding from all instruments that Rome could produce – fifes, harpsichords and four-stringed lutes as well as the voices of a choir.*

Princes and cardinals gave lavish banquets for Vittoria Colonna d'Avalos the Marchioness of Pescara, who had become the centre of conversation. She was enjoying great personal success and sometimes she would be asked to recite her poetry, which she did.

While Vittoria stayed on in Rome, Ferrante journeyed to the coronation of Charles V at Aix-la-Chapelle, and then accompanied the emperor on his visit to Henry VIII of England, where Charles paid homage to his aunt, Catherine of Aragon – and to Cardinal Wolsey. Catherine's marriage was going to have such influence on the history of both England and Rome, and indeed on the life of Vittoria for one, that it will be useful to dwell on the reasons that made this likeable and mistreated princess a pawn in current events.

The daughter of the Spanish monarchs, Catherine was quite a catch for England. After lengthy negotiations, Henry VII, a king who sat rather precariously on the English throne, secured her for his eldest son, Arthur, Prince of Wales. With the demure and shy Spanish princess, Henry not only consolidated the Tudor dynasty, but also kept France at bay. When, on 4 November 1501, the Spanish princess arrived in England, people lined the streets to catch a glimpse of the regal and horrendously devout princess and laughed at the oddity of her retinue's costumes. According to Spanish custom Catherine was veiled and nobody was able to see her face. Henry VII was worried: was she deformed? Scarred by smallpox? With a rude gesture, he pulled her veil off, revealing an extremely pretty face.

Arthur and Catherine, who conversed in Latin, seemed to get on, and they danced and laughed until, on 14 November, they were married with such pomp that the ceremony astonished even the Florentine ambassadors. After the ceremony, the young couple were undressed by their attendants and left together, naked in their regal bed. Six months later, Arthur was dead and Catherine, aged sixteen, a widow. It was then decided that the infanta should marry Henry VII's second son, the red-haired future Henry VIII, in spite of the fact that he was five-and-a-half years younger than Catherine, and her brother-in-law.

"I was a true maid without touch of man." The Spanish princess insisted that, at the time, she was still a virgin. At her coronation in 1509, when she was newly married to Henry VIII, she dressed in white. She maintained that Arthur had never ravished her; even later, when her royal husband, enamoured with Anne Boleyn, wanted to divorce her, Catherine never wavered. Although her nephew, Charles V, hardly knew her, he respected his close relative, the wife of a fellow monarch and a wise woman. We know nothing of their meeting in England; Charles who, beside his lands, had also inherited many disputes and wars with France, sought for an alliance with England. From 1519 to 1559, the Habsburg–Valois wars dominated Europe.

Europe's powers needed skilled diplomats; whenever Ferrante was not fighting, he was sent on diplomatic missions. Vittoria never saw him. Not that Ferrante was either diplomatic or skilled but he had become close to the emperor and was with him in 1520, the year of his coronation. That was the year in which Vittoria's father died. At this stage, Leo X, no longer on the side of the French, allied himself with the emperor. In 1521, Prospero Colonna and Ferrante d'Avalos were made joint commanders-in-chief of the imperial and papal armies. And it was time for Vittoria and Ferrante's adopted son, Alfonso del Vasto, to start on his military career. His father was in two minds: Alfonso was the only male heir of the house, but Vittoria appealed to him, "Take the young man with you! If he dies by misfortune, it will be a lesser evil than that the glory of your ancestors might be stained by the cowardice of its descendants." She presented Alfonso with a richly ornamented tent, decorated with dates – symbolizing growth – and a motto in Latin, which she herself had embroidered.

But embroidery was hardly Vittoria's concern; at that moment she was with-drawing within her own brand of religion, the kind of spirituality she was developing drove her to pray on her own and to form doubts on the kind of reli-giosity she had witnessed in Rome, at the papal court or during the superb religious rites she attended in Naples in the church of Santa Chiara where, on her way out, she would then see the destitute, the leper, the wretched. Now, as if God wanted to punish her, she received news that Ferrante had fallen ill, his health had never been good since he had been wounded and she worried about him. Even so once again he was on the battlefield where he beat the French and, in November 1521, conquered Milan. Later that year, in December, the pope's death was cheered as though it was a happy event. On 17 August, accompanied by Gian Matteo Giberti, the new pope, Adrian VI, arrived from Spain. A wise, conciliatory man, he was the last non-Italian pope until Cardinal Carol Woytila was elected in 1978, 455 years later. The new pope was from Utrecht and had been Charles V's tutor; his Erasmian origins were calculated to establish a peace-ful cohabitation amongst the various religious tendencies and quarrels. Besides, Charles saw in Adrian the man who could overturn the corruption of the curia.

Ferrante d'Avalos and Prospero Colonna welcomed the new pope and asked him to give them absolution since they had incurred public censure. The pope refused to do so. In spite of the riches which came from the New World, Charles's many wars had bankrupted him and the badly paid imperial army had started ravaging Lombardy. Ferrante dashed back to Rome and to Vittoria whose mother had died at the age of fifty, following a pilgrimage to the Holy Mother of Loreto. "Even behind her severe looks a bright light hid", she wrote in a somewhat unin-spired sonnet dedicated to Agnes. Ferrante stayed at Vittoria's side for her mother's funeral at Albano and then, once again, left her alone.

In 1523, after a brief pontificate, the austere Adrian died. Most thought that he had been poisoned, which is quite possible since it was a popular method of changing the power structure, and not only in the Renaissance. Moreover, Adrian had been determined to pursue an independent policy and had angered the curia by being incorruptible. He had been Charles's choice, his candidate, determined to change the ways of the Church but on 19 November, another Medici was pro-claimed pope with the name of Clement VII, and then Charles V understood that not even the might of the empire could bend the corruption that had cracked the keys of St Peter.

Two days after Clement's election, anxious to keep on good terms with the new pope, Vittoria wrote to her friend Gian Matteo Giberti a high official in the papal office. "Tonight I heard the hoped-for news that His Eminence Your Cardi-nal has been elected pope." In a convoluted and formal manner, she asked him to kiss His Holiness's feet on her behalf. A month later, she wrote again, this time addressing herself directly to the pope. Ferrante was in Lombardy; she, alone, spent the winter at Arpino, a d'Avalos fief, but a very small fief. By springtime

1524, she had moved to Marino, the Colonna castle where she had been born, staying with her brother.

Giberti sent her some madrigals written by Pietro Aretino, one of which praised Giberti; the others extolled Vittoria. "Our Messer Aretino showed me well how to achieve two great successes: to lift the level of his verse so much that his mind could sing your value and without lowering it give mine a little nobility, without taking any worthy praise to the first Madrigal" (26 May 1524). Giberti, a skilled politician and, by then, a very powerful man, held Vittoria in such confidence that he wrote to her disclosing the papal policy and this gives us an idea of the esteem in which Vittoria was kept, if politicians like him would discuss their actions with her in writing.

The new pope began to look on the imperial presence in Italy with suspicion; he preferred the lesser evil of the French and once again the papacy switched sides. But to go against Charles V was a great mistake, his power was too great. Feeling strong, Francis I himself descended upon Italy and put Pavia under siege. On 24 February, the two armies clashed: the imperial army with Ferrante broke through the French cavalry; the French king, his horse killed, went on fighting desperately. "All is lost except honour", the French king was to write to his mother in one of the most quoted sentences ever. Francis Valois was taken prisoner; 10,000 soldiers died. Letters from the pope were found in the French camp and the angry emperor realized the extent to which Clement had been in league with the French and determined to punish the traitor. In the meantime, taking advantage of the great confusion, de Lannoy, one of the Spanish commanders, took away with him the greatest prize, the royal French prisoner, and sailed off to Spain.

Ferrante, bleeding from three wounds, had given Charles V a vital victory. Angered to see his prisoner – an immensely prestigious catch – taken away from him, he wrote to the emperor (12 May 1524), "I was greatly amazed by the fact that the viceroy did not inform me." But Charles suspected Ferrante and was on Lannoy's side. On 26 May, the emperor, maybe wanting to show his gratitude, but not directly to Ferrante, addressed a letter to Vittoria, from Madrid:–

Very serene and dear relative.
When We received the news of the great and memorable victory, which Great God gave Us against the French in Lombardy, the sound of your name is to be added to the many other things pleasing to Us ... since you come from a root and belong to a family that to Us and to Our ancestors in all times rendered uncommon services; and you are united to a husband to whose valour and experience in matters of war, and to his happy way of managing them, We owe in great part the overmentioned victory ...

The emperor called her "relative" and he mentioned her family, not Ferrante's.

Vittoria, who hoped for the reward that Ferrante longed for – a wealthy fiefdom with a grand title or a cardinal's hat for Alfonso – wrote back to the emperor, a letter that was a work of sublime diplomacy. In fine style she asked his most powerful majesty to reward her husband: "I do not know what is to be most valued, either to receive the prize from you, such a great Prince, or the glory of one who says he is indebted to us." In fact, Charles had richly rewarded Lannoy but not Ferrante, who had enormous debts. Constable Bourbon warned Ferrante and the emperor: "In Rome, as elsewhere, they are beginning to plot."

Ferrante's rage at the poor reward he had received in exchange for the victory that had cost him his health was well known: Girolamo Morone, Chancellor of Milan, approached Ferrante to win him over – the Italian barons and the pope feared Charles V. Gian Matteo Giberti, Vittoria's friend, was in charge of the secret negotiations. The plotters, headed by the pope, the Venetians, and Morone, thought that the moment had come to get rid of the Spaniards: the imperial army, without pay or food, was oppressing the population; the north of Italy was sacked and ravaged every day; the populace was likely to revolt against the Spanish yoke.

Morone offered Ferrante the crown of Naples in exchange for the command of the Italian forces that would oppose the imperial army. Trembling at such a thought, in one of her many letters to Ferrante, Vittoria wrote:–

> Titles and kingdoms do not add to true honour without virtue and without principle, which alone enable a name to reach posterity untarnished. I do not desire to be the wife of a king, but I am proud of being the wife of the great captain who helped the greatest of kings with his bravery at war, and even more showing magnanimity in peace.

But few of her letters have reached us, only those which were intercepted by imperial spies.

Even if his contemporaries suspected that Ferrante was tempted by Morone's offers, he informed Bourbon of the plot. On 30 July, Ferrante wrote to Charles: "I don't like these practices. But since necessity dictates it and this case requires it, I rejoice in serving Your Majesty, certainly not without shame, because I well see that I sin against somebody in order not to sin against the one to whom I am most indebted."

Ferrante did not feel indebted to Charles, but feared the emperor and also hoped for the long-awaited reward. Besides he had listened to Vittoria's advice. Ferrante also warned Charles of the imperial army's unpopularity in Italy. "There is nobody here that does not fear Your Majesty's greatness, nobody who does not abhor the weight of his army." The dukes of Ferrara and Milan were against the emperor, he reported; likewise Genoa, Florence, Mantua, Lucca and Siena. "You have no friends and only a few servants who are tired and discouraged."

On 22 October in Novara, weak, "tired and discouraged", Ferrante called for Chancellor Morone who came to his tent and from whom he once again extracted every detail of the plot. When Morone left, he was arrested. Ferrante gave immediate orders to secure the imperial hold on the rebel cities; with his infantry and horsemen he occupied Milan. Venice, the *Serenissima*, informed its ambassador in

London (4 November): "*Il marchese di Pescara* left Pavia and reached Milan on the evening with 200 lancers and a large quantity of horsemen, 3,000 soldiers, and 18 cannons. At once he went for the duke [Sforza], advising him that he had come to occupy the city and the castle in the name of the Emperor." The Sforzas' brutal and beautiful castle – one of Leonardo's first achievements, built in the middle of Milan, a walled-in fortress with moats and sixty-two drawbridges, 1,800 machines of war, 1,000 mercenaries in times of peace, and four times that number in times of war – surrendered. By moving so swiftly, Ferrante had secured Italy for Spain.

Vittoria, at Marino, followed her husband's victories and wrote letters to the pope, whose hopes to redress the balance of power were now shattered, and to Giberti, Clement's agent in the alliance against Charles. She ignored the fact that she stood on opposing ground to them. Morone signed a confession; on 26 November 1525, Ferrante wrote to the emperor begging him to spare Morone's life and ordered that the chancellor's possessions should not be confiscated. But Ferrante had been so weakened by his wounds that, feeling the end was near, he sent a messenger to Vittoria, asking her to join him. She hastened northwards, but the news of her husband's death reached her just north of Rome, in the papal city of Viterbo.

He was thirty-six. Immediately, gossip spread: Ferrante had been poisoned, maybe by order of the pope but it is unlikely; by that stage Ferrante was weakend by his wounds and was ill. But even Ferrante's contemporary biographer mentions poison. Ferrante left all his wealth to Vittoria and their adopted son, Alfonso del Vasto who, with the emperor's consent, inherited the title of Marquess of Pescara. After a grand funeral in Milan, Ferrante's body was sent to Naples, but the monument for which Ariosto had written an epitaph was never built. His body is still in a casket, in the sacristy of San Domenico Maggiore in Naples, waiting to be sent to Spain for burial, a torn flag and a sword (the one he took from the King of France, at the battle of Pavia) still hangs from the dusty casket.

"If ever a desperate person lived in torment and pain draped in black sorrow, in a black cloak, that is I who live only by tears," lamented Vittoria. She returned to Rome, distraught, and joined the convent of San Silvestro in Capite, a church closely linked to the Colonna family. The pope, by now the enemy of the imperial forces, weak and undecided, helpless and isolated, was no friend of any Colonna. In a letter (7 December 1525), he forbade the nuns of San Silvestro, on pain of excommunication, to permit Vittoria to take the vows – her sorrow might have made Vittoria take too swift a decision. The real truth was that Clement did not want Vittoria around.

At the same time, Ascanio Colonna advised his sister to leave her convent, and to leave Rome, at once. So she fled to Marino, where the Colonnas, in league with the emperor, were preparing an attack against papal Rome. That was Charles's revenge against Clement's plotting. On 20 September 1526, Pompeo Colonna (a cardinal) put the Vatican under siege with an 800-strong cavalry and 3,000 soldiers, calling themselves the liberators from the tyranny of the pope. As the Vatican was sacked, the Roman populace, and even the papal militia, soon joined in; Clement took refuge at Castel Sant'Angelo. Soldiers looted the palace, the sacristy and the church.

Vittoria grieved. Life had become insufferable without her husband. She wrote: "That I may always think of him, or weep, or speak of him!" As the Colonnas became the worst enemies of the papacy, again she moved southwards to Aquino, then to Naples, and then, as Naples was once again threatened by the French, to her *"caro scoglio"* at Ischia.

In April 1527, a naval battle in the Bay of Salerno broke out between the Spanish and the Genoese fleet. Vittoria's only remaining brother Ascanio and Alfonso del Vasto were taken prisoner by the Genoese. Vittoria sent her brother medicines and money, and to Giberti she wrote interceding, begging. But how could she pacify two fiercely opposed factions – the papacy and the Colonnas? And she wrote a great many sonnets, describing herself as a lonely woman, a melancholy bird. Ischia became "a horrid and solitary rock" where she hid herself from those she loved and from herself as well. She would never see her husband ever again; at least when she had been left alone she knew he was alive, she knew he would come back to her. Finally the pope signed a peace treaty with the emperor, but it was too late.

In the spring of 1527, the imperial troops mutinied. They ravaged every territory they passed. Twelve thousand hungry Lutheran *Landsknechts*, without pay, joined them, and both descended upon Rome, which was the seat of that pope who had betrayed their master. To many Lutherans, Clement was the Antichrist; they burnt his effigy and declared Luther the real pope. George von Frundsberg from Tyrol, their commander, said, "The pope is the emperor's worst enemy and had begun the war. For the honour of God he must be hanged." Certainly Charles intended to punish the pope by turning a blind eye to his army's actions, but he miscalculated the mood of his unpaid hordes. On 7 May, 40,000 mutinous men forced an entry into Rome and, for eight days, massacred, plundered, tortured.

The assault on Rome started in the morning, from the heights behind St Peter's. A dense mist, almost a fog, enveloped the city. The Spaniards and the Lutheran free-lancers advanced, hidden by an opaque light. The imperial army was under the command of Constable Bourbon, who died in the first assault. They started by attacking the clergy and Church property; when they had finished, they went on to loot private houses and kill common people. Women suffered most because almost all were raped. The historian Guicciardini suggested that the Spaniards were the cruellest and greediest; but there were Italians, too, in the mutinying imperial army. The most violent period of the sack took place from 6–14 May, continuing for another month.

All the hatred of Europe against the Church exploded: friars and priests were beheaded, "many young nuns were raped and taken prisoners". St Peter's was turned into a stable. "All sins were committed in Rome", a contemporary wrote, "sodomy, simony, idolatry, hypocrisy, fraud. Surely what happened has not been by chance, but by the judgement of God." In the hot mid-June, the imperials left the capital as the plague exploded, lasting until the autumn, when the troops came back to Rome for the winter. During this time, property suffered; entire libraries, furniture and valuable objects were burnt to keep the army warm.

When the Medici pope, wearing the clothes of his major-domo, made his escape to Orvieto, he was reached by an embassy from England; the pope's authority was needed for Henry VIII's divorce from Catherine of Aragon. But Catherine was Charles V's aunt and Clement could only make vague promises; he would have liked to befriend Henry of England but he was a virtual prisoner of the emperor.

Then the plague took yet another vengeance on the capital: another 20–25,000 people died; two-thirds of the city was left in ruins. The sack of Rome was seen as the end of a great age: the time of the arts, of beauty, of the Renaissance, was no more. The previously happy-go-lucky Sadoleto, who witnessed the sack, wrote, "If, through our suffering, a satisfaction is made to the wrath of God, if these fearful punishments open the way to better laws and morals, then our misfortune is not the greatest ... before us lies a life of reformation ..."

Vittoria Colonna, distraught, was at Ischia with Costanza and her brother's daughter, called Vittoria after her. Dressed in black, her head covered with a veil, she fasted; she was in no mood to see anybody. There was another reason for Vittoria's despair: as mentioned earlier, her brother and adopted son had been taken prisoner by the Genoese. She wrote to Andrea Doria, the Genoese commander, asking him not to give in to French demands, but to keep her relatives as his own prisoners in Genoa. She was writing feverishly, making politics, begging, travelling.

She wrote and wrote, to quench her despair, as she herself said; she still mourned Ferrante, but also lamented the fate of Rome, of Christianity, of the role played by her house; she grieved, bewailing her sad fate. "I write in order to give vent to my extreme sorrow." Why would not death come to her? For the first time Vittoria, such a religious soul, even thought about killing herself. Whether she knew it or whether she ignored it, a new chapter was to open, a new pope was going to change her life and the Renaissance was closing its doors on Rome.

Tullia and her mother had also arrived in Rome some time in February 1527: they were escaping from Siena, upon where the imperial army had recently descended, looting and causing famine. The two women did not imagine that they were leaving the First Circle of hell for the very Pit. They witnessed the sack of Rome and saw the soldiers loot house after house, torturing people until they confessed where they had hidden their gold, plundering private houses, from the richest to the poorest. Giulia lost what she had slowly accumulated: all the money and jewels that she had brought with her from Siena, hoping to secure her treasure were stolen. Who could ever have imagined that the mutinous forces would dare to break into the sacred city, and that the emperor would let them sack Rome? There was no way and nowhere that mother and daughter could escape rape, theft and humiliation. If Giulia had dreamt of saving her Tullia (then about seventeen) from treading her own miserable path, now that the two women had lost everything there was no alternative.

The sack of Rome marked lives, especially those who were physically and spiritually weak, and those belonged to women, of course.

~❦ CHAPTER SIX ❦~

Vittoria, giulia and tullia (1527–38)

Despite Vittoria's state of despair, she was still capable of rational thought and determined to use it for good works, to help others. But how? Now even the Mediterranean was dangerous, not only because the Ottomans dared to raid the Italian coasts, but because the French, helped by the Genoese, were threatening Naples, and even Ischia, Vittoria's "beloved rock". "Of all the nobles of this kingdom ..." wrote Gregorio Rosso, a contemporary, "some went to Salerno, some to Ischia, in the household of the Marchese del Vasto, his beautiful wife, Donna Maria d'Aragona, and the learned Marchioness of Pescara, Vittoria Colonna, and the Duchess of Amalfi and the Princess of Salerno, Lucrezia Scaglione, beautiful and 'fast'."

Lucrezia Scaglione, the wife of Paolo Carafa and the mistress of the Viceroy of Naples, was indeed fast; Charles V said "although she was not born a titled lady, among all those dames she was famous and celebrated and treated herself as if titled, courageous, of excellent conversation and beautiful!" Vittoria Colonna wrote an epigram about her but none of her epigrams have survived.

After so many tragedies (the mutineering armies had sacked half of Italy as well as Rome), after the realization that the Italians had lost their status and independence, many felt disgust for the past, for their carefree way of life, their lack of spiritual direction. Friends rallied together. Vittoria received a letter from Castiglione who forgave her indiscretion with his manuscript. After all, so much had happened, they were all miserable victims of events:–

> *I have not dared to write to Your Excellency for a very long time, feeling that what I said could only give you the keenest pain. Now that such crushing calamities have overwhelmed us, and we are all in misery, I feel that it is our right, and perhaps our duty, to forget the past and open our eyes to spiritual things. At least we may try and rise out of the mist of human ignorance to the furthest point of which our imbecility is capable, and recognize that we know nothing.*

Vittoria wrote to Castiglione twice. In her second letter, she asked him to forgive her; his worry that she might be angry with him was unreasonable. It was he who should be offended with her.

Vittoria mentioned Giovio, from whom she had commissioned a biography of her husband, which he had just had completed. He sent it to her with a long letter written in Latin: "If there is something, Vittoria Colonna, that is the foremost wish of your very honest life ..." it was that the memory of her husband should never die. He ends in fine style: "Being an excellent woman of virile mind who, besides the flow of prose, competes with the best poets in writing verses ...", stressing the "virility", that is, the masculine strength of Vittoria's intelligence. In the new mood of the times, Vittoria's honesty was extolled: many contemporaries praised it in verses, from Giano Anysio to Luigi Tansillo in "Apologia pro mulieribus". She became a symbol of the new intellectual woman, no longer just a prominent aristocrat but a serious thinker.

She was a woman alone, now, with the responsibility of an adult son and little money to keep her small retinue. But her loneliness was dispelled by close friendships which she made with the women of Naples most of whom seemed to be looking for a spiritual leader. The wave of repentance had followed the time of overstated enjoyment and a real backlash was reaching everyone, Vittoria included.

Protestantism had become a source of political trouble and it was well known that the emperor was concerned by the threat of schism. Outside Italy, 10,000 sheets were being printed every day of a book which bore the title *The New Testament in German, at Wittemberg* (*Das Newe Testament Deutzch, Vuittemberg*). Martin Luther had translated the Bible into the language of his countrymen, and 3,000 copies appeared in September 1522. In eleven years, fifty-eight editions were published; in spite of decrees, which ordered copies of the book to be burnt in a number of German towns, the Bible became vastly popular. The revolutionary element was the translation in the vernacular; this meant that the voice of God was now available to all, not through the interpretation of the clergy, and not on specific days and in specific places, but by anybody, and at no cost. It was soon to appear in French and Italian.

Even if hostile to the Lutheran revolt, Charles V wished to see the Church of Rome reform itself and since the Turks were threatening Europe and the empire, Charles resuscitated the old concept of the crusades – this time as a mechanism of defence rather than aggression – turning his attention to the might of Suleiman. Charles, whose empire had come to him through dynastic accident, thought of himself as the head of a united Christendom; if the pope did not see eye to eye with the emperor over his role, the emperor would make him, by force. Clement concluded a peace treaty with the emperor and he had to grant an official pardon to the Colonnas.

This meant that Vittoria could return to Rome. In 1530, we find both her and Tullia in Rome. In spite of the sack, the capital was still a rich ground for a courtesan because it was inhabited by men on their own – clergymen, travellers, pilgrims and ambassadors. Tullia's mother had initiated her daughter ("because of

La piu bella e piu fauorita donna del gran Turcho dita la Rosa

In Venetia per Mathio Pagan in Fre zaria non per insegna la Fede[...]

13. La Sultana Rossa, Roxelana

This Circassian woman, who was a mere concubine in Suleiman's seraglio, won his attention and became his favourite wife. She prompted her royal husband to have his eldest son executed so that their son could inherit the crown, inducing the female poet Nisai to write: "O king of noble blood is this justice?". As a political woman, she corresponded with other rulers in the West. (Anonymous woodcut published by Mathio Pagani, Venice, c. 1550)

14. Suleiman the Magnificent

Suleiman was born in Trebizond. He captured Rhodes and, in 1525, responded to the appeal of Francis Valois. From a prison in Pavia – the King of the French had been captured by Vittoria Colonna's husband – Francis suggested that Suleiman attack the Habsburgs. The siege of Vienna in 1529 gave Europe a frisson of fear. (Anonymous woodcut published by Mathio Pagani, Venice, c. 1550) need", as Tullia was to say later) and set her up in splendour, not as a courtesan *"della candela"*, but in a palace, with six servants.

Vittoria's gloom was lifted by seeing her Roman friends and also making new ones, like Reginald Pole, the English bishop of royal descent, and Juan Valdés, the bearded reformer who had arrived from Spain. Jacopo Sadoleto, who, twenty years earlier, had loved Imperia to distraction, had changed into a grave man, but regretted the time of the *accademie*, of gaiety, of pagan aesthetics, of humanism: "Oh, when I think back to those days gone by, when so many of us gathered together", he wrote in a nostalgic mood to a friend, "and how often I remember those suppers … when we held meetings with so many brilliant friends … And how, after our banquets, more spiced with wit than gluttony, we used to recite poetry and make speeches …" All that had evaporated in the new mood, after the sack. It was as if the Italian Renaissance had been punished for being innovative, searching, and lay.

Anachronistically, Tullia tried to recapture those days by establishing a salon where there was dancing and singing alongside debates on Plato and Petrarch. To dispel the gloomy times music was much in vogue, with the *frottola*, a song which could be sung by one voice alone, and also the madrigal, another form of secular music. Tullia, dressed in her rich clothes, would entertain her guests with such music after a meal, helped by her servants. We may note here that in spite of the fact that both Tullia and Vittoria had servants, neither possessed slaves, although the Portuguese had been selling them to rich Romans for the last sixty years. Pope Innocent VII had received a gift of 100 Moorish slaves and had distributed them as gifts but the Church disapproved of this commerce in human flesh. In Venice, it was considered elegant to have a Moor, possibly a child, as a page, and many courtesans liked to be escorted by a Negress whose dark skin would offset the fairness of their own.

Wealthy people who had to keep up appearances had quite a sizeable staff. When travelling, Vittoria had to "borrow" or employ six or seven soldiers. A court, on the other hand, kept large numbers. At Urbino there was a staff of 355 people, including forty-five counts of the duchy, seventeen lesser noblemen and gentlemen, five secretaries, twenty-two pages, nineteen grooms of the chamber, nineteen waiters at the table, twenty-one footmen, five cooks, fifty stable boys under five masters, and 125 lackeys. The duchess (this was at the time when Urbino was ruled by Vittoria's uncle) had seven ladies-in-waiting. A court of this kind also offered many temporary jobs – Mantua employed 800 people. There was the category of the "familiars": *familiari*, those servants who were close to the intimate moments of their employers, such as footmen, pages, liveried helpers. The lowest of all categories were the runners: *galoppini*, men whose job was to run around with daily commissions. Clothes were still magnificent and the colours and designs emulated the rich textiles worn by the Byzantines. Clothes also described the social stratum of the wearer.

While Vittoria now shunned fine clothes, Tullia spent time and money buying brocades and raised velvet printed with motifs of gold; merchants and traders would call at her house, carrying fine cloths from the East, and they would show them to the enchanted courtesan, surrounded by her servants, her mother and her friends. Tullia also bought incense to burn in the house, extract of roses from Persia and semi-precious stones such as turquoise to sew on her bodice. The traders also offered silk ribbons of delicate colours, which her maids would intertwine among the locks of their mistress's celebrated hair.

The Renaissance invented fashion; that is, clothes which shaped the body and attracted attention to it, in contrast to the flowing robes of medieval times. Unlike today when everybody wants to conform and buy the same clothes, women then sought for individuality. Even tights had a different colour for each leg! A dress revealed the culture, the status, and the personality of the wearer. Materials were opulent: silk damasks, velvets and brocades, embroidered with gold and silver threads. On the other hand, being so rare and expensive, the fabrics revealed the social strata of their wearers at a glance. There was an immense difference in appearance between paupers and the rich: even shoes gave away those who walked on the muddy streets of cities. Somebody like Tullia would wear silk shoes, usually embroidered and sometimes bejewelled, often on very high heels or, rather, "platforms". Her dresses would have full skirts with high waists, and puffed sleeves. Necklines were low – chaste women would cover them with silk scarves – and bodices very tight. Clothes were particularly refined in Florence.

According to Mary McCarthy and others: "The Florentines in fact invented the Renaissance which is the same as saying that they invented the modern world – not of course an unmixed good." A rich Florentine, Filippo Strozzi, a Renaissance dandy, arrived in Rome and was admired for his original interpretation of fashion, for his gaiety and wit. Strozzi, a nobleman and a musical scholar, who was married to Clarice de' Medici, was in Rome on a secret political mission. He was hoping to gather help and fight the imperial army and the Medici rule. Florence had rebelled against the rule of the Medici but had been recaptured with the help of the Medici pope and of the imperial army.

In his youth, a republican, a free spirit, Strozzi had been an enthusiastic frequenter of many Florentine courtesans and, on this visit to Rome, he met Tullia and soon moved into her house. While he wrote, Tullia would play for him and, since she was an accomplished writer, she also helped him with his letters; he shared confidential matters of diplomacy with her. But Tullia frequented many powerful people who would have liked to know what the Florentines were up to. "Why do you write to me with Tullia next to you?" a letter from Florence addressed to Strozzi read, and, "I don't want you to read my letters when she is around. Loving her as you do – because of her spirit (since her beauty is not great enough to justify it) – I don't want you to put me in a position in which she can harm my reputation with those I write about." Indeed, Tullia chatted a great deal in her amusing salon, so much so that gossip about her had reached Florence. Or was she also a part-time spy, as courtesans often were? It is possible, as we shall see later.

She was becoming the toast of Rome, mainly because she was reviving those happy days which, outside her drawing-rooms, had otherwise disappeared. Young men, younger than Tullia – "those beardless men" – seemed to be particularly attracted to her salon with its atmosphere, partly sensuous and partly intellectual.

Indeed, six of them, hearing that "their" Tullia had been slandered by a group of aristocratic youngsters signed a long and slightly sarcastic document asserting that "The Most Illustrious Signora Tullia" was full of virtues and was "the best woman of the present, past, and future times". If they were to hear anything to the contrary, they were ready to fight for her and they challenged "any envious tongue" to a duel. There were many such tongues and, more than envious, they were prim. The new mood was reformist, religious, and sombre, and there was hardly any room for a courtesan who talked about Petrarch. Filippo Strozzi was one of the signatories of the gallant declaration in Tullia's defence. She was such an accomplished musician! Together they would sing, and music was a strong bond between them.

A further letter from Florence, written in the same hand as the one asking him to read his letters in private, warned Strozzi that to fight duels for such a woman as Tullia was not worthy of him: "Settle your affairs soon and come back." And so he did. One can only wonder if Tullia then missed Strozzi. He was rich, elegant and witty, but Tullia had trained herself not to fall in love with anybody.

Another rich young man spent a great deal of money on her. "Tullia played with him unmercifully and never gave herself to him making him suffer a thousand trials." What was it that captivated so many? She looked graceful and danced beautifully. She played hard to get and it was difficult to gain admission to her salon; a man needed a special introduction, and even then it was not certain that Tullia would be willing to sleep with him, although she accepted presents. Tullia, "monster, miracle, sibyl", in spite of being a courtesan, was aloof.

But with the renewed religious fervour, superstition was growing fierce. Tullia's detractors spread the story that she used magic formulas to bewitch so many so totally. A monk described in detail how Tullia, dressed in black, a vermilion ribbon round her forehead, would wash her hands thrice in pure water and then, throwing salt on the fire, would repeat some magic formulas. Novellas which attacked her began to circulate. "By selling herself to men and masquerading under false pretences of literary gifts and intellectual interests, Tullia attracted and seduced not only the young", wrote Giovan Battista Giraldi, "but also learned men of mature age". Austere intellectuals were made to dance the pavan just to amuse her, and, even after that, she would refuse them her body! he added. But Ippolito de' Medici, young and very handsome, thought otherwise:–

Se'l dolce folgorar dei bei crin d'oro
e'l fiammeggiar dei begli occhi lucenti
e'l far dolce acquetar per l'aria i venti
co'l riso ond'io m'incendio e mi scoloro ...

If the sweet blazing of her fine golden hair
and the flaming of her fine glittering eyes
and her sweet silencing breezes in the air
with her laughter which makes me burn and pale ...

Ippolito de Medici was expected to marry the young Isabella Colonna, step-daughter of Giulia Gonzaga. He was a dashing young man with thin moustache and a carefully trimmed beard, who loved dressing up in different styles and had himself portrayed by Titian as a Hungarian captain, in lush red velvet and a plumed hat, and, as Vasari noted, "in a second portrait, wearing armour".

A musician, a poet, a womanizer, he was the grandchild of Leo X and the cousin of Clement VII being the illegitimate son of Giuliano de' Medici, Duke of Nemours. Both popes loved him: Leo had himself portrayed with Ippolito as a child by Raphael. Clement made him cardinal in 1529 and, soon after, vice-chancellor of the Church, adding that he was doing so "judging that he soon will quieten down and acquire a gravity of soul", a piece of papal wishful thinking. When Ippolito met Giulia Gonzaga, the young relative of Vittoria who might have become his stepmother-in-law, he fell in love with her. It was not the same kind of sensual love that attracted him to Tullia, profane love; it was spiritual love, real, deep, all-embracing love. But Giulia was somewhat frightened by men and at this time she left her marvellous castle of Fondi, a medieval structure on a peak, protecting a lovely village, to be with Vittoria in Naples.

Vittoria was desperately searching for peace, which she sought in Ischia and then travelling to Naples, to Rome, to Aquino, to Orvieto, where she stayed at a convent for a few months. Always on the move, she became very close to Giulia Gonzaga, a relative through Giulia's first husband. Giulia, who was born in 1513, was twenty-three years younger than Vittoria. She had married Vespasiano Colonna, Count of Fondi, Duke of Traetto, when she was only fourteen, and was left a widow at the age of eighteen. She lived at Fondi, a lovely and rich town situated between the frontiers of the pontifical estate and the kingdom of Naples, where the best *mozzarella di bufala* comes from, and there she received the most celebrated poets and writers. In fact, she kept the same company as Vittoria, but, unlike Vittoria, she was unbelievably beautiful. Her looks were celebrated by Ariosto in *Orlando Furioso*:—

... ecco chi a quante oggi ne sono, toglie,
E a quante o greche o barbare o latine
Ne furon mai, di quai la fama s'oda,
Di grazia e di beltá la prima loda;
Giulia Gonzaga, che dovunque il piede

Volge e dovunque i sereni occhi gira,
Non pur ogn'altra di beltá le cede,
Ma, come scesa dal ciel, Dea l'ammira.

There is the woman who, for grace and beauty, erases all others of the present and of the past, Greeks, Barbarians, Latins whose fame had reached us; no other woman in beauty surpasses Giulia Gonzaga who, wherever she goes and wherever her serene eyes look, is admired by the goddess, Venus, descended from heaven.

(*Orlando Furioso*, C XLVI)

Ippolito de' Medici asked Sebastiano del Piombo, Michelangelo's best pupil, to portray his beloved. The painter wrote (8 June 1532): "I think I'll leave tomorrow from Rome in order to go to Fondi to portray a lady, and I think I'll stay fifteen days." He finished the painting within a month, "which as it came from the celestial beauty of that lady, from such a skilled hand, was a divine picture", Vasari commented. After Ippolito's death, this portrait was given to Catherine de' Medici, Ippolito's cousin who had loved him. Although there existed many portraits of Giulia, they have suffered the same fate as Vittoria's; towards the end of her life, Giulia Gonzaga was considered even more heretical than her distant relation and friend, and many of her portraits were burnt.

In Vittoria, Giulia saw a spiritual guide and a source of authority; together they discussed religion and reform, an all-embracing issue. Both were mystics; together they would go to listen to Juan Valdés's sermons in one of Naples's main churches, or on the seafront at the Riviera di Chiaia where the reformist friar lived, and they would then ask him questions. By 1533, Juan Valdés was established at Naples, where he made over 3,000 converts. Valdés, a follower of Erasmus, preached against corruption and simony; but he condemned Luther for his separation from the Church of Rome. Valdés wanted to reform mankind, not ecclesiastical life, and denounced a form of religion based on observing the outward rituals. Like his twin brother Alfonso, Juan Valdés was a humanist and his followers were consequently amazed when the wrath of the Spanish Inquisition began to fall on them. His brother, who was secretary to Charles V until his death in 1532, tried to shelter Juan from the Dominicans and the Inquisition, which in Spain (though not yet in Italy) had reached the peak of cruel obscurantism. But when he was to be tried by the Spanish Inquisition (he was probably condemned for heresy *in absentia*), Juan Valdés fled to Rome, where he was welcomed by the pope and by his then secretary Pietro Carnesecchi. Then the friar went to Naples, where he assembled around him the most devout and intellectual group of reformists. For a time, moderate reformers such as Valdés met with no serious opposition in Italy. But ideas travelled; the commercial links between Germany and Venice meant that Luther's ideas spread like fire; and Lutheranism, being a less aggressive heresy than Calvin's, was more attractive and hence potentially more dangerous. The University of Padua became a centre for reformist missionaries and the duchy of Ferrara, as we saw earlier, a haven for Protestants.

Naples, too, was a similar shelter, in spite of the fact that the ultra-reactionary and powerful Carafa family was Neapolitan and, of course, in spite of the dominant Spanish hand which pressed for the introduction of the Inquisition.

In Naples, Valdés preached and discussed important matters with a group of learned ladies: besides Vittoria and Giulia, the Duchess of Amalfi, Princess Caterina Cybo, and even the sister of the Grand Inquisitor of Spain, Alfonso Manriquez de Lara. It was a moment ripe for mysticism: the Ottomans were threatening Europe, the sack of Rome could not be forgotten, the pope had lost England and the independence of Italy.

This was also a time of revival of the religious orders: some took monastic vows but joined no house, like the Theatines founded in 1524 under the patronage of Bishop Gian Piero Carafa, a "hawk". Others, like Contarini and Pole, were the "doves", conciliatory in mood towards the Reformists. But all knew that the dishonesty within the papal curia, the sale of benefices, corruption of monastic orders, dispensations granted for money, sale of licences – simony, in short – had to come to an end. On the other hand, as long as the Basilica of St Peter was under construction, there was no other means of collecting the massive amount of money required.

It was the need for a spiritual religion rather than the dissatisfaction with the Roman Church that inspired Vittoria and her clan to follow Valdés and then Ochino. One day, Giulia Gonzaga had gone to listen to the friar and then had walked away from the church with Juan Valdés, to whom she talked about her feelings. It was Valdés himself who transcribed their dialogue:–

> Giulia: *Inside myself I feel a battle. Friar Ochino's words fill me with awe for hell. Ochino gives me a yearning for Paradise, but at the same time I feel love for the world. How can I evade this conflict? By compromising with both tendencies or by erasing one of them?*
>
> Valdés: *This anxiety is a sign that God is returning to you. My only fear is that you are seeking to regulate your Christian life so that those who are around you are not aware of the change in you. You have to choose between God and the world. Love God above all else and your neighbour like yourself.*
>
> Giulia: *But I've always heard that only holy vows lead to spiritual perfection.*
>
> Valdés: *Let them talk. Monks are perfect Christians only if they love God.*

Not all clerics loved God, Valdés seemed to be telling Giulia. And salvation, he added, sprang from faith, from the word of God: the scriptures.

Vittoria, too, felt a great need to return to the source, to the lost purity of religion. As she wrote in one sonnet, she believed she had been "informed" by the very word of God, by scripture:–

> Me reformó la Man che formó il Cielo
> E si pietosa al mio prego offerse

15. *Giulia Gonzaga*, copy from Sebastiano del Piombo
Sebastiano painted Giulia in the summer of 1532, commissioned by Ippolito de'
Medici, Giulia's lover. Known as one of the most beautiful women of her time,
Giulia courted the Reform and was condemned by the Inquisition. At Ippolito's
death the painting was sent to his cousin Catherine, Queen of France, who had
always loved him.

Che ancor lieto ne trema ardendo il core!

The Hand which formed the Heaven reformed me
And so pitifully responded to my prayers
That joyfully my heart, glowing, trembles.

From then onwards, Vittoria's "sun"; who had been her husband or maybe what she had imagined him to be, gave way to a deep religious vein.

While these women, almost all of them widows, gathered round Valdés and Ochino, Tullia was doing so well in Rome that she bought herself a property in the Campagna Romana, the dream of every courtesan. She did not care about religious problems: Tullia had shared her bed with too many clerics not to feel a total contempt for the Church; her consolation was her ephemeral success in music and poetry – in which she wanted to excel. In this way she kept her integrity and independence, and she did not fall for any of those young men who adored her so.

The young Cardinal de' Medici had disappeared from Tullia's circle: whenever he could, he rushed to Fondi to see Giulia Gonzaga. In order to understand how deep his love for her was, Ippolito translated the second book of the *Aeneid* and sent it to her with a loving dedication; because his heart was on fire, like Troy, he, Ippolito, had worked on that text. If his sighs and tears had not yet succeeded in moving Giulia, perhaps Virgil could, on Ippolito's behalf. And perhaps by reading Virgil's description of Troy burning she might understand his pleading heart.

Ippolito de' Medici was not the only man who loved Giulia. Rich and famous for her beauty, her hand was sought by many. But her matrimonial experience with a man over forty and *infirmus claudius ac mancus* – weak, limp and without a hand – made her reluctant to risk any physical involvement with men. Although it was murmured (and written) that, when Vespasiano died, his wife was still a virgin, it was clearly not so. Giulia's disgust for any physical contact with men, even with a young man as dashing and enamoured as Ippolito, may be explained by the fact that at the age of fourteen she had been ravished by a man twenty-six years her senior. Luckily, Vespasiano was almost always away at war; luckily, he was too ill to make too many demands on her; and, even more luckily, he died four years after their marriage.

Giulia felt guilty for her relief at her husband's death; he left her with a step-daughter (the girl Ippolito was supposed to marry), a large property at Fondi and several other fiefs, a great deal of money and the title of Duchess of Traetto, although, like most women of her rank and time, Giulia was always known by her maiden name. As often as he could Ippolito would ride southwards to Fondi, where he would stay for two or three weeks at a time. Giulia and Ippolito would walk together and talk; both loved music and poetry. Ippolito would never find her alone: she was surrounded by a court of writers and poets of whom she was beginning to tire. Giulia and Ippolito became lovers.

Her beauty was too famous. Khair-ed-Din Barbarossa, the Turkish admiral, had established himself on the northern coast of Africa and had conquered Tunis in 1534 in the name of his master, Suleiman. On 8 August of that year, Barbarossa and his pirates landed at Sperlonga and, at night, climbed to Fondi. Barbarossa wanted to deliver the most famous of all Christian beauties to his sultan as the best flower of his harem. Swiftly and silently, Barbarossa encircled Giulia's castle with 2,000 men; "flying, one could say, they arrived there and broke her door", wrote Giovio. They took Fondi so much by surprise that Giulia just had time to flee, "half naked", as the bishop tells us. On her horse, "having glimpsed her enemies", she fled to the mountains. Furious at not finding the beauty in her bedroom, Barbarossa and his men looked for her everywhere in the neighbourhood. Just outside Fondi there was a convent of twenty nuns, where the pirate, confident of finding Giulia, led his men. But when the infidels found no trace of Giulia Gonzaga, they questioned the nuns, who were so frightened as "to lose their breath" and were unable to speak in order to answer any of the questions. They were all raped and then killed. The Saracens looted, destroyed a great funeral monument in the cathedral next to Giulia's castle, and many inhabitants were taken away to be sold as slaves. While this familiar but gruesome scene was taking place, Giulia was still riding through the night, across the wild, hilly terrain, towards Campodimele, another of her fiefs, where she arrived at dawn, looking like a pagan nymph, her hair in disarray, a few clothes hiding her young body.

The pope received the news with horror and ordered that his army should leave at once and attack Barbarossa. Ippolito, who had listened to the messengers describing his lover's adventure, begged the pope to put him in command of the armed squad. But when Ippolito and his men arrived at Fondi, Barbarossa and his men had moved elsewhere. Formally, Ippolito handed the keys of the town back to Giulia: how wonderful it was for him to face her wearing full armour. She recounted to him what had happened and thought about her adventure with awe at having averted being raped a second time. Like a Mozartian heroine, she had narrowly escaped being abducted to Suleiman the Great's seraglio. It was an adventure everybody gossiped about, and which inspired Ludovico Ariosto and Bernardo Tasso in their poetry. To be locked up in a seraglio would have been death to a cultivated soul like Giulia's. She was one of those women sought after not only for her beauty, but for her scholarship and conversation.

Giulia's adventure became legendary but the story that the duchess had had a young page killed because he had seen her naked was apocryphal. One poet who told the story in a long eulogy ended by addressing her directly: "Why do you want to spend your youth perpetually as a widow, alone and without pleasure? Listen to my reasoning"; she was – he added – like a wild vine which would entwine the elm. And that elm, whom the pope affectionately called "mad devil", was still hoping.

Ippolito had gathered around him a noisy, amusing circle of Roman youths; he loved games and the theatre – he had many talents, but none for spiritual devotion. Giovio informs us that Ippolito kept "an infinite number of fine dogs and expensive horses" and often, when hunting with his friends, would have a table laid out in the middle of a wood near a spring of fresh water, where a lavish meal would be offered to all. Although he was rich, he often ran into debt. "He loved the extravagance of having in his court barbarians of more than twenty languages. Among these were Moors from Barbary born from the blood of lords ..." and even Tartars and Indian Moors and Turks, "wondrous at managing arms in hunting so that in daytime and at night he had them all to guard his person ..." His cousin the pope disapproved of Ippolito's exhibitionist show of worldly pleasures and thought of sending him to Hungary (for this reason, Ippolito had himself portrayed by Titian in the costume of a Hungarian captain); but Cardinal Ercole Gonzaga thought that it would be foolish to send Ippolito "to the discipline of the emperor which is grave and serious". Ippolito toyed with politics, but like his cousin, was indecisive and prone to change sides. At one moment he acted for the republican Florentine rebels who tried to get rid of Alessandro de' Medici, Ippolito's despotic cousin. But at a certain moment he decided to keep out of the whole messy and dangerous situation, and took holy orders. Giulia would never have consented to marry him and he could have enjoyed her love in any case. In fact, the Medicean pope had insisted on making Ippolito a cardinal. Clement now concentrated his attention on the last Medici, the pale and rather plain twelve-year-old Caterina de' Medici; indeed many thought that Ippolito had been made a cardinal because he was a serious suitor for Caterina, who was destined for higher things. Ippolito, Alessandro and Caterina de' Medici had grown up together and she had always loved her elegant cousin since her tender years. But the pope wanted to strengthen the Medician house by arranging a marriage with a son of the house of France. Alessandro was to marry Charles V's natural daughter. In exchange for Ippolito's agreeing to accept the cardinal's hat, Clement VII settled all Ippolito's debts, "which are of great sum". And Ippolito promised never to meet Filippo Strozzi again; the two had been seeing each other, laughing, whoring, and plotting.

In the hot summer of 1535, Ippolito de' Medici arrived at Fondi; he was joining Charles V in Tunis for the "crusade" against Barbarossa. He stayed a few days with Giulia and then proceeded towards Itri, another of her fiefs. On 2 August he was seized with a high fever, and on the following day, as his pains grew worse, he sent a messenger to Giulia, begging her to come to his bedside as he feared he would die without seeing her once again. She rode from Fondi, on the old Appian Way, up the mountains of Itri. And on the 10 August, towards midday, according to Giovio who was with him, "this talented young man of nobility, of learned intellect, of beauty of face and splendid with an illustrious life" died; but "death

16. *Ippolito de' Medici in Hungarian Costume* by Titian
Ippolito loved dressing up in different styles. Musician, poet, womanizer, the
grandchild of Leo X and the cousin of Clement VII, Ippolito was an illegitimate
son of Giuliano, Duke of Nemours.

was less harsh because he was near Donna Giulia who was with him extremely and virtuously courteous". Although Giulia was Ippolito's lover, she still seemed distant from the attractive man who had loved her so.

We don't know what Tullia felt when she heard of Ippolito's death; she probably did not grieve about her clients because she did not allow herself to love them, but Ippolito was special, young and handsome, gifted as a poet, boisterous and elegant, a true son of the Renaissance. Because she had been so exclusive and then had accepted the German in her bed for a week, Tullia was disliked by those who had not been welcomed to her salon. Moreover, the atmosphere in Rome was becoming oppressive and no longer so welcoming to courtesans. Tullia decided to leave Rome and covered up her flight by saying that she was going to visit Bologna. She had another reason for leaving Rome: she was pregnant by whom we don't know and probably she didn't know either. Instead of going to Bologna, she went with her mother to Adria, where Penelope was born. In order to save appearances, the little girl was passed off as her sister and given the surname of d'Aragona, in spite of the fact that Cardinal Luigi d'Aragona had died sixteen years earlier. This, of course, caused further ridicule and attacks on Tullia's snobbery. When the child was a few months old and the situation seemed calmer, Tullia had to resume her profession: she could not afford to retire.

She moved to Venice, a city where the influence of the Church was relatively slight, and rented a palace, which Tullia decorated with Flemish tapestries, and leather worked with gold. She bought Turkish carpets for the floors and Bokhara rugs to cover the tables; the furniture was inlaid or carved, and precious bibelots – Faience dishes, Venetian crystal, silver vases – made the rooms look like those of a patrician. The Venetians had invented a new object, the mirror. The novelty was the use of mercury which made the reflection so much sharper to the consternation of those who – like Tullia – could now detect the first lines disfiguring her alabaster complexion. There were paintings and armour, finely bound books, and on the tables, beautifully arranged, her musical instruments, including the lute (whose sound was considered to be aphrodisiac) and mandolin. Outside every window that overlooked the Grand Canal she arranged vases of flowers and plants, and also cages of birds. In the hall there was an elaborate majolica cage of monkeys and other cages with parrots. Tullia had good wines and rare foods: Venetian cuisine was celebrated for sophisticated recipes imported from Byzantium. At any time, Tullia was able to improvise a rich meal for an important guest and his retinue.

However, Tullia could not entertain in the same manner as dukes and princes, with tables with three tiers decorated with statues made of coloured sugar – "painted so that they looked real". In one such banquet, for example, forty-eight chandeliers had been hung from the ceiling and 104 napkins folded in different shapes (as the Chinese still do for special banquets). Knives were laid, but forks, which were rare and sophisticated objects, were brought by the guests or, rather, by the minority who chose to use them. Next to each napkin there was an assortment of different kinds of bread, and flowers made of gold and scented silks. Each guest's hands were washed with scented water. The first course of dishes was vast. There were different salads, with radishes and large lemons, anchovies, red radish sculpted in the shape of human figures or animals, ham, tongue (with a sauce of sugar and cinnamon), meatballs made of boar – which was common at the time – and fried fish with bay leaves. Some dishes were served in individual *piattelli*, one for each guest, others in twenty-five larger dishes. This must have been a kind of *hors d'oeuvre*, because the second round was called *vivanda* and consisted of larger, more important dishes, such as sugared capons, quails, different sorts of liver, pheasants roasted with oranges, onion pies, trout, and eel cooked in almond pastry, among other things. Music was the most important ingredient. So, while the guests helped themselves, Madonna Dalida, accompanied by four voices, sang songs written by Alfonso della Viuola. Then came the turn of a male voice, with five other male singers. There was also an orchestra of five viols, one lute, a clavichord with two registers, one large and one medium flute. A course of ten different dishes was then served, on twenty-five plates (fried brains, sweetbreads cooked with sugar and cinnamon, capons in the German style, with sweet wine, carp, rake, large shrimps fried with vinegar). While this *vivanda* was consumed, four "very fine" voices sang madrigals.

Venice was the very heart of good cooking and Catherine, future Queen of France, was to take some of the best Venetian chefs with her to Fontainbleau, thus starting off the greatness of French cuisine; in turn the sophistication of Venetian recipes came from refined Byzantium. It was – and is – an amazingly beautiful city, born out of the sea, from the foam, like Venus, but born for commerce not love: "The Venetians were not sentimental, they were efficient" writes Mary McCarthy in *Venice Observed*. "… At the age of twenty-five a young aristocrat was introduced into the maze of duties and ceremonies … Dress was prescribed for the nobility, though some of its members were very impoverished; beggars dressed in silk – the compulsory material for nobles – were a common sight in Venice."

In the freer atmosphere of Venice, Tullia became well known, but not popular. There were too many rivals. Her intellectualism irritated some and attracted others. It pleased the mature Bernardo Tasso, the father of the more celebrated poet, Torquato. Bernardo himself was not only a skilled poet, but also a good negotiator employed for diplomatic missions and delicate affairs. He fell in love with Tullia and she used him: as she was losing her youth, she needed a famous writer to extol her gifts – and also to help correct her own poetry. The best advertisement for herself came at the moment when it was really needed: a "dialogue", a form of journalism much in vogue at the time, written by a humanist who taught at Padua, in which Tullia and Bernardo were described while discussing the essence of love. These dialogues always featured real characters who were seen

17. *Santa Cecilia e santi* by Raphael

Raphael underlined the mathematical and philosophical nature of Music, depicting her beside Pythagoras, together with the great philosophers in his School of Athens (stanze della Segnatura). He also made a point of dividing instruments into "sacred" and "profane" in his *Santa Cecilia* (1515). While some musical instruments are ready to be played for the saint's nuptials, at her feet lie the flute, the triangolo and a viola da gamba, symbols of earthy vanitas.

talking in formal language about fashionable subjects, such as profane or spiritual love, relationships between men and women, and aesthetics.

In Tullia's dialogue she is often portrayed in the role of a superior lady. While for Bernardo Tasso love is "nothing else but the desire for something that exists or seems to be desirable to the beholder", for Tullia it must be a mixture of physical passion and intellectual communion. Later on she comes down to earth: "I know what I am and I know what I ought to be to become worthy of you. But I will change my way of life and be the woman I would like to be, or die in the attempt." A third voice gave Tullia consolation by saying that "it is natural for a woman to lead the life of a courtesan, and those who do not, disobey the laws of Nature." Even God was on the side of the courtesans. That stirred Tullia into protesting: "If you knew the servility, the vileness, the sadness and inconstancy of such a life, you would blame anyone … who says that it is a good thing and makes amends for it." So Tullia was prepared to tell how awful it was to pretend love and desire, to be a prostitute even if the noun of courtesan made it more palatable. It was humiliating, sad and she knew that her path could not change. At least she was able to write. Indeed Tullia's poetry was also praised in this text; she would be remembered by future generations.

Needless to say, the pretentiousness of Tullia's role in this text irritated not only the other Venetian courtesans but also those who had not been captivated by her. Pietro Aretino made it his business to spread about Venice all the gossip that Rome knew well (the equivalent of Il Pasquino in Venice was Il Gobbo – the hunchback – a statue near the Rialto); to praise a woman like Tullia, Aretino said, was to offend all virtuous Venetians. She wanted to appear like a princess, a muse, a nymph, while she was nothing but a hypocrite. In another dialogue, called *The Reasoning of Zoppino*, a daughter asked her mother why some who had come to Venice had not enjoyed the success that they expected. To which the mother answered crudely that men loved "a bottom, breasts, and a body that is firm and soft, from fifteen to sixteen years old, and not over twenty, and did not affect Petrarchian rubbish." The printed insults became the talk of the town. Venice was also the city where Veronica Franco lived; not only a famous courtesan but a fine poet, Veronica had been "visited" by the French king and an English duke – both got their Terza Rima in exchange for their aristocratic attentions. In fact, Venice appreciated those courtesans who could sing and write poetry, it could be said that the city not only was proud of them but traded on them since *La Serenissima* taxed these women very heavily. But times were changing, even in Venice.

Because the top courtesans were close to affairs of state, ambassadors reported on their movements: where they went, how many servants followed them, how many pieces of luggage they carried when they entered a city with their cavalcades of liveried gentlemen, how much money they had. This was due not only to an acute love of gossip (there were no newspapers), but also to the fact that the courtesans were regarded as potential spies. For example, did Tullia use the

18. *Tullia d'Aragona* (*A Young Woman with the Holy Lamb*)
by Alessandro Bonvicino, il Moretto

In trying to conform, Tullia d'Aragona became a loser; but she shone for her appetite for life, for never giving up when surrounded by unrelenting personal attacks, and, in her moment of passionate despair, she produced poetry which has given her a place in the history of literature: no good anthology of Italian poetry fails to include some of her love sonnets.

information she had extracted from Filippo Strozzi's letters? The anonymous correspondent, who, as we saw, was writing to Strozzi in Rome, seemed to suspect Tullia of spying for the imperials against the rebels. Strozzi, who was married to Clarice de' Medici, had now fled from Florence and was also in Venice; he could no longer bear the cruel rule of Alessandro de' Medici, whom he had helped to bring to power; indeed, he was organizing an army to fight Alessandro, his depraved relative who was eventually assassinated by Lorenzaccio de' Medici, the subject of a play by Alfred De Musset, "Lorenzaccio".

Although often one against the other for obvious commercial rivalry, the Venetians had asked the Florentines to come and teach them; in that the Medici were wonderful, old Cosimo, Lorenzo the Magnificent and, even more so, his son Piero encouraged "their" painters to go and spread the Florentine word: they were not jealous of the people they had themselves nurtured, often at their own expense. From Giotto to Sansovino, Venice was amazingly enriched by Florence. The Florentines brought painting, sculpture and architecture to Venice – in effect they brought the Renaissance. In Venice those forms merged with the Byzantine inheritance and Arab culture. But Venice kept the flame burning because, as the Venetians themselves said, their republic remained the only corner of Italy free from Spain, and that's why Spain and the Holy See hated it so and always tried to destroy *La Serenissima*.

It was through Venice that the new method of painting in oil spread to the rest of Italy, probably through Van Eyk and then Antonello da Messina. With Giovanni Bellini and his pupils, Giorgione and Titian, the Venetian school became sublime. Venetian women spread on those magnificent canvases, more sensuous than their Florentine counterparts, their blonde hair entwined with pearls whether they represented Venice, the Virgin Mary, a courtesan or a peasant girl. In Veronese's frescos at Maser, the lady of the house is watching us from the cornice of a door, a woman who talks to us within her domestic world.

On the other hand when Veronese was called by the Inquisition to justify his vast depiction of *The Last Supper* (now called *The Banquet in the House of Levi*) he had to answer impossible questions. Why were there dwarfs, buffoons and dogs, German warriors and other mundane things at a meal where the Lord was also depicted?

For example, one of the questions to Veronese was:–

"Do you not know that in Germany and in other places infected with heresy it is customary with various pictures full of scurrilousness and similar inventions to mock, vituperate, and scorn the things of the Holy Catholic Church in order to teach bad doctrines to foolish and ignorant people?"

"Yes, that is wrong but I am obliged to return to what I have said, that I am obliged to follow what my superiors have done."

"What have your superiors done? Have they perhaps done similar things?"

"Michelangelo in Rome, in the Pontifical Chapel painted Our Lord Jesus Christ, His Mother, St John, St Peter and the Heavenly Host. These are all represented in the nude – even the Virgin Mary – and in different poses and with little reverence."

Veronese's painting was as lay as the meals of Roman cardinals. And the Inquisition might have wanted to tame Venice itself rather than Veronese, since the republic was eternally disobedient to the Holy Father's command. They were also suspected of Calvinism. "*Cosa vuol dire calvinista? Siamo cristiani quanto il Papa e cristiani moriremo a dispetto di chi non lo vorria.*" (Calvinist, what does that mean? We are just as good Christians as the Pope and Christian we shall die whether they like it or not.) Thus Leonardo Donato, a trader, rebuffed the charge of heresy that had been put upon *La Serenissima*.

Another ferocious attack was directed against Tullia. The *Tariff of the Whores in Venice* consisted of a dialogue between a foreigner and a native who knew that city of women; they gossiped about the qualities of the several courtesans: Tullia, the Venetian said, "was the most abject of whores" – and that was the most offensive definition for somebody who had striven to appear a poet and a courtesan at the same time. Tullia was humiliated; luckily she had Bernardo Tasso to defend her with his pen. But the publication of the dialogue between Tasso and Tullia had been motivated by the fact that the lovers were parting; the poet was going south as secretary to the Prince of Salerno. When Tasso left in 1537, Tullia lost an important supporter, but a poor one (and she was very interested in money). Deprived of her prime literary defender, Tullia decided to leave once again; Ferrara,where we met her first, a rich, liberal court, was a natural choice.

Tasso went to Salerno, where he saw Vittoria Colonna and, in Fondi, he was a guest of Giulia Gonzaga. And he, too, fell for her. Giulia's mouth, "has more beauty and colour than pearls and rubies", her cheek was "a crimson pomegranate scattered on the top of a tiny hill of white, freshly fallen snow". And her hair!

> Il biondo, crespo, inanellato crine
> che con soavi errori ondeggia intorno
> mosso dall'aure fresche e peregrine
> né d'altro mai che di sé stesso adorno …

> *Her fair, curly, undulating hair*
> *which waves with fetching disorder*
> *moved by the fresh wandering breezes*
> *never adorned by anything but itself …*

In 1535 Filippo Strozzi had fought with the Florentine rebels and been taken prisoner. Tasso was now sent on to Spain, to try to negotiate his release. Cosimo de' Medici, the grandson of Caterina Sforza, succeeded Alessandro de' Medici. He was the son of a mercenary leader, Giovanni delle Bande Nere, Caterina's third husband and her real love, but was not part of the original line that could be traced to Cosimo de' Medici il Vecchio. In the opposite camp, the imperial forces were led by Alfonso, Vittoria's son, who treated his prisoners well. He refused Cosimo de' Medici's request to hand over the Florentine rebels, saying that he did not want to deliver men to see them tortured and hanged. In fact, Alfonso gave his prisoners their liberty and helped them financially if they had to pay ransoms. Filippo Strozzi was tortured but, a prisoner of the imperial forces, was not executed. The once happy, rich, elegant Florentine was waiting in prison, but Tasso was unsuccessful in his efforts to have the man released. Vittoria Colonna wrote to Alfonso, who had become captain-general of the imperial forces in Italy (11 September 1537):–

> *Once Filippo Strozzi lent me a certain amount of money; although I gave it back to him at once, I still feel obliged to him. I would be grateful if, still serving His Majesty and honouring Your Lordship, he could be helped …*

But her plea did not save Filippo Strozzi who, the following year, was found in a pool of his own blood. He had committed suicide. Those who visit St Maria Novella in Florence can admire his tomb, one of the finest and most elegant of Renaissance times, watched over by Ghirlandaio's finest frescos, all of them pregnant with meaning and metaphors.

While serving the Prince of Salerno, Bernardo Tasso repeated his visits to Giulia at nearby Fondi. He desired her, and he dedicated a book of poetry to her:

> *… To your rare virtues is added that divine beauty*
> *which Heavens never gave to any other …*

She was accustomed to breaking all hearts; even Valdés had been overwhelmed by her. "In Fondi, I spent one day with the lady who should be the lady of all the world," he wrote to Cardinal Ercole Gonzaga, "although I think that Our Lord has not thus decided so that we can all enjoy her divine conversation and kindness, which are not inferior to her beauty." But others could not tolerate Giulia's coolness, and Giovio wrote that "Donna Giulia is insane to endure in her rigidity and lonely life …". Giulia had other worries, and asked Valdés whether she should join a monastic order. In 1536, she eventually retired to the convent of St Francis in Naples, where she was to spend most of her time. But she did not take holy orders.

While Giulia was preoccupied with her inward religious search, Vittoria Colonna was on the move, writing letters on behalf of the Capuchin friars, who had been threatened with closure. She was vexed by her brother Ascanio's refusal to give his daughter Vittoria in marriage to the Prince of Sulmona, son of the Viceroy of Naples. It was Charles V's wish; the emperor, who loved the young prince, was rumoured to be his real father. After first consenting, Ascanio changed his mind; Charles was indignant "and waited for a better and more opportune time to take revenge on him", wrote a contemporary.

The elder Vittoria pleaded with Ascanio in a very fine letter. She writes as an elder and wiser sister who begs and does not order, reproaches and teases her brother for the excessively high esteem in which he holds himself. And she wrote (at the end of 1535 or beginning of 1536): "I cannot refrain, brother, from regretting that Nature made me a woman and took away from me the right to perpetuate my House ...". She reminds him of his wrongs: "I don't know by what whim you fail to comply with the marriage to Sulmona, as you already promised the Emperor." Vittoria goes on to detail to Ascanio the advantages of the match – Sulmona was rich and loved by the emperor (whom she calls "Caesar" or "Il Brabante" or "Padrone" – the Lord). Ascanio owed it to his daughter to marry her off, but if he was refusing her to the emperor's protégé,

> *are you thinking, brother, of giving her to the sky? It is a long way to reach. Are you thinking of giving her to the Lord of Hades since you always talk to spirits? That road is barred ... What is your intention, brother, I wonder? Maybe to marry her to our king: but he has the empress in his heart. To Philip, his successor?*

Vittoria reminded her brother that, ultimately, weddings, love, procreation, are the same for all (perhaps young Vittoria did not fancy the Prince of Sulmona), "the knot is the same and by the same silk woven." If Ascanio was to decide otherwise, "I prophesy turbulence and disgrace and this will be because Caesar will no longer help you."

Charles's vengeance or, rather, total lack of protection in the wars which were to follow between Ascanio and the papacy was, in fact, to destroy the power of the Colonnas. And it is mainly from this letter, written in an intimate style, that one can appreciate Vittoria's affectionate contempt for her lightweight brother who was the only heir of the Colonnas of Paliano and Marino. It is also a letter which shows a mature political mind, and – as Giovio commentated – a virile streak.

Vittoria Colonna was accorded the honour of a visit from the emperor: it was a noble gesture to visit the widow of his former captain. The daughter of a family who had served him, she was a woman ten years his senior, a poet who had addressed sonnets to him, expressing faith in the "proud eagle" of the Habsburgs. How interesting it would be to know what they said to each other, whether they talked French or Italian, or indeed Spanish, Latin or Flemish, how informally they behaved towards each other. (Charles always called Vittoria "relative".)

In Vittoria's eyes, the emperor was the symbol of Christendom, the man who had defeated the infidels and could enforce reform on the Catholic Church: he was a man of God. Did she talk about Ascanio's mishap? She would certainly have discussed the misfortunes of the Capuchins, but it is unlikely that the emperor opened his heart about the ecclesiastical subjects which, on the other hand, were the main reason for his forthcoming visit to Rome and to the new Farnese pope, Paul III. Vittoria persuaded the emperor to listen to friar Ochino preaching and Charles was "moved by his words".

Charles V left in the company of Vittoria's adopted son, the Marchese del Vasto and spent a night at Marino, Vittoria's birthplace. He then entered Rome, the city that his army had sacked seven years earlier. The pomp and honour with which Charles V was received had never been accorded to anyone before. Surrounded by his cardinals in full consistory, in an unprecedented act of courtesy, Pope Paul III went to greet Charles V on the steps of St Peter's, which was then undergoing its long transformation from ancient basilica into the building it is today.

Facing the new pope, Charles chose to speak Spanish and made a thundering attack on Francis I, the French king. There was a personal rivalry between the two kings, and this speech was Charles's way of announcing the renewal of warfare against France. "Let us decide the quarrel man to man", Charles said, "with what arms he pleases to choose – in our shirts, on an island, a bridge, aboard a galley moored in a river. If my hopes of victory were no better founded than his, and my resources no more certain, I would instantly throw myself at his feet and, with folded hands and a rope around my neck, implore his mercy!" The pope was astonished at such a tirade and did not know how to answer such an improper speech from the emperor, who was visiting Rome officially and had been received with much honour. In the event, Paul made a short placatory speech and dissolved the assembly.

In Rome, Charles – who was thirty-five at the time– lived at the Belvedere, the marvellous villa built by Pollaiuolo, frescoed by Andrea Mantegna, which we can still see in the gardens of the Vatican. Here he received the Roman nobility, diplomats, spies and generals of the army. Charles feared a schism and decided that reform of the Church had to be faced and that a council should take into account the grievances of his northern subjects. Unwillingly – because to take the initiative showed weakness – Paul III published a bull in which he called for such a council. He raised several men to the College of Cardinals – most of whom were moderates, known critics of the Church of Rome – and instructed them to prepare a plan for reform. Among these men were Gaspare Contarini, Gian Piero Carafa, Jacopo Sadoleto, and Reginald Pole. The members of the *Consilium* belonged to "the Oratory of Divine Love" founded in 1517, a voluntary association which bound them to a strict observance of Christian worship. Judging the society too liberal, Carafa left it and helped to found another religious order, the Theatines, which was later joined by a Spaniard, Ignatius de Loyola.

In a short span of time, the commission of critics produced their report; the famous *Consilium de emendanda ecclesia* ("Advice on the Reform of the Church", 1537) concluded that the popes, believing they owned the Church, had sold the Church's offices, appointments and benefices. Too many abuses had resulted. The critics also demanded censorship and control over public disputations: Erasmus's popular book, *Colloquia*, should be banned from schools. On the other hand, they did not seem to understand or come to terms with the Protestant reformers' main point: man's direct contact with God, the priesthood of all believers – a revolutionary point for the faithful, who until then had to find God through intermediaries, the pope, the clergy.

The commission's statements shocked the curia and the holy men were accused of being the tool of the Lutherans. Paul III was in difficulties; after the sack the Vatican had been left with little money and the war against the Turks cost a great deal; in 1537, more than half of the papal income still came from the sale of licences and exemptions, which had so shocked the Protestants and which the *Consilium* had condemned. Vittoria was also confused by what should have been left to the spirituality of the faithful.

When Vittoria Colonna left Ferrara in 1537, she wrote, "I shall pray God that He may return me to His delightful Ferrara with Your Excellency my lord, and with the Excellency of Madam and your divine children." While at Ferrara, Vittoria had written to Margaret Queen of Navarre, another reformer who was under suspicion of Protestantism. Violent sermons had been directed against her from French pulpits. Margaret (1492–1549), who was two years younger than Vittoria, composed dramatic poems condemned by the Sorbonne as heretical, on themes from the scriptures to be acted by her court, and she protected many Lutherans.

"*Serenissima Regina*", Vittoria wrote. She wished that her majesty might come to Italy. "I will speak of it to Renée of Ferrara, whose good judgement is shown in everything, and to the Reverend Pole, whose conversation is celestial ... and I will speak of it to the Reverend Bembo, always labouring in the vineyard of the Lord, and also to many others, whom I have no time to enumerate." The Queen of Navarre answered the "*Illustrissima Marchesa di Pescara*", signing herself "your good cousin and friend". She is flattered to be compared to Vittoria, although only in her faith can she compete with her, not in her writing. But they should work together towards the triumph of the reformed faith, she adds, "Ours is a friendship which fame began, and which has been much increased by our correspondence. I, more than ever, desire to receive them and am, still more, so adventurous as to hope that in this world I may hear you talk about another world ..." But they never met. Instead, a collection of Vittoria's own poems, which she had sent to Margaret, were intercepted by spies and shown to Francis I: they were opposed to the Catholic religion, the French king was told. But "His Majesty burst out laughing."

The weather in Ferrara was bad for Vittoria but what really motivated her hasty departure was the fact that friar Ochino fled to Lucca; Renée could no longer protect him. Nor could Vittoria who was heavily compromised, having persuaded the Duke of Ferrara to give him a palace for the new order of the Capuchins. In Lucca, an openly reformist city, Vittoria spent many pleasant days in the company of Pietro Carnesecchi, the Florentine nobleman, "one of the Pope's great favourites", writes Benvenuto Cellini.

After Clement's death, Carnesecchi had left the Vatican and had followed Valdés in Naples, before travelling to Florence (since Cosimo de' Medici was one of his close friends), and from there "to the Baths of Lucca where, for my good fortune, I was going at the same time as she [Vittoria Colonna]; so I had the chance of being in an even closer familiarity and service to her, which continued until the very last moment of her life."

Tullia, however, remained at Ferrara because she had found another man to take the very same role as Bernardo Tasso – as bed companion and public relations officer – Girolamo Muzio, the famous poet of the Este court, dedicated poems in praise of her sexual embraces; some of the poems, although very frank, were read aloud in the presence of the chaste Vittoria. One example was: "Come, beautiful Nymph, and between your soft arms gather he who with open arms awaits you with desire, and welcome your ardent lover in your womb with joy!"

For three years, Muzio remained Tullia's lover and, just as she had with Filippo Strozzi, she seemed to share a pleasant conjugal life with the poet. He was "so amusing in his conversation and so ready with a joke that it was a pleasure to hear him". Muzio would have to pay in order to make love to her unless she had quarrelled with another lover, in which case she would give herself to him for free. He would also teach her tricks which were useful for her career, "things so rare and marvellous that you can't imagine!". And she cultivated him because he could otherwise have written some horrible things against her, as Pietro Aretino had. Literary friends were all-important; they took the place of the media today: to make enemies of them was fatal for a courtesan. "Writers like this, it pleases them to paint white black, and to show people in a bad light, not because they deserve it but for their personal amusement or advantage," Tullia wrote. And it was worth her while to spend so long with a poet who wrote of her eyes:–

> .... occhi belli
> occhi leggiadri, occhi amorosi e cari
> piú che le stelle belli e piú che il sole.

> .... *beautiful eyes*
> *pretty eyes, amorous and dear eyes*
> *lovelier than the stars and the sun.*

But Tullia had to leave Ferrara when she became pregnant with Celio a little boy who was immediately dispatched to a wet nurse. Penelope, smuggled as a younger sister, remained with Tullia. In Ferrara too the appeal of her novelty was fading. For a while she disappears from pamphlets and "dialogues" – but only for time.

While Giulia Gonzaga was in a convent in Naples and Tullia was having a baby somewhere in the north of Italy, Vittoria Colonna, once again back in Rome, met the eccentric Michelangelo Buonarroti. The two felt the shock of recognition, and loved each other intensely.

CHAPTER SEVEN

Vittoria Colonna and Michelangelo

In 1538, when they met for the second time, Michelangelo was a mature man of sixty-three, and Vittoria was forty-eight. They had changed since their first encounter many years before during the carefree rule of Leo X. At that time they had hardly taken any notice of each other, although each knew of the other. Vittoria, after all, was one of the foremost poets, the friend of many of his friends; and Michelangelo had been recognized as the greatest painter, architect and sculptor of his age, a superhuman being who had painted the creation of the world and other scenes from the book of Genesis, and the prophets of the Old Testament and the pagan sibyls on the ceiling of the Sistine Chapel, working flat on his back on a high scaffold, assisted only by one paint-mixer, the famous Urbino.

But now, after many political and personal upheavals that had profoundly changed them both, these two famous people met again and felt a mutual attraction, a communion, an uncommon reciprocal devotion. They fell in love passionately and Michelangelo wrote of and to Vittoria: "No! It is not a mortal object that struck my view when for the first time your eyes fixed on mine ..."; "in that woman for whom I forgot all, I admire the work of the Creator; and my love, she knows it well, has no other object"; "Who is going to defend me against the light of your beautiful face, against the splendour of your eyes from which love throws its darts?" He envied her hair, "whose blonde halo laced with flowers encircles her charming head and can enjoy the pleasure of being near her sweet forehead."

Theirs was an affair conducted publicly, in the sense that it was spied upon with enormous curiosity and interest – Michelangelo had always been homosexual and Vittoria overwhelmingly chaste. It was a platonic affair, but all the same it was full-blooded and passionate. They could hardly keep away from each other, and Michelangelo, by then almost a recluse, always responded to her. Their correspondence grew so frequent as to lead Vittoria to beg him to write less, otherwise neither would have time to work. He never tired of declaring to her and to the world how much he loved her, what an astonishing chance it had been to know her soul, to be able to have contact with her. How conscious he was of her talent – and of his own – is shown in the epitaph which he wrote for Vittoria soon after her death:-

> Forse ad ambedue noi dar lunga vita
> posso, o vuoi nei colori, o vuoi nei sassi,
> rassembrando di noi l'affetto, 'l volto;
> secché mill'anni dopo la partita,
> quanto tu bella fosti, ed io t'amassi,
> si veggia, e come a amarti io non fui stolto.

> *Maybe to both of us I can give lasting life*
> *in painting or in sculpture*
> *by copying the looks and the face of each*
> *so that a thousand years after our deaths*
> *how beautiful you were and how much I loved you*
> *shall be judged – and that I was no fool in loving you.*

What Vittoria thought of him and told him to his face we know from a verbatim account given by a Portuguese painter – "You have the merit", she said to Michelangelo,

> *of being generous with prudence, not profligate with thoughtfulness. So that your friends think more highly of your disposition than of your works; while those who do not know you think highly of what is less perfect in you, and this is the work of your own hands. As for me, I think you worthy of no less praise for the way in which you keep yourself to yourself, avoid useless chat, refuse to paint for whatever lord seeks you, because in the whole of your life you have produced only one work.*

Vittoria was referring to the grandiosity and eternity of the Sistine Chapel (she had not seen his Florentine works) in discussing the essence of being a painter: by then, he had started to paint the end wall of the chapel.

Both Michelangelo and Vittoria were extraordinarily energetic; both shunned worldly company and both were eccentric. Vittoria then had taken to wearing the habit of a Franciscan monk – that is, the poorest kind of dress in a sombre colour. Michelangelo no longer took any personal care, his beard was left to grow grey and disorderly. He was a man of medium height, his nose was broken, the result of a blow he had received in his youth. The son of a Tuscan magistrate of small nobility, he had a terrible temper and was feared for his *furie*: he was probably a manic depressive.

"In particular he loved the Marchesa di Pescara", Condivi, Michelangelo's disciple and first biographer wrote:–

> *of whose divine soul he was enamoured, by whom he was overwhelmingly loved too; of whom he still keeps many letters, full of honest and sweet love and of those thoughts which used to rise from her soul. He wrote for her more and more sonnets, full of intelligence and sweet desire. She often moved from Viterbo and from other places where she*

had gone for duties or to spend the summer, and came to Rome with the sole goal of see-ing Michelangelo.

Michelangelo expressed himself in the "fourth art" – which for Vittoria was the first – and was a greater poet than she, more powerful and inventive, free from the literary conventions by which she was bound. Her poetry flows better, her language is easier, but her thoughts are less complex and interesting. When writ-ing verse, Michelangelo ignored the accepted restrictions and invented new ones; at times he respected the rhythm of the sonnet, but at others his poems consisted of as few as two lines, without rhyme. His poetry had the virility of his sculpture, to which he often compared it. Sculptured forms were latent in a piece of stone, Michelangelo believed, and just as he liberated statues from stone, so he could free the verse from the thought of the mind. Vittoria's influence had moulded him into a better man, he wrote, through all the processes of sculpting his soul.

Michelangelo was almost the first man, the first lay figure to be close to Vitto-ria for many years; she had been surrounded by bishops and friars. Like her, he had suffered. In the previous year, his father had died – the father he worshipped; and almost at the same time his brother had died of the plague, in his arms. Flor-ence, his Florence, had died too. When the city expelled the Medicis, Michelangelo had taken an active part in the revolt and had taken charge of Flor-ence's fortifications. He was a republican and opposed to the rule of the Medici family which, once again, had been imposed on Florence by the combined efforts of the pontifical and imperial forces. When the exhausted city finally opened its gates to the besieging army, and the bell of the popular council was taken down from the Palazzo dei Priori, Michelangelo expressed his powerless rage in his work, which became darker, angrier, stronger, and mystical.

Most of the rebels were harshly punished, but Michelangelo was pardoned and allowed to continue his work in the Medician sacristy of San Lorenzo. When he was in Florence, the Medici pope, Clement VII, had met Michelangelo and asked him to return to Rome to finish the Sistine Chapel. Michelangelo was considered by Clement and others to be the greatest sculptor of his time, maybe the greatest of all time, and a genius in the arts of painting, drawing, architecture and poetry.

After the restoration of the Medicean rule in Florence, Michelangelo felt no reason to remain in Tuscany: "I have no friends, I need none; I wish for none." In 1534 he was back in Rome, where he was to spend his last thirty years. His first commission there was to fresco the huge wall behind the altar of the Sistine Chapel with *The Last Judgement*. In the capital he saw few people and terrified everybody with his moroseness and temper. Even the pope was afraid of him. He took offence easily, was intolerant with his intellectual inferiors – who constituted the majority; women he found lightweight and boring, a waste of time. He was secretive and depressed, and seemed to be in his element only when confronting a piece of marble or choosing colours to grind. And yet everybody wanted to meet the living legend.

One such person was Francisco de Hollanda, a Portuguese miniaturist and author who had been sent to Rome by his king to copy the best paintings and meet the great men of the Renaissance. He spent the spring of 1538 and the following year in Rome, and described some of his encounters there with a freshness rarely found in formal letters. Of course, most of all, he longed to meet the famed and difficult Michelangelo. A noble Sienese, Lattanzio Tolomei, thought that the best – and possibly only – way for Hollanda to meet the great man was through Vittoria.

One Sunday de Hollanda went to visit Lattanzio Tolomei:-

> *I was told that he left word that I should join him in the church of San Silvestro on Monte Cavallo where, with the Marchesa Pescara, he was listening to the reading of the Epistles of St Paul. Madonna Vittoria Colonna, Marchesa di Pescara, sister of Signor Ascanio Colonna, is one of the most excellent and famous women in Europe, which means in the world. As noble as she is handsome, she is an expert in Latin culture and full of intelligence; she possesses all qualities and virtues which adorn a woman. From the time of her heroic husband's death, she leads a modest and withdrawn life. Weary of the brilliant life she formerly led, she devotes herself to Jesus Christ only and to deep studies, supporting many needy women, a model of genuine Catholic piety.*

The church of San Silvestro on the Quirinal Hill (also called Monte Cavallo, the horse's hill) was among the oldest in Rome; its gardens were almost attached to the Colonnas', whose large palazzo stands at the foot of the hill. In that garden Vittoria often used to meet her friends after the sermons and readings which took place in the church. They would sit in the shadowy place, when the pink sky was reflected in the fountain, to discuss the arts and sciences and gossip gently. Opposite the bench where they sat, there was a low wall covered with ivy. At times, Valerio Belli, the stone cutter, joined them, and also Sebastiano del Piombo, the painter, both friends of Michelangelo. They would talk until late and somebody would then accompany Vittoria back to her convent at the foot of the hill. On that evening, after the reading of the Epistles was over, the group remained inside the church, conversing – it was too hot outside.

When the reading was over, looking at de Hollanda and Tolomei, the marchesa said, "If I'm not mistaken, Messer Francisco would rather listen to Michelangelo on painting". Vittoria was teasing the Portuguese (whom she later mistakenly called a Spaniard). She knew that he was longing to talk to Michelangelo. De Hollanda's account continues:–

> *"Madam", I replied, "Your Excellency seems to entertain the opinion that everything which is not painting and art is foreign and unintelligible to me. It will certainly be very pleasing to hear Michelangelo speak, but I prefer Fra Ambrosio's exposition of the Epistles of St Paul." I spoke with some pique. "You need not take it so seriously," said Tolomei, "the Marchesa certainly did not mean that a man who is a good painter is not good at anything else. We Italians rank too high for that. Perhaps the*

words of the Marchesa were intended to intimate that, besides the enjoyment we have had, hearing Michelangelo speak today is still in store for us." "If it be so," I replied, "it would be after all nothing extraordinary, for Your Excellency would only be following your usual habit of granting a thousand times more than one ventures to desire." The Marchesa smiled. "We ought to know how to give," she said, "when a grateful mind is concerned and here especially, when giving and receiving afford equal enjoyment."

One of her retinue approached as she called, "Do you know Michelangelo's dwellings?" Her friend lived not far away, in the shallow valley between the Quirinal and the Capitol:–

"Go and tell him that I and Messer Tolomei are here in the chapel, where it is beautifully cool: the church too is private and agreeable; and that I beg to ask him whether he is inclined to lose a few hours in our society and to turn them into a gain for us – but not a word that the gentleman from Spain is here with us."

After a few minutes in which none of us spoke, there was knocking at the door. The servant had met Michelangelo close by, as he was on the point of going to the Thermae. He was climbing the Esquiline road in conversation with Urbino, his colour-grinder, and fell at once into the snare. The marchesa rose to receive him and remained standing for some time until she had made him sit:–

At first we were all silent; but the Marchesa, who could never speak without elevating those with whom she conversed, and even the place where she was, began to lead the conversation with the greatest art, about all possible things without, however, touching, even remotely, on painting. She wished to give Michelangelo assurance. She proceeded as if approaching an unassailable fortress, so long as he was on his guard.

And then they talked about paintings and painter, their relationship with the public, their responsibilities: religious images were so important at that time, the mysteries and dogmas of religion being imparted visually through painted images, that the responsibility of the image-maker was enormous; it was he who must endeavour to project a mystical, spiritual approach. They talked about the merit of drawing as opposed to painting, comparing the Flemish to the German and the Spanish to the Italian school. Michelangelo complained that painters often had to waste their time with people who sought their company for nothing but amusement:–

"Art belongs to no land, it comes from heaven," he said. It was not the subject of a painting that mattered, but the laborious perfection that could awaken piety, because, he believed, perfection was divine. "A good picture is nothing but a copy of God's perfection, an imitation of His paintings."

Then Tolomei told that Emperor Maximilian once pardoned a painter who was about to be executed, saying:–

"I can make earls and dukes, but God alone can make a great artist." Michelangelo said, "I assure you that the very Holy Father often displeases me by asking me why I don't appear more often, although I think I serve His Holiness better by staying at home than going to see him if it is only for silly concerns. And then I have to say to the Pope that I prefer working for him in my guise rather than being all day long in his presence, like so many do."

Then Vittoria talked about a project of hers:–

"His Holiness has gracefully consented to my building a convent near here, on the hill, close to that ruined porch from which, they say, Nero watched Rome burning. The footprints of such a cruel man would thus be erased by virginal women. I do not know, Michelangelo, what shape and proportion to give to such a building and on which side to place its entrance. Wouldn't it be possible to use part of the ancient building for the new one?" "Yes, Madama, certainly," Michelangelo answered. "The porch which is on the ground, in ruins, could be used for the steeple."

This answer was delivered with such promptness and such a serious face that Tolomei could not but remark it, after which, the great man added:–

"I think that nothing could forbid Your Excellency to build a cloister. When we leave we could, if you like, have a look at the place, I can make a few suggestions."

Annoyed by the fact that Michelangelo had not even looked at him, de Hollanda said that often the best way to pass unnoticed was to be very close to the person one would like to be noticed by. Michelangelo apologized: "Forgive me, to tell the truth I had not noticed you since I had eyes only for the marchioness." De Hollanda then asked whether he could join their company on the following Sunday:–

She acceded to my request and Michelangelo promised to come. Then he was the first to rise and the Marchesa stood. We accompanied them to the gate. Tolomei left with Michelangelo and I with La Marchesa from San Silvestro up to the monastery where they keep the head of St John the Baptist, and where she lived.

On the following Sunday, the Portuguese started off towards that enchanted garden, and on his way spent some time admiring the crowds: Margaret of Austria, daughter of Charles V and widow of Alessandro de' Medici, was marrying the pope's grandson, the young Ottavio Farnese. Triumphal carriages descended from the Capitol hill, horsemen were dressed in bright colours and ladies of the nobility glittered in their rich carriages; the display of pomp astonished the Portuguese envoy who then climbed the Quirinal hill, where once again he found Michelangelo and Tolomei sitting in the gardens behind the monastery, under the shade of the laurel trees; but Vittoria was not with them. Being a Colonna, she had to be present at the wedding, something which she had forgotten on the previous Sunday. She had left word that she would join them on the following Sunday. But there ends the "letter" that this special envoy – who thought that Michelangelo was the greatest painter who ever lived, followed by Leonardo and then Raphael – sent to his king.

They were difficult times for both Vittoria and Michelangelo; the painter had lost all illusions; even his family, which he had loved, had rewarded him badly. Aware of his genius, Michelangelo had lost faith in it. His lost humanism was turned into spiritualism by Vittoria, who also saved him from total bitterness; her intellectual greatness is witnessed by the adoration that such a man felt for her:-

> Ben puó talor col mio 'rdente desio
> salir la speme, e non esser fallace;
> ché s'ogni nostro affetto al ciel dispiace,
> a che fin fatto avrebbe il mondo Iddio?
>
> Qual più giusta cagion dell'amart'io
> é, che dar Gloria a quella eterna pace,
> onde pende il divin, che di te piace,
> e c'ogni cor gentil fa casto e pio?
>
> Fallace speme ha sol l'amor, che muore
> con la beltá, c'ogni momento scema,
> ond'é soggetta al variar d'un bel viso.
>
> Dolce e ben quella in un pudico core
> che per cangiar di scorza o d'ora strema
> non manca, e qui caparra il paradiso.

My hope can sometimes ascend with my burning desire, and not be false; for if every one of our desires is unacceptable to heaven, to what end did God make the world? What more righteous cause have I for loving you, than to glorify that eternal peace, from which what is divine and pleases in you, that makes every heart chaste and holy? Only the love that is tainted with false hope dies with beauty which lessens every moment, for, in this way, it is subject to the changing of a fair face. Sweet is that love in an innocent heart which does not fail for altering of features or the last hour, and it savours paradise here.

There was a warm side to Vittoria's character that is difficult to find in her journals or in her often tediously chaste letters. The great love that she inspired in Michelangelo betrays not only her strength and wit but also her weaknesses, for which he reproached her. Like most homosexuals, Michelangelo was attracted by the intellectual side of Vittoria's character. She must have been delectable to be with, exact in the choice of her words and attentive to what she was saying; and apart from Michelangelo, who had fallen in love with her, Vittoria was surrounded by the close friendship of some of the greatest men of her age.

Vittoria was conscious of Michelangelo's love for her and, as we saw in de Hollanda's description, she behaved in a feminine way, showing her audience that, were she to desire it, she was able to produce Michelangelo; and she could even make him socialize, she could distract him from his all-absorbing work on *The Last Judgement*. It is interesting to note that Vittoria asked her servant not to mention the presence of an intruder – de Hollanda – as she guessed that Michelangelo might have felt that she wanted to show him off to one of the many who longed to set eyes on him. Vittoria drew him out slowly and carefully, not making him feel the centre of excessive attention. She admired the genius of his creativity, but she loved the man; she discussed with him the connection between the inner force of the creator and the object of the creation. By improving his spirituality – and with the help of God – Michelangelo would reach the sublime, because he was sublime.

In one of the many sonnets dedicated to her, Michelangelo addressed himself to Vittoria: her immortal soul had come to earth straight from heaven, to which it would eventually go back, in order to please and heal and honour the world with its presence. That is what made him love her so, not so much her outward good looks, her serene face; his love clung to what was going to live forever, like her virtue, rather than to what was due to die and rot. God showed Himself to him in no other object but her; and that was what he loved, her mortal and graceful body, because God mirrored Himself in her. And again, he showed his mystical love for her by going back to his favourite image:–

> Si come per levar, Donna, si pone
> in pietra alpestre e dura
> una viva figura,
> che la più cresce, e più la pietra scema;
> tal alcun'opre buone,
> per l'alma, che pur trema,
> cela il soverchio della propria carne
> con l'inculta sua cruda e dura scorza.
> Tu pur dalle mie streme
> parti puó sol levarne,
> ch'in me non é di me voler ne forza.

Lady, just as one supposes a living figure to be contained within the hard stone, so as to draw it out, and it gradually emerges as the stone flakes away; so the surface of our flesh with its unworked, rough, hard skin hides deeds worthy of the soul. And you can draw these from my outward parts, you alone, as in me there is neither will nor strength of mind.

With Vittoria, Michelangelo shared a belief in a purer and more direct contact with God than that offered by the Catholic Church: Michelangelo had never had a high opinion of the clergy or of the papacy. To de' Medici, when he was still a cardinal and was soon to become Clement VII, Michelangelo had written "now if the Pope is issuing Briefs licensing people to steal, I beg your Most Reverend Lordship to get one for me, since I am more in need of it than they are ..."

Neither Leo nor Clement sat down when speaking to Michelangelo, fearing that, although unasked, he would sit down as well. And if Clement conceded that Michelangelo could keep his hat on in the papal presence, it was because the pope knew that he would do so anyway. Once, offended by something that Pope Clement had said, Michelangelo left Rome there and then. "If His Holiness wants me, he may seek me elsewhere." The pope sent five couriers after him with the order: "Return immediately on pain of our displeasure." To which Michelangelo answered: " If I were undeserving of your esteem yesterday, I shall not be worthy of it tomorrow."

Everybody feared Michelangelo's temper, his eccentric loneliness, his wish to paint alone, in secret, in order to surprise with the strength of his work when it was completed. Indeed when *The Last Judgement* was shown to the public, it created a sensation: its style and message were so different from the frescos on the ceiling, majestic and harmonious, that Michelangelo had painted years earlier, in a different political and spiritual context. In the images of *The Last Judgement* the crowd of saints inspired fear; the sweet, virile humanity of a young Christ contrasted with the wretched brood of muddy, stinking humans.

With Vittoria, Michelangelo discussed *The Last Judgement*, the concept he was brooding over secretly: he wanted to express the meanness and fragility of human life, and his sinful, tormented self. He even allowed her to come and see the Sistine Chapel while he was painting. Vittoria would come to St Peter's accompanied by one lady-in-waiting or by her secretary. She was the one person with whom the silent, morose painter would communicate; in his own eyes, she was his equal in intellect and his peer in spirituality, while most of the others who crowded the papal court and the capital were perverse social climbers. And he painted her likeness; Vittoria lent her face to the queen of the vast celestial crowd, standing just behind the strong, youthful Christ, looking away from the cardinals and those popes who were — and are — elected in the Sistine Chapel. Michelangelo himself painted his own likeness in St Bartholomew's discarded skin. The martyr had been skinned alive.

Michelangelo was going to give something to Vittoria: a surprise, something inspired by his sublime love for her. "Signora", he wrote,

> *before taking all that Vostra Signoria has often wanted to give me, in order to receive it less unworthily, I want to make something for you with my own hands. As I have seen that the grace of God cannot be purchased and that to keep it badly is a very grave sin — I say it is my fault, and that I accept what you give me willingly, when I shall make something for you, not to keep in my own house but for your house, so that I can be with it too and I shall think I am in Paradise; for which I shall feel more obliged — if I can be more than I am to you, Your Excellency.*

Enticed by curiosity, Vittoria got to know what it was that Michelangelo was preparing for her; a drawing of a crucifix. But the gift never came, and Michelangelo never mentioned it again. Vittoria asked Tomaso to make enquiries; annoyed, even angry, Michelangelo wrote:–

19. *The Last Judgment* (Vittoria Colonna as The Virgin Mary) by Michelangelo
Almost uniquely, Vittoria was allowed in and out of the Sistine Chapel while
Michelangelo was painting. The two exchanged letters and saw each other regularly. With Michelangelo there was a strong affinity and a mutual respect but also
love, as witnessed by his poems dedicated to her and his letters. She died in his
arms.

Signora Marchesa, As I was in Rome you need not have asked Messer Tomaso with regard to the crucifix and place him between you and me, your servant, to ask for my services in this way. I wanted to do more for you than for anyone else in the world; but you know how hard work is burdening me and this made it impossible to show this to Sua Signoria. I know that you are familiar with the saying "Amor non vuol maestro" [love does not want a master] *and also "Chi ama non dorme"* [who loves does not sleep]. *It was unnecessary to make enquiries through others, and although it seemed as if I had forgotten it, I wanted to surprise you. My plan is now spoilt. Mal fa chi tanta fé si tosto oblia* [Wrong is he who forgets so soon such great trust].

Michelangelo was hurt by the fact that Vittoria should send a third party to enquire, as if distrusting his word and acting behind his back. How could she ever have thought that he had forgotten? A man like him does not forget, especially when he loves a woman like her. As we saw earlier, when she failed Castiglione, Vittoria was prone to this kind of gaffe, because of her enthusiasm and her sometimes uncharacteristic impatience. In any case, Michelangelo took offence easily. And he might have been irritated by another letter from Vittoria, short and casual, which could have been sent just before Michelangelo received Tomaso's enquiries. Alas, most of their letters are undated. This one reads:–

Cordialissimo mio signor Michelangelo, I beg you to send me the Crucifix for a while if you have almost accomplished it, because I would like to show it to some gentlemen from the Very Reverend Cardinal of Mantua, and if you are not working today, you could come and talk to me at your ease.

How could she take him for granted and be so offhand and ask him to show the finished or unfinished crucifix to the chatty court of a cardinal?

Unfortunately, Michelangelo's crucifix has disappeared; there is only a trace of a drawing (to which Condivi refers) of a serene-looking Christ. At a later date (July 1543), in a letter to Michelangelo, Vittoria refers to the image of Christ as "that you painted so well ... in my 'Samaritan'". This is clearly a painting which Michelangelo gave to her and it could be the work to which these letters refer. When Vittoria received the preparatory sketch for the actual painting, she marvelled; it was accompanied by an evasive letter. She answered:–

Unique Maestro Michelangelo and my very singular friend, I have received your letter and looked at the Crucifix, which crucified all other representations I know in my mind. A better, accomplished, a more alive and finished image cannot be seen, and certainly I could never express how subtly and wonderfully it is made. For which I do not want to hear it from others; but then, please, explain it to me: does this belong to others? Never mind! But in case you have sold it and you want some of your pupils to copy it, I shall talk it over with you, because, knowing the difficulty of imitating it, I would prefer that your pupil would make something different from this. But if it belongs to you, you must forgive me if I do not return it to you. I have examined it well, by candlelight and with lenses and mirror, and I've never seen a more perfect thing.

This letter is not entirely clear: presumably she was uncertain – or pretended to be – whether the drawing was a present or just for her to look at; because of the little squabble caused by her letter, Michelangelo sent her no explanatory word with the painting. Presumably he did not tell her that the drawing (or was it a painted sketch?) was a preliminary for the finished picture which was to come – at least he could enjoy the expectation of that surprise for his impatient lady! It may have been the drawing Condivi refers to, not the finished painting (although the object she admired was so "accomplished and fine"), otherwise Vittoria would not mention the fact that a pupil could not make a copy of it.

When Michelangelo sent her the finished painting, she wrote him a letter, apologizing for her previous rashness:–

> *Whatever you make excites a strong judgement from whoever is watching it; and in order to enhance this experience I talked to you about expanding your perfect creation with goodness; and I see now that omnia possibilita sunt credenti [all is possible to the believer]. I had great faith that God would give you supernatural inspiration while you were making this Christ. Then I saw it, and it was so wonderful that my expectation was exceeded in every way; then, becoming spirited by the miracles that had happened, I desired that which now I see wonderfully finished; in every way it reaches the highest perfection and nobody could hope to achieve so much. And I tell you that I am very happy that the angel on its right-hand side is more handsome because Michael will place you, Michelangelo, to the right of the Father on the day to come, and for this I do not know how to serve you in any other way but to pray to this sweet Christ, whom you painted so well and perfectly, and pray you that you should command me as your own thing in everything and for everything.*

Michelangelo's friendship, love and attentions had not distracted Vittoria from her multitude of commitments: she had her estates to administer, she was maintaining much correspondence, and she was promoting the Reform. She acquired a secretary, Giuseppe Jova from Lucca, whose father had squandered his family's fortune. But she did not use him for private letters, such as those she wrote to her adopted son or to Michelangelo. Alfonso del Vasto had fallen in love with Laura di Monteforte, a young married lady who lived at Ischia, and for three years "he neither touched nor caressed his wife". We saw how del Vasto had been asked by Vittoria to intercede in favour of Filippo Strozzi, the Florentine nobleman who committed suicide. Vittoria had probably written that letter to the captain-general of the imperial army in Italy on Michelangelo's request; Michelangelo was a friend of Strozzi and of the Republic. Watching in agony as so many of his companions were tortured and dispossessed, he expressed his tormented love for Vittoria and his tormented soul in a sonnet which betrays his convoluted feelings, his philosophy, and a new kind of modesty about his limitations as a creator – and as a man and lover:–

> Non ha l'ottimo artista alcun concetto
> c'un marmo solo in sé non circoscriva

col suo soverchio; e solo a quello arriva
la man che ubbidisce all'intelletto.

Il mal ch'io fuggo, e'l ben ch'io mi prometto
in te, Donna leggiadra, altera e diva,
tal si nasconde; e perch'io più non viva,
contraria ho l'arte al disiato effetto.

Amor dunque non ha, nè tua beltade,
o durezza, o fortuna, o gran disdegno,
del mio mal colpa, o mio destino o sorte,
se dentro del tuo cor morte e pietate
porti in un tempo, e che 'l mio basso ingegno
non sappia, ardendo, trarne altro che morte.

The best artist has not one idea that a piece of marble, still unworked, could not contain within itself; and that potential form is realized only by the hand that obeys the intellect. The evil I fly from, and the good I promise myself are likewise hid in you, proud, divine Lady; and to my life's impoverishment, my art is opposed to the desired result.

So Love is not to blame for my plight, nor your beauty, nor the hardness of things, nor chance, nor great scorn, nor is my destiny or fate, if within your heart you bear at the one time death and pity, and my miserable wit does not know, in spite of passion, how to draw anything from you but death.

The poetry he addressed to her was quite different from the conventional tone of contemporary sonnets in which hair was golden, eyes shone and women's teeth glittered like pearls; Michelangelo's passionate confessions astonished the world: the wild genius, the reclusive genius loved the most virtuous woman!

It was now Vittoria's turn to suffer from political events. There was one unsettled score between her brother Ascanio and the emperor; besides, Ascanio, unable to understand the times, still behaved as the mighty Colonnas had always done, forgetting that the family had become a vassal of the emperor – in all but name – and had no power against a Church whose pope was now related to Charles V.

Refusing to buy salt that had been highly taxed by the new Farnese pope, Ascanio disobeyed the law by purchasing it elsewhere; some of his men were imprisoned. Like all papal vassals, Ascanio was ordered to obey. He refused, and when summoned to appear for judgement on 25 February 1541, he swore that he was faithful to the Church, but did not appear. Thus started *La Guerra del Sale*, the war of the salt. Pier Luigi Farnese, the pope's son, took charge of an armed squad which was to show Ascanio Colonna – and other possible rebels – what it meant to disobey the pope. Vittoria's feelings for her brother were mixed, but she never forgot that he was the head of her family. *"La casa Colonna è sempre la prima"*, she wrote to him – the house of Colonna is always the first. But she knew that nothing good would come from a quarrel with the Farnese and, after Ascanio's refusal to marry his daughter to Charles's protégé, her brother could no longer count on the emperor's protection.

Diplomacy was needed, and patience: Job's patience, she specified. She approached the emperor and his ambassador in Rome who, together with the Viceroy of Naples, was trying to reconcile the two parties. Ascanio did not want to appear in the pope's presence, fearing to be taken prisoner: the fiefs of the Colonnas would have been put to good use by the many Farneses whose appetite for land was equal to that of their Borgia and Medici predecessors. And Paul III, like all popes before him, was anxious to free the papal territories from the strategic belt of the Colonna fortresses which could endanger Rome by cutting off its route to the sea.

Vittoria was in Rome, still spending her Sunday evenings in the company of her *singolarissimo amico* Michelangelo, when she wrote to her brother, who was between Paliano and Marino: "It is difficult to understand this Pope, but take care that all you do should be with His Majesty the Emperor's service in mind." He should consider apologizing – but with honour – she suggested. Ascanio was busy gathering troops from his fiefs in Campania and Lazio. Vittoria left Rome, the seat of the enemy, returning to the convent of St Paul at Orvieto. She took with her two maids, Prudentia and Chiara di Nobilione, and two menservants. The Governor of Orvieto went to visit her, since she was an honoured and celebrated lady. But his visits were not only motivated by courtesy. The governor kept Cardinal Alessandro Farnese informed. Vittoria had received a messenger from Cardinal Fregoso and letters from the emperor and the Marchese del Vasto; Charles V advised Ascanio to give in to the pope's demands. The emperor, who wrote from Regensburg (Ratisbon), disliked the idea of a new civil war in "his" Italy: the disobedience of one subject could be an evil example to others, and it had to be punished. At Regensburg, where, in his continuous search for religious unity he was talking to the Diet, Charles had apparently thundered against Ascanio Colonna: the emperor disliked him. The emperor wrote to Vittoria:–

Illustre marchesa Our friend,
We have seen your letter and the services that We and Our ancestors have received from the Colonnas are such that they cannot be forgotten, and We shall always keep them in mind as they deserve in order to look and favour the conservation of your house. But now, as you with your wisdom can judge, those means which Ascanio used in the present issue have passed the limits of reason and honesty ... As you will hear from the Marquess Our ambassador, all the same We shall take care that the matter is solved in a friendly way and the calling to arms stopped, and all those troubles which could derive from it, especially to your estates, to the public wealth and to the peace in Italy.

In another letter to Vittoria, also written from Regensburg, the emperor Charles stressed that Ascanio had to be brought to reason. Messengers brought letters to Orvieto from everywhere: Ascanio Colonna's salt business was becoming an international affair. The wise Cardinal Contarini, also in Regensburg, requested a meeting with Vittoria: only she could persuade Ascanio to realize how dangerous it was to come to a confrontation with the pope. Contarini was told that Vittoria had written to her brother several times and that there was nothing more left to be done.

In another letter Vittoria informed her brother that he was in danger: "God may guard you and may He, with all His goodness, take all the ills away ... but such a war, for 30 cows, was it needed?" This referred to the fact that Ascanio withdrew his cattle from Vatican soil. Charles's ambassador received orders to let things go their own way. Vittoria was discouraged. On 9 March 1541, Ascanio wrote to his sister: she too was to abandon all diplomatic efforts. Ascanio's wife, Giovanna, and his children left for Ischia, where they were welcomed by the ageing Costanza; the old, respected princess died a few months later.

War was to break out between the Farneses and the Colonnas. "In spite of some excuses offered from the imperial side", Cardinal Farnese stated in a letter, "*il signor Ascanio*" should have paid for the salt, and he could only avoid the war by sending his eldest son as hostage, going away from Rome as an exile after appearing in person and giving away two of his fiefs chosen by His Holiness; the Church, the cardinal added, knew that a turbulent vassal had to obey. There was "no peril for this See", he added. Indeed what could the Farneses fear? The pope's army was superior to that of the Colonnas; the emperor, now the pope's relative, was on his side.

The rapacity with which the Farneses took advantage of Ascanio's mistake was reminiscent of earlier Renaissance times. From their fiefs on the southern and western side of the capital, the Colonnas blocked Rome from Ardea to Nettuno, on the coast, up to the Equi and Ernici mountains. But the papal army was quick to counter-attack: Rocca di Papa fell at once to the undisciplined force of papal mercenaries who then proceeded to march against Paliano, the main fortress of the Colonnas. Fighting like a demon, inside the fortress, outside in the village, Ascanio Colonna resisted for two months. During this time the mercenaries raided neighbouring villages, and it was so difficult to keep any discipline among them that a force of mounted police was sent from Rome. In the meantime, other fortresses had fallen: Gennazzano, Cave, Ceciliano, Scurcola. Vittoria lamented the fate of her land, the place where she had first seen the light:–

> Veggio rilucer sol di armate squadre
> i miei sí larghi campi, ed odo il canto
> rivolto in grida e 'l dolce riso in pianto
> la 've io prima toccai l'antica madre.

I see the country of my people rekindled with armed squads and I hear singing turn into screams and sweet laughter into tears where I first touched mother earth.

On 26 May Paliano fell. The Governor of Orvieto came to see her with the news: "Possession comes and goes", she answered. "What is important is that lives should be safe." In fact only seventy survivors were still defending it; all the others had died. Vittoria witnessed the power of the Colonnas disintegrate once and for all: she was too intelligent not to understand this and, in spite of her belief in a better world, she suffered for the fall of her family from temporal power. All of Ascanio's possessions in the pontifical lands were confiscated, his castles razed to the ground; with a few of his loyal supporters, Ascanio took refuge in his Neapolitan fiefs, outside the grasp of the Farneses.

Michelangelo was too involved in his work and in his spiritual traumas to take an active interest in the collapse of the Colonnas: probably he had never met Ascanio and, had he done so, he would not have thought much of the man. Michelangelo continued writing to Vittoria, and for her:–

> Per esser manco, Alta Signora, si degno
> del don di vostra immense cortesia …

> *In order to be worthy, noble lady,*
> *of the gifts of your immense courtesy …*

She sent him all her sonnets; he bound them together in beautiful leather and kept this book as his most precious possession. He also kept and bound all her letters from Orvieto and Viterbo, as he told his nephew. In the poetry that Vittoria sent him, she sought for the peace of spiritual guidance from God. But life was becoming difficult for her, and not only because of Ascanio's disobedience to the pope.

She moved to Viterbo, a city governed by the English cardinal, Reginald Pole; Michelangelo was in Rome. But she would travel to see him and in this she showed that she needed him. It is in fact unthinkable that the two friends did not discuss the major items which were troubling Vittoria's life. "I ask you, high and divine woman, if the repented sinner has less glory than the proud just", he wrote. To him she was the source of bliss, a kind of Holy Mother.

The Inquisition, however, was of a totally different opinion.

CHAPTER EIGHT

Women and the Inquisition

The pope conferred on the Englishman, Cardinal Reginald Pole the governorship of the Patrimonium Petri, centred around Viterbo, the oldest of the Papal States, known as the Patrimony. The Cardinal d'Inghilterra was to live in Viterbo, a beautiful city, a day's journey north-west of Rome and his only duty was to administer justice.

Pole lived in a fine palace, attracting Valdés's supporters, whose sympathy for reformist ideas was, in some cases, Protestant. The Viterbo group became well known, and suspect: they were devout enthusiasts of ecclesiastical reform; friends and guests and visitors and servants participated in endless and passionate debates. This is why Vittoria followed Pole there a month later and took up residence at the convent of St Catherine: she was to remain at Viterbo for three years.

All over Europe, women from the nobility and the gentry were rallying to the Protestant cause. Tall, with a long nose and very thin lips, Jeanne d'Albret (1555–72), wife of Antoine de Bourbon and daughter of Margaret de Valois, Queen of Navarre, was a staunch Protestant and turned her kingdom, Navarre, into the heart of the Reformation. The battle for the faith, which coincided with the battle for women's rights of education, freedom of speech, and independence, united people from different social strata. But what is important to our story is that the spiritual force was that of womanhood.

The emperor called for a "religious colloquy", a conference, a meeting – a diet – between Protestant and Catholic representatives, on German soil at Regensburg. The Protestants' chief representative was Melanchthon; the Catholics', Cardinal Contarini, one of the four members of the Sacred College recognized in Germany, he was Vittoria's friend, a "dove". There was initial agreement over the question of justification by faith, which made Contarini hopeful. Justification by faith was the main theme of Valdés's preaching – and of Ochino and Pietro Martire Vermigli, also known as Peter Martyr. According to Valdés, and to Luther, faith in Christ meant salvation. On the other hand, if salvation could be achieved by justification – faith through Christ – what need was there of the sacrament of confession? But the "hawks", led by Cardinal Carafa, objected to what they labelled *sola fide*. An accommodation still seemed possible. Enthusiasm reigned among the moderates, the "doves", for a compromise (Contarini, Sadoleto, Vittoria Colonna, Pole, Giberti, Carnesecchi, Morone, Fragoso and others). Then came a breakdown of agreement on items like celibacy, the juridical structure of the Church and papal supremacy.

The last hope of achieving unity by negotiation was dashed and the diet ended in July 1541, the two sides having reached no agreement. It was terrible news also for Vittoria who had contemplated going to Regensburg, and might have even been there in order to influence the "doves".

In August, very thin, if not emaciated, Vittoria left Viterbo and returned to Rome for a short visit; the Colonna palace, the huge building whose gardens still stretch up towards the Quirinal hill, was deserted, her family exiled. There she received visits from a few friends; from them she heard that Ochino was in Milan enjoying immense success, to which she said, "Please God that it may continue." Valdés then died; his group, in which Giulia Gonzaga figured so prominently, was dispersed and did not know where to go, where to gather. Somehow they all needed a figurehead; for a short while Vittoria filled that gap but she wanted Reginald Pole, in whom she had put her trust, to guide her and her group.

Vittoria had met Cardinal Pole, who was eight years her junior, earlier on in her life, but it was at Viterbo that they became intimate friends. When Pole had opposed Henry VIII, he had fled to Italy, where, anyway, he was at home: he had been educated at the University of Padua. His mother, the Countess of Salisbury, Margaret Plantagenet, had been executed in 1539 because of her son's opposition to Henry VIII's divorce from Catherine of Aragon. On that occasion, Pole wrote to Vittoria that when Henry VIII had "sentenced her to death, that is, to life eternal", in his heart it was Vittoria who had replaced his mother. Indeed, Queen Mary Tudor had been placed in the care of the Countess of Salisbury and the royal baby's wet nurse had been Katherine, wife of Leonard Pole.

Reginald Pole himself was the grandchild of the Duke of Clarence, whose two brothers had been kings. He had met Sadoleto, Pietro Bembo and Contarini when he was a student in Padua and Sadoleto thought that Pole was "a man of unshaken constancy and of virtue of the most superior order ... his conversation was above the ordinary sort of men, and it would be a strong heart that would not soften in half an hour of his talk." He was also a close friend of the most intellectual of the group, Contarini, and, like him, had been made a cardinal with the group of reformists in December 1536. But Pole did not believe in religious controversy; he supported ecclesiastical authority.

Until then, influenced by Ochino, Vittoria was going through another spiritual crisis. Like many of her circle she believed in justification, the earning of salvation not by deeds but by faith, and she was reading "dangerous" texts. Pole advised, and even teased, Vittoria: she was to abstain from excessive mortification, discard some books which only confused her. "After being advised by the cardinal that she rather offended God than the reverse by treating her body with such austerity and rigour ... she began to desist from that very austere mode of life, reducing her mortifications little by little to a just and reasonable mean", Pietro

Carnesecchi was to recount. Presumably by mortifications, Carnesecchi meant rigorous fasting and self-inflicted corporal punishment. He added that the cardinal was not only a friend of Vittoria, but honoured her like a mother. Vittoria herself wrote to Giulia Gonzaga, "I owe the health both of my soul and of my body to Cardinal Pole – the former was endangered by superstition, the latter by misuse." Pole also stressed that Vittoria should not probe into doctrinal problems – she was not up to that. Nor was he: "If only Contarini were with us!" he used to say at times. He would talk about religion with Vittoria and give her advice, but Pole was a man who preferred to sit on the fence. Vittoria, who was growing more and more attached to him, insisted that he should come and visit her often.

The Viterbo court was crowded with fervent visitors. The intellectuals, of whom Pole said, "Vittoria is the centre", dined together discussing the latest events. Pietro Carnesecchi was at Viterbo for a year. But doom hovered over them; the failure of the Diet of Regensburg had brought distrust on those who had sought an accommodation with the Protestants. Contarini was amazed and angered by the way in which many regarded his efforts to find a common ground on the doctrine of justification. On the other side of the fence, the chief "hawk", Cardinal Carafa, conferred about, "what we have heard about the things of Ratisbon". And Viterbo, the capital of the moderates, was already considered to be Protestant, if not heretic, because of its affinity with Luther's views.

Calvin's preaching had not only conquered Geneva but was reaching Italy, and the whole papal effort was put into halting this spread. These new ideas were, in effect, political, and can be better understood by us if we associate them with the similar fire that burnt over the better part of Europe when Socialist ideas conquered the nineteenth century. These were ideas that spread to all classes – which is why they were fought with hatred. In the Italian north, the *spirituali* used preachers like Ochino and Peter Martyr Vermigli, who were extremely popular with the masses, to battle against heresy, but, in the eyes of the "hawks", these preachers were suspect. Cardinal Carafa, a noble Neapolitan, inflexible, gloomy and unforgiving, declared that the whole of Italy was infected with the Lutheran heresy.

Even if Contarini had used Ochino to win back Calvin's congregations, on 15 July the Benedictine friar was invited to go to Rome in order to deal with "matters of importance". Six days after receiving this summons, the pope issued the bull *Licet ab initio*, establishing the Roman Inquisition tribunal under Cardinal Carafa. Not even waiting for funds, Carafa, at his own expense, set up a palace for the Inquisition to hold proceedings. At that time, Ochino was in Verona with Bishop Giberti, preaching to enthusiastic crowds: to put it mildly, he was in no hurry to go to Rome. On 27 July, a papal brief again ordered him to Rome and so he set out on his journey but, on his way, he stopped in Bologna to see Contarini who was very ill. What the two said to each other is impossible to know. This was an important meeting since, a couple of months later, the Inquisition wanted to prove that Contarini had persuaded Ochino to flee, hence the whole Viterbo group – Vittoria first of all – was guilty.

From Bologna, Ochino reached Florence and visited Peter Martyr, who had also been ordered to appear before the consistory court. Peter Martyr told Ochino that had he gone to Rome, he would have faced death. Therefore, on 22 August, from the convent of Montuorghi near Florence, Ochino wrote to Vittoria in an agitated frame of mind:–

> I find myself here outside Florence in no small trouble of mind, having come with the intention of going to Rome although many people dissuaded me from doing so. But, understanding better every day the way things are, I am persuaded by Peter Martyr and others not to proceed; because I could not but deny Christ or be crucified. The first I will not do; the second, yes, but with His grace and when it shall be His will. I have not now the spirit to go voluntarily to death. When God requires me, He will know how to find me anywhere ... After this, what more can I do in Italy? ... On the other hand, think how hard it is for me to act with all these considerations. I know you will think so. The flesh recoils from leaving everything behind and thinking what they will say. I would welcome the opportunity to speak to you, to hear your opinion and that of the Rev Monsignor Pole, or to receive a letter from you.

If Ochino thought that his flight would cause uproar and would damage his protectors, he was understating the scandal that his – and Peter Martyr's – flight produced. It was a catastrophe. The apostasy of Ochino, the Vicar-General of the Capuchins, together with that of Peter Martyr, confirmed Carafa's suspicions. It was even thought that Vittoria might follow Ochino's example. She had written several "Protestant" sonnets, like the one in which she had doubted the sacrament of confession: "We must not, like our forefathers, lay our sins on others, but with kindled hope and true penitence, avoiding priestly robes, declare our sins to Him alone." That was the reason for her torments: she had reached the conclusion, like many of her circle that the Protestants were in possession of the true faith.

In fact, while she had been at her closest with Ochino, Vittoria had been a Protestant "without knowing it", as Cardinal Carafa put it. On the other hand, the confusion in the Church was grave; after the sack of Rome, the plague, the ravage of the many armies, simony, corruption, there had grown a deep disgust with the clergy's corruption, and the determination of the papacy to keep spiritual and territorial power within its hands, which – it pretended – were the hands of God. Many were drawn to those ideas that Calvin and Luther had written down. The Church of Rome had written nothing; no one knew what to believe or disbelieve. The pope – and, even more, the emperor – had been striving for an impossible reunion with the Protestants. Only the Diet of Regensburg had spelt out to most (but not to the emperor) that an accommodation with the northern heretics had by then become impossible. In effect, Regensburg tacitly recognized that the faith of Luther and Calvin was already different – something that the moderates had not understood, but people like Carafa, the Inquisitor-General, and Loyola had.

Although told not to think about theological matters, Vittoria could not ponder on the themes that were shaking her group and herself. On the state of the Church, in fact, she had written sonnets which had shocked some, although she innocently composed them with the fervour of a reformist, of one who wanted to see the Church in a healthier state:-

Veggio d'alga e di fango ormai sí carca
Pietro, la rete tua, che se qualche onda
Di fuor l'assale o intorno la circonda
Potrá spezzarsi e a rischio andar la barca.

Peter, I see your nets so full of weeds and mud,
Now, that if a wave clashes
Your boat from outside or surrounds it
It could break and be destroyed.

Bernardino Ochino fled from Florence to Ferrara where, with the help of Renée d'Este, and also with the help of Vittoria's brother, who lent him a horse, he crossed the frontiers and reached Geneva. Peter Martyr, who had fled from Lucca, wrote to Cardinal Pole just before reaching Zurich, condemning the evils of the papist religion. Eighteen monks from his monastery followed him into Switzerland; many more were jailed.

Ochino's flight decided the fate of the moderates: he had been so well known; larger and larger crowds had become familiar with his preaching. Carnesecchi, who was at Viterbo at the time, said that in Vittoria's eyes "the decision he had taken was condemned and detested, although beforehand she had always revered and respected him". It was a shattering setback; Rome was resolved now to proceed against those suspected of heresy. Vittoria and her circle "... were all stricken with fear".

In order to justify his flight, Ochino had sent Vittoria his book, a pamphlet. Pole advised her to send it immediately to Cardinal Cervini (later Pope Julius III), a Curial "hawk", in order to clear herself. But from the date of Ochino's flight, Vittoria and her group, still too powerful to be persecuted and prosecuted, in the secret of the inquisitorial records were described as heretics. To Cardinal Cervini Vittoria wrote: "I have today received the enclosed with a book, which I send to you." In her postscript she added a comment on Ochino's letter: "I grieve exceedingly that while he thinks to excuse himself the more he accuses himself; and that when he believes to be saving others from shipwreck, the more he exposes himself to the floods, being outside that ark which saves and secures."

She too felt exposed. Some of the moderates, like Contarini, had died or were to die soon, the remaining exponent of the *spirituali* being Pole, whom Carafa saw as an adversary. And Carafa had a more formidable character than Pole. The Inquisition to fight heresy, over which Carafa presided, was empowered to cross-examine anyone. Modelled on the Spanish Inquisition, the reformed Holy Office looked with suspicious eyes upon any intellectual. The real enemy to the new doctrine was a thinking woman, a literate and emancipated woman; that kind of person had to be eliminated. The embodiment of that woman was Vittoria, a dangerous example.

This was the end of the Renaissance. Culture, once beloved and fostered by the papacy, opened the way to dangerous freedom; ideas were the weapons of revolt and had to be suppressed. Then – as now – knowledge, culture, intellectual curiosity became suspect, even dangerous to oppressive regimes: knowledge leading to engaging the mind into reasoning, culture into wanting to know more, intellectual curiosity sharpening the appetite for information, fact. Ignorance was considered safe and political oppression went hand in hand with the congregation of the Inquisition. A monk-like, tall, emaciated figure – the kind of Grand Inquisitor of Verdi's opera *Don Carlos* – Carafa despised moderation and worked by persecuting and implanting fear. He even proceeded on a secret instruction against Vittoria's brother: "Ascanio Colonna, himself taught by Ochino, Pole, and by his sister, the Marchioness". There were various secret inquiries going on into the "Valdesian group at Viterbo", which had been penetrated by spies.

With the death of so many of her friends (Giberti also died, not yet fifty), Vittoria clung to Reginald Pole. He reassured her: faith alone could save her, but she should go on with her "works", prayers, penitence and confession. She wrote many letters, most of which have disappeared, especially those which reached the Inquisition, whose papers were destroyed by a popular revolt in 1857.

On 20 July, Vittoria wrote to Michelangelo who, in spite of his isolation, should be considered part of the circle of the *spirituali*. Her letter was addressed to "My more than magnificent and more than dearest Messer Michelangelo Buonarroti":–

Magnifico Messer Michelangelo, I haven't answered your letter before as yours has been, one can say, an answer to mine, thinking that if you and I go on writing to each other, as I am obliged by your courtesy, I shall have to leave the chapel of St Catherine, without being with my Sisters at the ordained times, and that you would have to leave the chapel of St Paul, without being there from morning to night, all day with your sweet discourse with your paintings – as I think that their likenesses talk to you as those beings who surround me talk to me; so that we shall fail – I the wives and you the Vicar of Christ. Knowing well of your firm friendship and very secure affection, I cannot confirm the arrival of your letter; I prefer to wait with a settled mood for a more important occasion on which to write to you, praying that God, of whom you talked to me with such a loving and humble heart, that I may find you on my return with His image so renewed and for real faith in your soul, as you painted it so well in my "Samaritana". And I always send you my best and to your Urbino.

There must be some coded message in this letter, which certainly fell into the hands of the Inquisition. With it, she sent him three sonnets. Michelangelo sent her back some of his short stories. At this time, during her despair and gloom, he became particularly affectionate and caring. As he was to say much later, writing to a friend of his, Father Giovanni Benedetto Battucci (1 August 1550): "I send you some of my short stories, those I used to write for the Marchioness of Pescara, who loved me very much, and I loved her no less. Death took away from me a great friend."

Rome was too dangerous for Vittoria, although she did not realize how much. In her convent she led a life of partial retirement, as many noblewomen did when they retired to a nunnery, unable to maintain a palace on their own. She went out to visit friends, and friends came to visit her. Vittoria, who was with her servant Prudentia, went on writing letters and poems almost feverishly, but then she fell ill. A friend wrote to her doctor saying that her soul was ill; what Vittoria needed was a doctor for her gravely depressed state. Another sent a letter to her doctor in Viterbo: "I beg you, Master Giuseppe, use every care for the health of such a noble lady ... Here you have to concentrate all your study, pour all your knowledge."

She was extremely depressed: her son was going through a period of disgrace with the emperor, her brother was exiled, she, labelled as a heretic, had never felt more isolated. On 22 December she wrote to Cardinal Morone, one of the *spirituali* who was later to be accused of heresy together with Cardinal Pole: "You have witnessed the chaos of ignorance in which I was, the labyrinth of errors in which I wandered, my body perpetually in movement to find repose and my soul ever agitated in its search for peace." It was true, she had stopped her frantic travelling, she had resigned herself to writing and praying. Of her life in Viterbo she wrote to Costanza d'Avalos, sister of her adopted son, whom we met as a follower of Valdés in Naples. Some of her letters to Costanza are exclusively involved with religious considerations of a very orthodox kind – the cult of Mary, the reading of St Augustine: Vittoria knew that spies would read the letters written by one woman suspected of heresy to another. Even in better times Italy was crowded with spies paid to intercept all correspondence: Isabella Gonzaga used to write two versions of the same letter – one sent openly for the spies, the other being the real and secret letter.

Not that prostitution was considered as dangerous as culture but courtesans were rich and, with the loss of revenue from the north of Europe, the Church was intent at finding other sources of income. The hand of the Inquisition was felt on matters not only of faith but also of morality: from a socially recognized position, courtesans and prostitutes were to become outcasts. In 1543 Venice, under papal pressure, legislated against courtesans wearing the same robes as gentlewomen. "It is ordered that no prostitute living in this land may wear gold, silver and silk, with the exception of their bonnets – which may be of pure silk – they may not wear chains, pearls, rings with stones or without stones ...". They could not possess rich furnishings or tapestries, but only rugs from Bergamo or Brescia, and if they were to contravene these particular sumptuary laws they would be deprived of their possessions and fined 100 ducats, half of which would go to the anonymous informers, the other half to charity. If the informers were slaves, they would be freed. One of the reasons for these sumptuary laws was inflation; people spent too much, the luxury which the courtesans displayed was a bad example to others and, by fining them and forbidding them to buy clothes, jewels, tapestries, the authorities thought they could put a partial stop to the excessive expenditure of most citizens.

Anonymous letters poured in: many described how they had seen a prostitute in church dressed like a married woman. Following the victory of Carafa's "hawks", in many cities courtesans were not allowed to go to church except at stated hours, they could not go to Mass on feast days, and they could go to confession only between 3pm and Vespers, so that their presence should not "contaminate dignified ladies". Prostitutes were to sit on the balconies of their houses displaying their bared breasts, their legs dangling down, in a humiliating – and uninviting – display of their profession. The Venetian "Ponte delle Tette", the Bridge of Tits, is still called after this forced custom. New institutes were opened to give shelter to young women who might have been attracted to dangerous paths: these places, a vast literature tells us, were nests of ignorance and exploitation. On the other hand, "the married woman", writes Cardinal Agostino Valier, "will attend to those domestic arts to which commonly women apply themselves like sewing, ironing and similar occupations, so that idleness, from which all evils derive, may never corrupt her." This was the type of woman the Inquisition wanted to protect: no nonsense about salons, writing and reading Plato, Aristotle and Petrarch. Men could just tolerate an intellectual like Vittoria Colonna because she came from the nobility and was chaste. But a Tullia, no. Some cities prescribed capital punishment for those who practised homosexuality, "that vice more usual among the *literati* and the clergy". In Venice until then transvestites went around the streets quite openly.

Most of Italy was either under the domination of the pope or that of the emperor. In 1545, the former addressed a letter to the ecclesiastical authorities in Ferrara to "institute a strict inquiry into the conduct of all ranks and, having taken depositions, applied torture, and brought the trials to a conclusion, to transmit the test to Rome for judgement." Spies were introduced in every house; the Protestant duchess, Renée of Ferrara, became a virtual prisoner in her palace, segregated from her family. In 1554 she was ordered to renounce her Protestant faith something that she did, but only formally. Even after that and after Ercole's death, Renée found herself surrounded by hostility, her own son Alfonso II (1559–97) treated her with fear and enmity – so much so that the duchess left Ferrara for her castle of Montargis in France, where she went on giving shelter to reformers fleeing Italy; she died in 1575. In 1560, the Reformed Church of Ferrara was dispersed, one of its preachers executed, and many others thrown in prison.

In 1546, trying to escape the hostility of the new laws, Tullia returned to Siena, (on paper an independent republic but occupied by the imperial forces) having married an older and poorer man. Silvestro Guicciardini was a "cover"; being married allowed Tullia to seem respectable and, for Silvestro, she was a goldmine. But the precaution of marrying was not enough: "*Meretrices* are also considered those who have a husband but are not with their husbands, live separately, and keep commerce with one or more men."

The following year Tullia was denounced as a prostitute and for not observing the law compelling *meretrices* to live in a special quarter of Siena; besides, her dress did not conform to the new laws. However, "the noble lady Tullia, daughter of the late Costanzo Palmieri d'Aragona and the wife of Silvestro Guicciardini", said the sentence of the Capitano di Giustizia of Siena, "has been unjustly defamed: she is entitled to dress and live as becomes an honest and noble person." Somebody must have helped her: we know very little about Tullia's life in this period since she had no "admirer" who wrote about her. She was no letter-writer either: Tullia survived on poetry about her or by her; in those troubled times few of her old friends and admirers wanted to receive her flattering sonnets or write verses in her praise. In August 1546, another anonymous denunciation was dismissed by the captain of justice.

As a writer Tullia had to be careful: for the first time printed words were being scrutinized. The Inquisition had not yet invented the Index, but some books were confiscated and burnt. There were trials against those printers who issued "guides" of courtesans and prostitutes, like Hieronimo Canepin in Venice. The *Tariffa* was seized and destroyed. In its rare (and filthy) poem, the *Tariffa* mentions Tullia. It tells the story of a foreigner who is in love, unrequitedly so, and in vulgar tones stops a gentleman, asking him how he could give vent to his unquenchable desire.

As the foreigner is impatient to find any "hole to fuck", the gentleman warns him that in Venice there are prostitutes in quantity, more than there are ants on the ground and flowers in April meadows and cows in the markets. The foreigner begs the gentleman to describe them to him, their value and their stories so that he may pick one from what he says. So the gentleman illustrates how there is one particular courtesan who asks for twenty scudi, and there is a Cornelia Griffo who, because she is well read, asks for forty.

Once, Lucia Alberi, he goes on recounting – who only took four scudi – was visited by a man who noticed a priest waiting for his turn. This man locked himself in the room with the prostitute and began to touch Lucia here and there, until his hand fell on "that natural hole" where the lady had plaited her hairs into braids. "Does this please my lord?" she asked, but the man's desire fled and he left the field open to the priest, who then performed a little black mass. Then it goes on:–

Talking about Tullia d'Aragona
who bores the pants off you
pissing out her knowledge of Helicon's fountains.
She wants ten scudos to take it from behind
and five in front, and you'll discard her
in favour of the biggest tart from any brothel.

Once again Tullia had to flee from Venice and went to Siena. But then Siena revolted against the imperial rule, many of Tullia's friends were killed and many fled the city. Outside its walls, corpses of tortured men and people hanged were left to rot in order to give an example to the rioting citizens. Tullia herself lost a great deal of property – her house was robbed several times – and, together with her mother and her daughter whom she still smuggled as her sister, but without her husband and son, Tullia left Siena for Florence. She arrived as a refugee, not as a grand lady.

The mere pretence of being rich and of keeping a salon, was a drain on her income. It is possible that her husband had taken what was left of her money and jewels, something he could legally do in any case and she was probably black-mailed. In short, when she arrived in Florence, Tullia was penniless; she had two children to support, an ageing mother, and she herself was no longer young. She needed to build up a new clientele and she had by now understood that she needed a literary sponsor, a well-known writer to extol her gifts, as Tasso and Muzio had done in the past. It was not easy during times as hard as these, but she thought of somebody whom she had already met in Rome and Venice.

Benedetto Varchi was a celebrity, ten years older than herself, a well-known literary figure. Tullia started bombarding him with letters and sonnets:–

Varchi, whose rare and immortal worth
fills every gentle soul with longing
why should I not – as I desire –
of your great knowledge fill my heart?

Varchi was living almost in exile, some distance from Florence in his country villa of Careggi; and because he was in trouble, Tullia's flattering letters, her poems, her attention stimulated his curiosity and pleased him. Hers, on the other hand, was a calculated operation. Varchi was in disgrace because the previous year he had been imprisoned and fined for raping a girl of nine; owing to Varchi's notoriety, the story had caused a huge scandal, and although Varchi's friends had procured him an official pardon, he felt more secure out of Florence.

Although practically a colony of the empire under the puppet rule of Duke Cosimo de' Medici, Florence had not yet promulgated any laws against courtesans. It was a rich city where some academies still thrived, like the Accademia degli Umidi. But ideas were no longer debated there. One of these academies was gastronomic: each of the twelve worthy members provided a new recipe, some of which, like those of the painter Andrea del Sarto, were very elaborate. It was called the Compagnia de la Marmitta (of the cooking pan). An average meal would open with a melon or salad, followed by minced liver or pigeon, cheese or fruit. But although they strived to recall the foundation of Plato's Academy where dialogues were debated by Socrates and his friends and written down by Plato, the substance was now very thin.

Tullia dreamt of opening a salon as she had in the past, but with a difference: this time it would take the shape of an *accademia*, a circle where items would be discussed by learned wits. This was important in Florence. Old Cosimo de' Medici, Lorenzo the Magnificent's grandfather, had invented clubs which celebrated Plato and Aristotle's writings in Greek and Latin, frequented even by the very young Michelangelo. But Tullia needed publicity. Without waiting any longer, Tullia wrote to Varchi asking him to do what she had always wanted from him, "with your pen raise my name out of the reach of the talons of importunate death". And he obliged by sending her the usual flattering poem: it was like being photographed by Avedon. Finely worded poetry, even if empty, gave a sheen of elegance, of prominence. And Tullia understood the times; she had to fight hard to keep earning her living as a courtesan, but pretending not to be one. Celio, her newly born son, was living with a governess who was expensive; Penelope was with her, growing prettier and prettier. When Varchi finally arrived in Florence, Tullia used all of her seductive powers and he fell for her: all the poems in her honour that she could have desired were produced by the mature *innamorato*.

At that time, a very different man, tormented by different worries, was also in Florence: Monsignor Carnesecchi, after his return from Viterbo, was not only deeply suspect but had no one to turn to. Most of the *spirituali* had died, Vittoria was ill, and Cardinal Pole did not share his ideas. At least in Florence Carnesecchi had a powerful protector in the Duke Cosimo de' Medici. Then, feeling he needed to talk, to confront his ideas and fears with somebody, he left for Fondi, knowing that Giulia Gonzaga was also an admirer of the reformers. When Pietro Carnesecchi arrived at Fondi and met that celebrated beauty, no longer young but still challengingly haughty, he fell in love with her: "I had started to love her for her human gifts; then our love had become spiritual and divine, in conformity to the religion we shared."

Giulia's life had also changed a great deal, as she revealed in a letter she sent to her cousin Ferrante on 23 February 1543. She started by apologizing for talking about her worries: after all, she and others had followed Valdés for fourteen years without any trouble:—

> *Now I am thinking that the strange ways in which that tribunal of the Inquisition acts are such that anybody – to get out of it – says not what he knows but what he thinks that those very reverend men {Cardinal Carafa and Cardinal Juan Alvarez de Toledo} would like to hear, and they have ministers very able to use persuasion; so it could be that some of those who said that they talked to me about something or mis-interpreted my way of thinking said things which in reality I know nothing about*

and could not hear of, because they behave very secretly and also, being of a good nature, I cannot understand what is wrong: and, if at times I have talked about religious matters, it was in order to understand them, never to deviate from what the Catholic Church teaches. But in these cases they say that even suspicion is enough.

Giulia then protested, saying that if the Church thought that Valdés's writings were evil, they should ban them and she would abide by the rules, even if she possessed no book by Valdés. Was this notion meant to reach those eyes which, in fact, read this letter? (It appeared, with many of Giulia's letters, at the Inquisition.)

Giulia goes on telling her cousin (who was later tried by the Inquisition), who had enquired about her state, that she had no idea of what she was being accused: she had only reasoned about religion with a few people; three at the most. Even after Ochino's flight, Giulia had naively written to her cousin Ferrante, also a follower of the Capuchin, saying that she "had always been a devout admirer of Friar Bernardino as I think many other women were, not because I held him higher than St Peter, but as he was a good Christian."

Carnesecchi found the palace at Fondi no longer full of poets and philosophers, but deserted. Clearly Giulia did not see why she was considered a heretic, or, from being the centre of a whole admiring group, why she was suddenly shunned. What had she said that was so terrible? Giulia had good grounds to protest: unless the Church was to spell out what was wrong, how could she be blamed for what in the immediate past had been acceptable? Valdés had been welcomed by Pope Clement; and Ochino admired by the emperor. Giulia was not as sharp as Vittoria, who understood that political times had changed, and that a new mood of reaction was under way. Whether Giulia succumbed at once to the younger and handsome Carnesecchi – whose portraits figures in a British private collection – must be left to our imagination. But at that moment they needed each other and had nobody but each other, so it was natural for Giulia to fall in the effeminate arms of Pietro Carnesecchi and for Pietro to give himself to the famous beauty.

In August 1544 Vittoria was better, and in September she returned to Rome. Reginald Pole left a month later because, in spite of his open mind and tolerance – or probably because of it – the pope had appointed him one of the presidents of a new council, which was to take place at Trent. The city of Trent had been chosen for yet another diet because it was within the realm of the Holy Roman Empire, but not too far from papal territory. Without Pole and her friends, there was no more reason for Vittoria to stay on in Viterbo, now threatened by the Turks. Barbarossa had taken the fortress of the Monte Argentario and Port'Ercole, where Agostino Chigi had once kept his fortune. It looked as if everything was collapsing around her. Vittoria took refuge in another convent, a very simple one, at St Anna de Funári. This convent of Benedictine nuns lay between the Tiber and the Capitol, on the ruins of the gigantic Roman Circus Flaminius.

It was one of Rome's poorest areas. The huge side walls of the circus were still standing and, under those, some merchants had carved out dark little shops, which gave the name to the street: via della Botteghe Oscure – of the dark shops. Vittoria was looked upon by the nuns with a certain suspicion: she had no friends among them; only Madonna Prudentia looked after her.

While Charles V had pressed the pope to open the diet, the "hawks" resolved to forget about appeasing the reformists, and to concentrate on finding written answers and laws for religious creeds. By doing so, they gave a statute to the Church of Rome. As Giulia had put it in her letters, nobody had so far stated what should and should not be accepted, what was heresy and what was not.

Carafa and Ignatius Loyola now planned for war; on the other hand, by giving Pole – the moderate – such an important role at Trent, the pope was hoping to attract the Church of England back to Rome. The ranks were divided: Carafa, appointed legate at the council and supported by Loyola's Jesuits, fought liberal opinions while the weaker moderates admitted some justice in the Protestants' claims. But the fanatics were more popular; if the Reformation had brought spiritual values to people like Vittoria and Giulia, it was depriving simpler people of the pomp they had so loved, of pilgrimages, of the worship of saints, or relics, the natural pagan trend of southern European religion.

The task of the Church was to define truth, Loyola said, therefore dogmatic definitions were needed. The pope too saw the Council of Trent as an instrument of this nature, but the emperor and the moderates still hoped to bring back the lost unity of the Christians. During the time in which the Inquisition was established, the pope had agreed that the Jesuits could take their vows of obedience, not to him, but to their founder, Ignatius of Loyola. (This was a rule broken only by Pope Wojtyla, who chose to appoint the head of the Jesuits himself, turning down the elected "black pope".) Loyola (1491–1556) was a short man, of bad health, black visionary eyes, silent and austere. He was slightly lame from a wound in his leg that he had acquired when he was a soldier in his youth in Spain. With the power of his amazing will he shaped the Society of Jesus to be a formidable army governed by military rule, tremendous scholarship and blind obedience. Such a man and such a system did not appeal to intellectuals, but was just what Carafa needed to wage war against Protestants.

By then Pole was regarded with suspicion by Loyola and Vittoria was judged as dangerous. Before going to Trent, Pole was in Rome working on the preliminaries of the council and saw Vittoria, who was worried and weak. Soon after, she went to visit Giulia Gonzaga for a month, but in the spring of 1546 Alfonso, Vittoria's son, died of fever. His last years had been difficult; he, too, had been under suspicion. Affected by all that was happening, Vittoria fell ill again. "I am extremely distressed to hear of the indisposition of the Marchesa di Pescara", a friend wrote. She received news from Trent: on 8 April, the council had affirmed that the Holy Bible was to be explained to the faithful only through the role of the clergy; Pole had opposed the decision. When the thorny question of justification by faith was to be debated, Pole – the advocate of toleration – realized that he was going to be overruled. On account of ill health he was allowed to leave. Pole should not have left the field free to his enemies, Vittoria thought. Carafa had rejected mediation; the property of the heretics should be confiscated, their books burnt, he said. No heretic should be tolerated at any court: those "pestilential weeds" were to be rooted out at whatever cost. Now the Inquisition was free to act.

From Padua, where he had gone to stay with Pietro Bembo, Pole wrote to Vittoria (4 October 1546). He started by saying that there was not much he could tell her in writing but that her messenger would "fill her up" with news: clearly there were items that by then even Cardinal Pole, one of the presidents of the Council of Trent, feared to put down on paper. He was very happy staying with Bembo, he said; he had a study for his own use, and a little garden: it was a blessing:–

> *Having told you this, I heard with greater displeasure than I ever felt about my own sickness about that of Your Excellency, which started from last August and continues to these days, nor am I unable to say anything, if not to shout to the doctor of the sky that He may deign Himself to be your doctor. Because I do not think that you have to take more medicines from the doctor on earth, except to take his advice about diet and good air in which, I beg you, follow his advice.*

Certainly the dark convent was no place for a sick, elderly woman. Michelangelo went to see her: he too had grown much older; recently he had been so ill that it was feared he was going to die. He had been moved to a healthier house than his own, to Palazzo Strozzi, a guest of Roberto Strozzi, son of Filippo, whose misfortunes we followed through the lives of Tullia and Vittoria. Roberto himself had fled to Lyons – a city which was called "the Florence of France", because many persecuted Florentines had taken refuge there; Michelangelo sent him a message, remembering his old friend Filippo. Another of Vittoria's visitors, Fortunato Martinengo, wrote of her (7 June 1546) to a third party: "How humble she is! How good! Without a precedent … I visited her often; and if I had not been afraid of being importunate, I would never have said goodbye." Her strength and mental reasoning were amazing. She talked so intelligently that "I shall at least be appeased by having met and having become the admirer of the most famous and worthy woman who is alive today."

As she told Michelangelo, Vittoria was finding it difficult to write, to concentrate: "As in your case sculpture mirrors the goodness of Him who made you the only master sculptor, you will understand that I thank only the Lord for my almost dead writings, and I offended Him less by writing than I do now with my idleness." From her cell at the convent, she heard that Ochino had joined the Calvinists; Carafa was proved right. Clouds crowded, denser and denser, over her. Her only remaining paladin, Michelangelo lent his own copy of Vittoria's poems to as many friends as possible so that, he said, her poetry would be known and printed *"in modo che per tutti ci sono in stampa"* – so that they would be printed for all.

Things were not so hard for Tullia who, in Florence, had succeeded in establishing her academy-salon; where she entertained men such as Don Luigi da Toledo, who was none other than the Duchess of Florence's brother, his son Pietro, and Niccoló Martelli, a man who had written a letter to Michelangelo praising his *Last Judgement*. On particular days Tullia's academy would debate themes such as the purity of the language and Varchi, who was jealous of her other clients, would still do her the favour of correcting her poetry. Niccoló Martelli extolled Tullia by comparing her "to the April sun that melts the frosts of winter", meaning that hers had been a welcome cure for the boredom of Cosimo de' Medici's Florence. Her flesh was alabaster and pure snow, he wrote to her, and he hinted at her diet – Tullia must have laboured to preserve her looks (6 March 1546). But, as usual, Tullia had detractors as well. Alfonso de' Pazzi nicknamed her "the courtesan of the academicians" and Varchi was so teased that he fled, writing her a farewell poem in which he accused the nasty gang of detractors. Another poet, Alessandro Arrighi, put the clock back a few decades and addressed Tullia's rare beauty, "which has not yet been equalled in the world."

Everything was going well for Tullia, until the wind of change reached Florence: in October 1546 Cosimo legislated against courtesans. In future they were to posess no jewels, no silk, and "the *meretrices* should wear a veil, or cloth, or a handkerchief, or some material on their head that has a stripe a finger wide, in gold silk, or other yellow material, so that it should be seen by everybody, under pain – if they do not obey – of ten golden scudos, in best gold, for each time."

An anonymous letter reached the magistrate: a prostitute named Tullia d'Aragona was not conforming to the new laws. She could no longer go out; how could Tullia be expected to wear the horrible yellow stripe, which would label her as a common prostitute? Tullia never thought of herself as a *meretrix*. How could she hold the refined "lessons" in her academy and receive her noble friends? She was desperate: her world, so laboriously created, had collapsed.

It was not only women who were alone in the tempest of the Inquisition, now that Florence was becoming as reactionary as Rome. Indeed Monsignor Pietro Carnesecchi received his first summons to appear before the tribunal of the Inquisition. He was examined by Juan Alvarez de Toledo but Cosimo de' Medici intervened and the charges against Carnesecchi were dropped, this time. The whole of Tuscany, once the very home of the Renaissance, once so carefree, so joyous, was now strangled by fear. In Lucca, where the silk manufacturers' "middle class" had welcomed the Reformation, Giuseppe Jova, Vittoria Colonna's former secretary, fell foul of the Inquisition. Jova, who came from the minor nobility, was quick to flee to Lyons where he joined the many Tuscan exiles. (He was later condemned to death *in absentia*.)

Back in Rome we find Vittoria so ill that she had to be moved to the Cesarini Palace, Giulia Cesarini being the only relative of Vittoria left in Rome. That was on the very beginning of 1547. She was housed in a comfortable room near an inner garden. On 18 February she made a will: her brother Ascanio, still in exile, was her heir; 1,000 scudi were left to each of the four convents where she had spent part of her life; 9,000 to Cardinal Pole; other sums to her servants and to the destitute. She begged the Cardinals Pole, Morone and Sadoleto (Bembo had just died) to be her executors. She left Michelangelo out of her will, probably because they had discussed it and he, having no heir and being very well off, would have wanted neither money nor the bureaucratic worries of being her executor.

A week later Michelangelo was woken in the middle of the night by a servant of the Cesarinis. When he reached the Cesarini Palace early in the morning, he found Vittoria near death. "Say a prayer for me", she asked him, "I cannot remember the words ...". He kissed her hand over and over again, crying. Later he wished he had kissed her forehead and her face. She died in his arms; she was fifty-seven. Her relative took her body back to St Anna's, waiting for Ascanio's orders: nobody wanted to be responsible for the corpse of a heretic.

But the old, enraged Michelangelo found no consolation: "After her death often he stood as if bewildered and as if he had lost his mind", his pupil, Condivi, described. And he himself wrote:—

> Quando il principio dei sospir miei tanti
> Fu per morte dal cielo al mondo tolto
> Natura, che non fé mai si bel volto
> Restó in vergogna e chi lo vide in pianti.
>
> O sorte rea dei miei sospiri amanti,
> O fallaci speranze, o spirto sciolto,
> Dove se'or? La terra ha pur raccolto
> Tue belle membra, e'l ciel tuoi pensier santi.
>
> Mal si credette morte acerba e rea
> Fermare il suon di tue virtuti sparte
> Ch'oblio di Lete estinguer non potea.
>
> Che spogliato da lei ben mille carte
> Parlan di te; ne per te'l cielo avea
> Lassú, se non per morte, albergo e parti.

When the cause of many of my sighs
Was taken from the world by heaven,
Nature, which never fashioned so fair a face,
stood ashamed and all who saw it, in tears.

Oh cruel fate on my loving desire!
Oh vain hopes. Oh emancipated spirit

Where are you now? Earth has already gathered
Your beautiful form and heaven your holy thoughts.

It was wrongly thought that untimely and cruel death
Could stop the power of your worth
Lethe's oblivion could not extinguish them.

Robbed of its prey, a thousand writings
Will record your fame; nor heaven could give you a dwelling
And a home, except through death.

Michelangelo alone raised his voice to claim Vittoria's eternal life through her work. He would visit those places where they had been together: "I often came to sit here because I love to relive my sorrows more than my joys."

On 27 February, two days after Vittoria's death, her will disappeared; she had wanted to be buried like her sisters at St Anna's, but she was not. The nuns did not consider it an honour to have the heretic's corpse in their church. They were ignorant, hostile, and they all became keen witnesses for the Inquisition. Two other executors, Bartolomeo Stelle and Lorenzo Bonorio, were left to sort out the risky business. Bonorio wrote to Ascanio in exile: "Her body is still in a casket sealed with pitch; it would be better if Your Excellency were to change it, if he wishes that her body remains here." There were frantic exchanges of letters. On 29 February, Bonorio wrote to Ascanio that, "having consulted the Very Reverend of England [Pole], they have started to make a proper casket." On 15 March, Ascanio was informed that, "We have followed your order for her body; it is in a casket sealed with pitch on three sides, the one above will be made in velvet." The casket was placed – but not buried – in the nuns' communal pit; a century later (29 June 1652) the pit was explored and a diary recorded that Vittoria's corpse "was in a casket of wood quilted in embroidered velvet ... on that occasion she was buried." Later, the floods of the Tiber reduced Vittoria's bones to mud – together with those of the other nuns.

Her mystical face, as portrayed by Michelangelo in *The Last Judgement*, lives on, watched by the thousands who visit the Sistine Chapel. But where are the two portraits of Vittoria which (an eye-witness recounts) Michelangelo kept in his house? Probably destroyed but, as Michelangelo wrote in his sonnet, "a thousand writings" rescued her fame, that fame which "they" were trying to take away. But propaganda is strong: even today Vittoria is often described as a tiresome woman whose only claim to fame was to have stimulated Michelangelo's imagination – and love.

Only one year after her death, she was examined by the Inquisiton: *"Marchionissima Piscariae filia spirituali et discipula Cardinalis Poli heretici."* The charges against Vittoria ran to three pages long.

the broken lute

While the Renaissance had taken women – some women – out into the world, the Counter-Reformation consciously set out to put them back whence they came: ignorance was a gift beloved by God; it gave shelter from temptation. The Italian woman had started reading far too much; now she was to go back to the medieval pattern whereby she saw few or no books, or even better was illiterate and unable to read at all. Before Gutenberg's invention, there had been no books, only expensive manuscripts, and the owners of these manuscripts could be kept in check. Ignorance was guaranteed to keep people weak and submissive. The massive literature written with women in mind which, following Castiglione's best-seller, *The Courtier*, was appearing all over Europe, was of a didactic type; it belonged to the "how-to" genre popular today: how to dress, how to educate, how to appear graceful, how to take good care of one's body by dieting and cosmetics, what manners were acceptable, how to converse gracefully (conversation being regarded very highly; Margaret of Navarre wrote that it was the "essential divertissement"). Not only were these books popular in Italy and France but also in England; 125 editions of manuals on how to sing and play were published in England between 1560 and 1640. People like Thomas Morley, William Byrd and Orlando Gibbons wrote songs and instrumental music for the virginals, the lute, the many viols; special music was written for dancing. A damsel in Robert Greene's *Never Too Late* "took a lute in her hand" and in the next scene a lady is sitting in her garden, "plaieng upon a Lute many pretie Roundelaies, Borginets, Madrigals ..." and, recapturing the mood of the Renaissance, she was playing "in honour of Venus". These were books and scores aimed at improving the woman's mind and condition and at distracting her from the home, breeding and praying. Both the Counter-Reformation and Calvinism – which often merged in their misogyny – condemned such books; religion, of course, was man's weapon. On the other hand, the many printing presses that had sprung up everywhere in Europe made it difficult to control which books were printed and sold.

The other kind of literature for women – having more time for leisure, women were becoming good "consumers" – was that of entertainment: love stories told with the purpose of amusing, like Ariosto's *Orlando Furioso*, Boiardo's *Orlando Innamorato* and Boccaccio's *Decameron*. But now it was also considered wrong for women to be entertained; the Calvinists had always thought so and the moralizing Catholics were copying the Puritans' worst excesses.

Music, which had been taught to every girl of the middle and upper strata, should no longer encourage dancing and flirting but go back to the Church. Music should inspire fear of God, glorify the Church, not the senses. Dances, songs, madrigals set the scene for amorous exchanges; lyrics which praised the female form were to be discouraged. Musical instruments had been used as symbols, as feminine symbols. Indeed the lute, considered to be an aphrodisiac instrument, was to be discarded, broken.

The status of the sitter in a portrait was readable by contemporaries because of the symbols used to describe the sitter's activities and, since the majority could not read, there were conventions. The lute, for one, was a symbol of pleasure, of cultured entertainment, it also described a courtesan. The ability to play a lute or any instrument of civilized life, was a sign of an educated mind, wrote Castiglione in *The Courtesan*. The painter Sofonisba Anguissola portrayed herself at the spinet and Artemisia Gentileschi with the lute which, like the spinet, was a metaphor for carnal love.

Painting was not usually considered suitable for a girl: there were powders to be mixed, ladders and scaffolding to be climbed; hands and clothes became dirty, and there was no time to arrange hair beautifully, or to look after the whiteness of one's hands. In fact, painting was taken up only by those who had no other choice, like Artemisia Gentileschi (1597–1652), who was a child of the Counter-Reformation. Raped when sixteen (a trial had divulged the scandal), she had been tortured in order to find out whether she was telling the truth. Because so much scandal followed her name, Artemisia could no longer live as a normal woman, marry and have children: that was an option barred to somebody with her past. So she chose a man's work and, like her father – at times better than her father – she became a painter, a job which she could exercise in northern Europe, far from the cradle of the Counter-Reformation. Sofonisba Anguissola (1528–1626), the daughter of a minor nobleman, was also trained to be a painter out of necessity – her father had six daughters and not enough money for six dowries. Besides, this was considered exceedingly eccentric by his contemporaries.

Music was more in tune with femininity; the famous composer and singer Barbara di Santa Sofia Strozzi is portrayed by Bernardo Strozzi with a viola da gamba and other instruments. Harmony and music were also symbols of accord between man and woman especially in the Flemish world; and Music was always depicted as a fair female together with Harmony. On the other hand Fury, Avarice, Cowardice and Shame were also portrayed as ugly or elderly women. That is to say that the very personification of the symbol is female: Peace, Charity and other capital virtues being largish, fatter females showing the generous nature of the particular virtue. Even the Church, the implacable enemy of the female sex, wherever depicted together with a city (like Venice or Florence and, later, nations, France, Italy, Britain) were idealized in female forms.

Raphael underlined the mathematical and philosophical nature of his female Music, depicting her beside Pythagoras, together with the great philosophers in his *School of Athens*. He also made a point of dividing instruments into "sacred" and "profane" in his *Santa Cecilia* (1515). While some musical instruments are ready to be played for the saint's nuptials, at her feet lie the flute, triangolo and a viola da gamba, symbols of earthy *vanitas*.

Vittoria was depicted holding some of her sonnets but Tullia who would have aspired to hold a manuscript, was to be admired with her lute. In a painting, a book or a manuscript represented learning. The petals of a dishevelled rose could be read as the disease of the person portrayed or her spent sexuality – the rose being a constant presence in the symbolism of all times. The rose was one of the many logos for sex in both literature and painting; Italian literature used it back in the thirteenth century (cf Cielo d'Alcamo, the Sicilian poet of Frederick II's circle) and again during the Renaissance with Poliziano and Lorenzo de' Medici, who exhorted young girls to gather their roses when in bud. The open rose symbolized the more mature female sexuality which eventually should be discarded; in the nineteenth century it became the camellia, (cf. *La Dame aux Camellias* and *La Traviata*). In Phoenician and Achaean times, the red rose was the symbol of Adonis loved by Aphrodite. The pomegranate (in Latin: *punica*) also had a Phoenician origin and was a Renaissance sign for sex. It sprouts from Dionysus's blood, its ripe fruit splits open like a wound and shows the red inside. The open fruit symbolized death and the promise of resurrection when held in the hand of Aphrodite; for the Renaissance it was the symbol of a woman just after the sexual act and it abounds in late Renaissance. It was also abundance; in her temple of Paestum, Juno was represented holding the pomegranate which is now in the hand of the Virgin Mary in the church that has taken the temple's place; the pilgrims who pray for fertility now are the same as the women who prayed to Juno-Hera. The slipper has another evident sexual connotation: Titian signs his name inside one in a painting where Tarquin is about to rape the naked Lucretia; Cinderella conquers her prince with the narrow slipper (*vulva*) and even Wagner in *Die Meistersingers* plays with this specific metaphor.

But symbols changed. What was easily understandable in Renaissance Italy was not necessarily so in the Low Countries; as we shall see in Chapter Thirteen, the wife of a burgher would require to be painted surrounded by objects depicting her wealth, so tulips and roses suggested wealth – not sex. The symbol for Christ in medieval times (a fish, a shepherd), or for life (a tree, a snake) was no longer recognized as such in Renaissance times. On the other hand, during the Counter-Reformation many "sexy" portraits were changed into images of saints and martyrs by merely repainting the symbol: off with the lute, the white dog, the rose, replaced by a wheel of St Catherine, the palm of martyrdom or a plate with St Lucia's eyes.

In Dutch painting the symbol turns into explicit and unsubtle description. For example, the brothel keeper mimics copulation, her dog licks her client's finger (Hendrick Pot). Mirrors are temptation, letters dreamingly perused by an elusive gaze (Vermeer) distant or unrequited love. The erotic symbols of the Dutch include oysters, ripe fruit and goblets waiting to be filled. Francis Bacon throws light on the immense difference of thought between the Renaissance in Italy and France and what happened in the North. In *New Atlantis* (1627) he states that man should look at the future, not to Plato and his philosophy; his is the idea of progress and progress is the future; in a nutshell, the story of what was going to happen.

In English Renaissance portraiture we can observe crowns and jewels as symbols of power but also empty backgrounds, celestial turquoise which enhances the face of the sitter – as if painter and lady sitter would not want to give anything away of their status but for their expressions – and the signature of the painter who, in Holbein's case, would have been enough to indicate the sitter's economic position. Strangely enough, although feared and hated by the narrower expression of the Churches, woman remained the representation of most images. The Counter-Reformation's anger expressed itself in a furious attack against the very representation of leisure and grace, and that was the lute. The *"juste-milieu"* (the denomination is Balzac's) discarded anything "different". And, since the lute was an instrument of pleasure and had that suggestive shape from which it took its profane symbol, it was the first instrument to be discarded as the representation of the sexually liberated woman. It combined sex with culture, music with physical love.

As we have seen, women's clothes were to be restrained, too, and statutory laws decreed this. They applied not only to women of doubtful morality. All were to conform and dress more soberly – a negation of individuality, of the Renaissance. This restraint of women was decreed partly to counter rampant inflation, caused by wars, low productivity and an increasing population but also to put them down.

As Tuscan bankers and merchants had already discovered, good business – that never flourishes under repressive regimes – was now to be found outside Italy: many left looking for trade and liberty. Those who did generally belonged to a middle class which was scared of the growing restrictions imposed by both temporal and spiritual powers. The atmosphere in Italy was becoming claustrophobic: the spirit of the Renaissance was leaving those shores but, by travelling north, it found a new way, and it lived a new life. Florence, once the very heart of the Renaissance, had become a shell empty of freedom and ideas.

In April 1547, Tullia d'Aragona was once again summoned by the Ufficiali d'Onestá: she had disobeyed the law by not wearing a yellow veil and she had persisted in using silk. Tullia found her admirable strength: she talked and wrote to her important friends and one of them, Don Pedro da Toledo, the nephew of the Duchess de' Medici, came to her aid. He advised Tullia to appeal to his aunt, accompanying her petition with poems composed for her by well-known writers. Tullia was so humiliated and depressed that she was unable to draft the letter to the duchess. Once again Varchi came to her aid: "Help me and save me with your wisdom, in making this appeal!" she wrote.

In the petition, Tullia stated that, owing to the present circumstances, she hardly left her room, let alone her own house. She begged the duchess to talk to "the Most Excellent and Most Illustrious Duke" so that she should not be forced "to observe the law about the yellow veil". Humbly she promised that she would wear simple clothes and that she would show herself in the streets wearing a cloak "in the Roman fashion", which was Spartan and simple. Cosimo read it and scribbled in his own hand on the corner of Tullia's letter, "*Fasseli gratia per poetessa*": reprieve her, since she is a poet.

In a small town like Florence, both duke and duchess could not but be well aware that Tullia was a courtesan, but she served a purpose in entertaining courtiers and foreign visitors. She was also known to possess the art of conversation – an esteemed gift which, as we can see from the many laboured and elegant dialogues published at the time, was difficult to achieve. Besides, the poems which Tullia had attached to her petition had been written by impressive names: Ippolito de' Medici, a kinsman of Cosimo's, Bernardo Tasso, Varchi and Muzio.

When Tullia received the official reprieve, she was jubilant. It read: "As the duke, with a special gift, desires to give tribute to the rare gifts of poetry and philosophy that are recognized with pleasure among the esteemed talents of the learned Tullia d'Aragona", she was to be exempted from observing the law, "and she is allowed to wear those clothes and ornaments which she pleases". But even the duke's special reprieve could not recreate her glittering academy. Besides, for the first time in her life Tullia had fallen in love, with Pietro Mannelli, handsome, fair-haired, and twenty-four years old. And she – she was nearing forty! The young man had other thoughts: although he did make love to her, he preferred younger ladies. Experiencing the agony of love for the first time, Tullia wrote poems straight from her heart; she would not send those sonnets to Varchi for correction – indeed at times their grammar falters, but they are beautiful and have resisted time, which has instead killed Varchi's heavy poetry. She had been like a nightingale, she wrote, flying among trees, free, ignoring the pangs of love; she had been gathering her trophies in the temple of Venus, but love had now made her a prisoner. Tullia knew that she no longer had the means to keep her man, the centre of her life. And she was alone, her "institute of culture" was closed, all those men from the nobility, who could at least have impressed Pietro, had been dispersed by the fact that she had been humiliated as a mere tart.

She was losing "her beautiful sun, maybe it was her fault, maybe destiny …":–

> Ma io, s'avvien che perda il mio bel sole,
> O per mia colpa o per malvagia sorte,

Non spero aver, ne' voglio, altro conforto.

But I do not hope to have comfort
if it happens that I lose my beautiful sun
either through my own fault or because it is my destiny,

She could not confess her distress to Varchi, or to her ageing mother; nor could she tell Penelope, whom she insisted on calling a sister.

In order to show that she really was a poet, Tullia felt that she had to publish. Besides, everybody seemed to be printing books and reading them. Tullia wanted to prove herself to her Pietro, but she also wanted to show her gratitude to the Medici, the rulers.

The Medici were suddenly closely related to the powerful house of France: in the previous year Francis, King of France, had died, and the new king's wife was Catherine de' Medici, who was half-French anyway. Conducting the ceremony in Marseilles, the dying, almost blind Medici pope himself gave the fourteen-year-old Catherine to Henri Valois, son of Francis I of France.

Working feverishly, in 1547, Tullia was able to publish two books, a *Dialogue* and a *Rime*. The dialogue was a long discussion about love in the abstract, which showed off Tullia's stylistic ability. Her *Rime*, on the other hand, consisted of her own poems and those addressed to her by the famous: it was reprinted four times in the century. The *Rime* was dedicated to Duchess Eleonora de' Medici (Venice, 1547), and the *Dialogue* to Duke Cosimo, to whom she owed her "liberty". "In me", she wrote in her dedicatory preface, hinting at what he had done for her, "the desire is very ardent to offer Your Excellency at least a small sign of the affection and servitude which I always felt towards your illustrious and very happy family, as to the obligations I have with it, particularly for the favours received from you." Of course, by reading such a dedication anyone who did not know Tullia's personal story would have believed that the Medici were her patrons: Tullia was skilled in such manoeuvres.

The story of this *Dialogue* followed the conventions of a semi-staged play. Her old lover and friend Muzio had seen to the publication of the dialogue, *On the Infinity of Love*. And this is the story, typical of the genre: at Tullia's house, some are debating the theme of love, and whether true love can end. Who knocks at the door? Our – and Tullia's – friend Varchi. Thinking that he has interrupted Tullia's fine reasoning, he apologizes, but she welcomes him. As he was walking towards her house, he caught himself pondering, "Poor me! Love takes me where I do not want to go, thinking of being unwelcome to the one I want overwhelmingly to please." He might suffer having to converse with Tullia, who is only a woman, she answers – and Varchi, she knows, thinks that "women are less worthy and perfect than men". Besides, Tullia says, fishing for compliments, she has no knowledge of style and language. Protests at her modesty (written by Tullia) fol-

20. Catherine de' Medici

Shown here with her daughters and daughters-in-law is Claude de France, first wife of Francis I of France, Valois, and Renée Duchess of Ferrara's sister. Catherine de' Medici is to her right in a white cap. From the age of six, Catherine was educated in Florence with her Medici cousins Ippolito and Alessandro. Many in Florence hoped that the two branches of the Medici family would join in marriage. But Clarice Strozzi died when Catherine was nine and the little girl was left alone to face the turbulence of the Florentine rebellion against the Medici rule. Her fortunes changed when another Medici was made pope and it was he who decided on the great alliance with the throne of France. (From a miniature in the Medici's Book of Hours) low: she! Tullia? The woman who has the finest style! Then they return to the previous topic: "vulgar" and "honest" – profane or sacred – love, a theme which painters like Titian had depicted famously. Dishonest love, Tullia says, belongs to base men who want to appease an animal desire and who, after having done so, often turn their love into hatred. Honest love derives from reason, as Petrarch and Bembo wrote, but also from fantasy. "It is true that a lover, besides a spiritual union, may desire a bodily one, to become as much as possible a whole with the loved object, and when the two bodies cannot penetrate one another, he can never extinguish his desire, and so his love is bitter." Varchi thinks that whatever Nature planned cannot be condemned. But what about those men who love other men? Tullia is enraged: "They do not follow Nature's order, and they deserve that punishment that not only is prescribed by clerical and divine laws, but also by human and civil laws." But why, Tullia asks Varchi, did Plato praise homosexuals? Plato and Socrates loved young men, but not physically, Varchi answers, and is scandalized at the thought that anybody could think otherwise. Can women be loved for their minds alone? Tullia asks. Oh yes, says Varchi.

Tullia's "debate" treated fashionable themes central to Renaissance life, love and its different interpretations. Sacred and profane love, in other words, platonic and physical love, were often depicted in painting and rendered in poetry. It is interesting to perceive how the Renaissance in Italy accepted and coupled both giving them a most attractive face. Titian, in his famous canvas now at the Borghese Gallery, represents both forms of love as attractive young women, one naked and the other beautifully dressed, leaning on the rim of a well – the symbol of knowledge but also as the source of life – thus representing the female soul and the female body. The two faces of love are equally extolled in poetry and litera-ture. Spiritual love, Plato wrote, could be as strong if not stronger and also as passionate as physical love, and certainly more enduring. The Italian Renaissance depicted the courtesan (not the *hetera*, the mere prostitute) as the acceptable and socially desirable model of physical love. It is only later that profane love takes on the darker tonality of sin, of the forbidden, of wrongdoing. It continued with the arrival of Folly, who interferes with the serenity of love affairs, as in Louise Labé's poetry or Bronzino's depiction of Venus and Cupid. (Folly, in the latter case, is present because the beautiful and mature woman is copulating with a very young boy.)

Ficino, who belonged to an earlier generation than Tullia, and who had been in Cosimo (the Elder) de' Medici's circle, believed that Platonism contained antici-pations of Christianity. Plato was the one writer who popularized the idea of spiritual love; the true love of a person prepared for the love of God; if the lover had learnt to transcend bodily desires and to focus on the soul, love turned into religious devotion. "The shadow of Plato hung over the science of the Renaissance as well as its poetry," writes Anthony Gottlieb. Plato's goal of using mathematics as the key to unlock the secret of nature had spread to craftsmen, musicians, gardeners and traders, as well as those painters who had studied the laws of perspective. And it had even penetrated the nature of love which was discussed in discourses, *trattati* and *dialoghi*. The search for the rules of perspective was very much an aspect of the platonic mathematical investigation. "Ah, Paolo", Donatello remonstrated to the painter Uccello, "this perspective of yours is making you abandon the certain for the uncertain." For Paolo Uccello's wife, it must have been like sharing the house with an overpowering mistress. Indeed he would stay up all night worrying about some problem of perspective and murmuring, *"Ah che dolce cosa e' questa prospettiva."* As she would beg him to come to bed he would repeat, "What a sweet thing is this perspective." Perspective, of course, being based on geometry and mathematics.

Beauty – a typical Renaissance theme – was central to the debate in Tullia's *Dialogue*, although, to judge from his portrait by Titian, Varchi was rather ugly. "... Love is nothing else but a desire to enjoy by union either what is really beautiful, or what appears to be beautiful to the lover", Tullia writes.

But Tullia's two books did not retrieve her social position, although she continued to pursue it. She even sent a sonnet to Cardinal Bembo, and hinted that she was thinking of taking the veil: the elderly cardinal did not even bother to answer. But she battled on, and around this time she started writing a narrative poem, *Guerrin Meschino*, based on a Spanish story. Not only was it a fashionable thing to do, but with it Tullia hoped to secure the Spanish Eleonora de' Medici's patronage. *Guerrin Meschino* was only published in 1560 after Tullia's death, when her manuscript finished up in the hands of a Venetian printer. In her foreword, Tullia explained why she had decided to write such a work. Much harm, she wrote hypocritically, had been done by indecent books. Boccaccio's *Decameron*, which was "dishonest and irreligious", and Ariosto's *Orlando Furioso* corrupted women, and such texts were not suitable "either for nuns, girls, widows or married women, or even for prostitutes, because it is not new for a woman, by want or some other misfortune, to fall into error with her body."

On the same subject, Robert Greene was writing in England, "Let her spend her time in reading such ancient authors as may sharpen her wisdom by their perfect sentences." On the other hand, Greene also objected to writers like Ovid, Apuleius, Aristotle, and to those love stories which could put women into temptation. In her foreword, Tullia was at least sincere about her past: "I, who in the early years of my life, knew more about the world than I would now have wished ...".

In spite of playing up to the new ideas, of keeping a low profile, and of having important friends, Tullia was forced to leave Florence and that was towards the end of 1548 or at the very beginning of 1549. The new hawkish wave could not tolerate the scandalous presence of a Tullia for long. In her finest poem, she bewailed her lost good looks and the great love whom she had to leave: "Where is, wretched me, that golden hair which Love – to catch me – made into a net?"

Before leaving with her family and her possessions, she addressed a last poem, a farewell, to Pietro Mannelli:–

> Ov'e', misera me, quell'aureo crine,
> di cui fe' rete , per pigliarmi, Amore?
> Ov'e' lassa, il bel viso, onde l'ardore
> Nasce, che mena la mia vita al fine?
>
> Ove son quelle luci alte et divine
> In cui dolce si vive e insieme more?
> Ov'e' la bianca man, che lo mio core
> Stringendo punse con acute spine?
>
> Ove sunonan l'angeliche parole
> Ch'in un momento mi dan morte e vita?
> U'i cari sguardi? u' le sembianze belle?
> Ove luce ora il vivo almo mio sole
> con cui dolce destin mi venne in sorte
> quanto mai piove da benigne stelle?

> *Woe is me! Where have my golden curls gone*
> *which Cupid made into a net to trap me?*
> *Where has it gone, the beauty of my face*
> *which showed that passion that will end my life?*
>
> *Where are those wide and divine eyes*
> *within which I lived so sweetly and, at the same time, died?*
> *Where is that white hand which, holding my heart,*
> *pricked me with sharp thorns?*
>
> *And those angelic words, where are they?*
> *Words that in a moment could give me death or life?*
> *Where are his dear glances? his alluring body?*
> *Where is my sun now speeding light?*
> *That sun which a sweet destiny chanced me to possess*
> *as if showered upon from the stars above?*

She wrote to Varchi, to whom she owed so much. "My dear Patron", she called him, and sent him gifts: a couple of doves, a bottle of Malvasia wine and one of water – a symbol of friendship – and an alabaster salt cellar. She was sad when she wrote her farewell letter to him and talked about death. But she warned him that, even from afar, she might have to send him some rhymes to correct – because he was her maestro. Humiliated, thrown out, challenged but not vanquished until the end, Tullia had every intention of going on writing.

We do not know whether Duchess Eleonora read the poems dedicated to her by Tullia, or whether Duke Cosimo read her *Dialogue on the Infinity of Love* – he was certainly not interested in pure love, but in a "dishonest" kind, as Tullia had put it, and certainly not in endless love although he was close to his wife Eleonora da Toledo. But he could be faithful to his friends. In fact, once again he sheltered the elegant Pietro Carnesecchi from the Inquisition that was raging in Rome.

By 1549 Tullia was in Rome, in a comfortable apartment but no longer in a house with a garden and room for servants. Penelope was almost fourteen and was, Muzio reported, a very beautiful girl who had already made some "conquests". She was already on the same path as her mother and grandmother, as some of Tullia's enemies had been quick to point out. Tall, trim and pale, aware of her destiny, Penelope was now the main breadwinner.

Her death on 1 February 1549, possibly of tuberculosis, left her mother with the sense of tragedy, of loss. She had been unable to provide Penelope with a dignified life, a dowry, and a husband. But we have no letters, no sonnets from Tullia, only a poem written by an anonymous friend and dedicated to "the little girl courtesan", which concluded that death might have been a better fate for a girl whose path was already so sad. Penelope was buried in the nearby Church of St Augustine: the inscription on her tomb stated that her "mother" Giulia, who was to follow shortly, and her "sister" Tullia, were in despair.

Tullia was left with little Celio whom she wanted to educate; he at least had a chance to escape his women's fate. But money was needed for education, for respectability, for anything and Tullia could no longer prostitute herself since she was beginning to be too old and too tired. In the past, when everything had gone wrong, Tullia had started all over again but this time her immense resilience broke down. She was now alone in a city which had changed dramatically.

Rome's politics depended on whichever pope was elected. When Paul III died in November 1549 it looked as if things could change because Cardinal Pole suddenly became the obvious candidate for the throne of St Peter. The fact that Reginald Pole almost became Paul's successor stresses that the climate of opinion had changed in Rome in many ways, for Pole did not belong to a powerful Italian family, nor could he have bought his way into the papacy, since he was not rich. As the leader of the moderates, Pole had Carafa and the Society of Jesus fiercely opposed to him. But he showed weakness when, having been named pope by acclamation, he stated that he needed to be elected in the proper manner, and gave his enemies time to mount a campaign which lost him the papacy and, eventually, also his cardinalship.

One could meditate on the many "ifs" of history: had Reginald Pole become pope, history would not have been the same. Women would have kept the position they acquired in the Renaissance, the Inquisition would have been tamed and, as the candidate of Charles V, Pole would have striven for the emperor's still-cherished dream of Christian unity. Besides, as an Englishman, he could have worked towards a rapprochement of his country to the Church of Rome. Instead the tide of the Counter-Reformation really started in 1555 with the election of Cardinal Carafa, who took the name of Paul IV: as Carafa became pope, Charles V abdicated in favour of his son. The emperor's vision was shattered by Carafa's presence on the throne of St Peter. Il Pasquino, always alert, commented:–

Figli, meno giudizio
e piú fede comanda il Sant'Uffizio.
E ragionate poco:
che contro la ragion esiste il fuoco.
E la lingua a suo posto
che a Paolo quarto piace assai l'arrosto.

Believers, less judgement
and more faith by the Holy Office is required.
And reason little
that against reason there is fire.
And keep your tongue tight
that Paul IV loves roasting people.

Cardinal Carafa was seventy-nine when he ascended the throne of St Peter and it was believed that he would die shortly. He did not, and his rule was violent and unrelenting – it was even said that by then Paul IV had become insane. He instituted the Roman ghetto where Jews were to be locked in every night, and had to wear a yellow hat. Booksellers had to send the lists of their books, and even private collectors were ordered to burn all those volumes that were considered dangerous, and these included even Cardinal Contarini's *On the Benefits Bestowed by Christ*. The operation was so successful that not a single copy of Contarini's book has survived.

As Pasquino has said, Paul IV loved roasting people: the *auto da fés* were held opposite the Dominican church and convent of Santa Maria sopra Minerva, near the Pantheon, and also at Campo dei Fiori: "Some are every day burnt, hanged or beheaded", a contemporary wrote. "Rome has not enough prisons to hold the people who were taken up in suspicion." In 1556 Pietro Carnesecchi was summoned to appear in Rome, but Duke Cosimo again protected him. Cardinal Pole was appointed Archbishop of Canterbury and moved to England; less than a year later, denounced by Rome as a heretic, he died a natural death just a few hours after Queen Mary (1558). At the same time and in Florence Carnesecchi was deprived of his ecclesiastical benefices, and just escaped the scaffold. When Carnesecchi heard of Reginald Pole's death, he wrote to Giulia Gonzaga:–

I have had news of the death of my very sweet lord of England which certainly hurt my heart, although I had already sheltered the pain with my imagination, knowing that he was so ill. I pray God that He may keep for me Donna Giulia, and if He wants to take her from me before time, that He would concede that favour He did to the cardinal of England, and that is that I too may follow my queen.

In this poetic way, Carnesecchi stressed that he loved her, and Giulia, moved, answered that his death "would have thrown her into such deep agony to make her feel love for nobody."

By then Giulia was over forty and alone in the middle of the tempest; she needed a man; perhaps Carnesecchi was the person. He wrote back to her immediately: if she were determined to love nobody, then he, who loved her so, would be desperate. Giulia replied in such affectionate tones that he answered, happy, full of elation. Her letter had given him tremendous joy, he said. He was the luckiest of men, one of the elect, although he wept when he had read of her desire to die. "They say that all the queens in the world would not be able to separate me from Donna Giulia and to make me give up the hope I have of seeing her again and of living with her that span of time which is left to me …". And in spite of the clouds of the Inquisition gathering over him he added, "… there is still some hope of seeing Naples again and of spending the last years of my life in the company of Donna Giulia …". The magnificent châtelaine and the pale Tuscan were lovers.

With the election of Carafa, harsher restrictions had been imposed on prostitutes. In 1562 a law forbade all prostitutes to be interred in chapels; they were to be buried in a special graveyard outside the walls of Rome. A very voluminous veil, much longer and heavier than that which Tullia had narrowly escaped in Florence – a kind of chador – was imposed on them. When Ghislieri, who had been Inquisitor-General, became Pope Pius V, a bull announced that within six days prostitutes were to leave Rome and within twelve days they were to be expelled from papal territory. Several courtesans left at once; poorer ones followed but without an armed escort, and were attacked by bandits who robbed them and threw them in the Tiber. Those who did not drown died of exhaustion.

But since prostitutes represented a considerable flow of money, Roman merchants sent forty delegates to speak to the indignant pope. Finally, after hearing of the many murders and of all those women who had been robbed – and of the considerable economic loss to the city – Pius V relented: prostitutes were allowed to remain, as long as they lived in a given district. So they remained closed in another kind of ghetto while society no longer accepted them; they no longer played any role in public life. Tullia had to move from via dei Prefetti near the Pantheon, and wear that veil which now sheltered an older face – her pearl-like skin was lined and yellowing. Celio had grown to be a young man in the medical profession, the only member of Tullia's family to have a real craft.

Rejected by men and fate, she turned to religion and joined the Company of the Crucifix; she dedicated herself to good works, to charity. The only thing that she was still able to do was to write, but no rhymes flowed from her pen. As she was getting lonelier and poorer, she moved to an inn in Trastevere, whose owner had married her maid Lucrezia. She brought with her some of her fine furniture to decorate two small rooms; and the only maid she could afford was Cristofara, a mere child.

When Tullia fell ill, Lucrezia and her husband took good care of her and Mastro Panuntio, the doctor, came to see her often. The scene is perfectly set now for the last act of *La Traviata*: the Renaissance Violetta is in bed, her maid Lucrezia-Annina receives the doctor who tries to cheer her up, while whispering to Lucrezia that the end is near.

But Tullia was older than Violetta, and there was no Alfredo to rush to her bedside. On 2 March the doctor advised calling for the notary Virginio Grandinelli, who found Tullia in her modest inn, in her grand green bed, dressed in black, her face still witness to her past beauty. Tullia, who could hardly talk, dictated her will and had just the strength to sign it: "*Io Tullia Aragona, manus propria.*" *Io*, in Italian, not *ego*, a slip of the pen for a woman who had prided herself on her fine Latin. The notary transcribed.

Her bedroom furniture was left to Lucrezia, including her beautiful bed, its green hangings, a pair of sheets, and a blanket. To her little maid, Cristofara, Tullia left ten scudi and a black dress. A new suit of black cloth was to be tailored for the good doctor who had looked after her in those last months. There were also charitable bequests; some – like the one to the nuns of the Convertite (the convent for penitent prostitutes) – were required by law: all prostitutes having to leave a fifth of their estate to that institution; to the monks of St Agostino she left half a scudo a year for a candle to be lit in front of her tomb. Tullia's residuary heir was her son, Celio. The remainder of her possessions were to be sold so that the proceeds could be invested and an income could then provide for Celio's further education.

On 14 March, twelve days after she had dictated her will, Tullia died, surrounded by those who still loved her – Lucrezia, Cristofara, and Matteo, Lucrezia's husband. Celio was not around and possibly was not even informed of his mother's desperate last hours; she would have been ashamed to show herself to him in such a state and maybe now that he had achieved a middle-class status, he was ashamed of her.

Tullia's possessions were sold but some of her jewels had to be given to her creditors. All others, including the false diamonds, fetched little. Among her things there was a harpsichord, a box filled with Italian and Latin books (some of them of music), and a lute, the instrument which she had played so well; but this lute, the records tell us, was broken. All this paraphernalia was sold for only twelve scudi to a merchant in second-hand goods.

Tullia was buried with her mother and "sister" in the most beautiful church of St Agostino, not far from via dei Prefetti, but shortly after her death the inscription which carried her name and that of the other two women, was erased, together with all mention of the once-extolled Roman courtesans. Tullia's memory now rested solely in what she had written – and what had been written about her.

Prone to follow the mighty in power, but ready to revolt against those who, by dying, could no longer retaliate, Rome rebelled in 1559 against Pope Carafa, as soon as he died. The Roman populace assaulted the Inquisition and burnt all the papers they found, then moved on to open the doors of prisons, liberating 400 men who had been sentenced for heresy. The wave of enraged citizens veered towards Santa Maria sopra Minerva, tried to burn the monastery and threw several monks out of the windows. Hundreds then rushed to the Capitol where they destroyed a statue erected in honour of Pope Carafa; over the severed marble head a Jew put the yellow cap that Paul IV had ordered the Jews to wear. At that sight, the mob became inflamed with renewed anger and pushed the head with its marble tiara to the ground, kicking it as far as the Tiber.

But there was no turning back from the prevailing mood of the time. The days when people, instead of kicking statues into the river, saluted the rediscovery of classic statues with processions and flowers belonged to the Renaissance; and the Renaissance in Italy was no more. Seven years after the Roman rebellion against Pope Paul IV, Pius V – the Dominican monk Ghislieri – demanded of Duke Cosimo de' Medici the person of Pietro Carnesecchi. Cosimo, who pined for the princely title of archduke, finally gave up his friend in exchange for the papal promise of the granducato. Cosimo asked Pietro Carnesecchi to dine with him and had him chained to his chair, then handed him to the Inquisition officers in Rome. Cardinal Bonelli, Pius's nephew, wrote to Cosimo in July 1566 saying that the pope was highly pleased to see that the duke had done his duty: "His Beatitude sends Your Excellency his very holy blessings, and promises to keep your service in his mind; and he also says that if many other Christian princes were like you in these parts, and from you would take example for the future, religious matters would take a better shape." On the corner of this letter, Cosimo dryly remarked "That will be all". Maybe he felt ashamed.

Just after Carnesecchi's arrest, Giulia Gonzaga died in Naples: Carnesecchi lost even the idea of her, the love of his life. He was the only moderate left: by punishing him the hawks would take revenge on the whole group. So he was thrown into prison and the trial that followed was as much against Pole, Vittoria Colonna, Giulia Gonzaga and Contarini as it was against him.

In November 1566, Carnesecchi was interrogated at length about Vittoria Colonna whose "heretical" letters and sonnets were part of the proceedings. He answered in a composed way, as if he trusted those who were accusing him. Asked when and how he had met Vittoria, Carnesecchi answered:–

I met and studied her – as the excellence of that lady deserved. The first time I saw her and kissed her hand was in Rome in the first year of Pope Paul III [1534] and that was since I had been introduced to her, if I well remember, by Cardinal Palmieri, who was a close friend of that lady. I met her again in Florence as she had come there in order to go to the Baths of Lucca where, for my good fortune, I was going at the same time; so I had the chance of being in even closer familiarity and service to her, which continued until the very last moment of her life. And then in the meantime I saw her often here in Rome and in Viterbo, at the time when I was a guest of the Cardinal of England – she having retired there to a convent whose name I cannot recollect so that she could, I think, pray and serve God in a quieter way than when she was in Rome.

Asked – in Latin – what the two of them discussed, Carnesecchi answered, "Spiritual matters, for hours." Carnesecchi was questioned on Vittoria's religious leanings. "She attached great importance to grace and faith. On the other hand, in her life and in her actions she showed that she kept works in great account, by giving a great deal of money to charity and being charitable to everybody." Having described Pole's sitting-on-the-fence theology, Carnesecchi – who at this stage was probably being tortured, because on the next item he "confesses" to the "sin" of some of his greatest friends – answered, "I cannot sincerely say if the lady was deviating from any article of the Catholic faith, even if I do not remember whether she opened her heart totally to me about such questions, that I may testify other than by means of conjecture, founded principally on the intimacy that she had with Friar Bernardino Ochino."

When Giulia Gonzaga's name was mentioned, she was accused of being "a person who was very friendly with you, who has been under inquiry and accused of heresy". The pope even demanded to see Giulia's personal papers and, according to the Venetian ambassador, said that "Our Beatitude, regarding those writings, said that had he seen them before her death, he would have burnt her alive!"

In May 1567 Cosimo wrote to Pius V asking him to be clement and free Carnesecchi after such a long imprisonment: it was a year since Cosimo had handed his friend over to the Inquisition. But in August 1567 Pietro Carnesecchi was instead convicted of holding thirty-four heretical tenets, "*heretiche erronee temerarie et scandalose*", and condemned to death.

On 1 October, very early in the morning, he was escorted to the bridge of St Angelo. It was a nasty day, drizzling. "He went fashionably dressed in a white shirt with a new pair of gloves and a white handkerchief in his hand"; the Florentine Serristori described the scene to Duke Cosimo, coldly, as if it were a common spectacle – which it probably was by then. In another account to Cosimo's son, Francesco Babbi wrote (1 October 1567): "On this very same morning at dawn that unfortunate Carnesecchi, accompanied by that friar, was taken to St Angelo's bridge, and there they were both beheaded."

The other letter-writer, Serristori, goes on:–

The execution took place so early not out of respect for him but, being the time of the Consistory, the cardinals were to be spared such an atrocious spectacle as they passed the bridge; but as it drizzled and the wood did not take fire, all the cardinals saw him, hanging from his feet, as naked as he was born. Even though it was so early I went, to see if he was to say something before he died. He showed a desire to speak, but he was not allowed to; only he recommended his soul to God twice, which we heard; he behaved without any cowardice ... After he had been decapitated, the Master of

Justice took his clothes away, as indeed what remained of his belongings were his by right, and pulled him by his feet to take him to the pole where he was burnt.

One year later Cosimo was rewarded with the title of Grand Duke of Tuscany which the Spanish court, however, did not recognize. It may be that, as he passed by Castel Sant'Angelo, Cosimo thought of the cost of that empty title. Pius V, too, was rewarded after his death, and made a saint. Thus, as usual, evil triumphed on earth and in heaven.

❧ CHAPTER TEN ❧

Women in france

The Renaissance travelled northwards to France, to England, and to the Flanders. The way had already been prepared by freedom and ease of communication, and by a keen and widespread acquisition of Italianate manners and culture. But, as new ideas were debated, another type of Renaissance flourished in the north with the spread of the Reformation. While in Italy those with enquiring minds were burnt at the stake and the economic situation barred the way to patronage, a certain amount of freedom and better economic conditions favoured France.

In 1567, the year of Carnesecchi's beheading, another Florentine, Tommaso Fortini, a lawyer who had fled to Lyons because of religious persecutions, found himself the heir of the estate of Parcieu which had belonged to Louise Labé, the great poet whom he had not deserted in the last years of her disgrace. Lyons was the French centre which had first inherited the spirit of that Renaissance.

Tommaso Fortini had become rich in Lyons, the city of busy markets and silk manufacturers, printers, bankers. A lawyer could make a fortune in a place where trade flourished, much to the astonishment and anger of the peasantry. Braudel quotes a Breton peasant, Noel du Fail, who, in 1548, was amazed to see such quick changes in society. There was a new intermediate class with which the agricultural labourer had to come to terms, and money – another novelty in those circles which had always used barter – was circulating fast:–

> ... Chicken and goslings are hardly allowed to perfection before they are taken to sell for money to be given either to the lawyer or the doctor, people almost unknown before now; to the one in return for dealing harshly with the neighbour, having him put in prison, to the other for curing him of a fever ordering him to be bled (which, thank God, I've never tried) or for a clyster.

One can see how the French lower class regretted the good old days before the rise of the merchants, of the small landowners, the notaries, the doctors – in short, of the middle class which was the backbone of Lyons's wealth.

Members of this class in France and elsewhere in northern Europe sympathized with the Reformation and often became Protestant; in the mid-sixteenth century, 15 per cent of the French population was Calvinist or, as they called themselves, Huguenot – because of an old legend of a King Hugo – and they were organized in 2,000 congregations.

The Reformation accorded a realistic position to women in the sense that they were seen as useful to society, not on its margins, but part of it. This also derived from the fact that the west of Europe was mainly ruled by women, as we shall see. In Chapter 31 of *The Proverbs of Solomon*, Luther gave a materialistic definition of the wife's role as a woman in whom a husband places total confidence. Although Luther did not credit women with any intellectual capacity, at least he recognized them as the companions of men. He himself did not want to marry because he thought he could be murdered at any time: on 15 June 1520, Leo X had excommunicated him with the bull *Exsurge, Domine, et judica causam tuam* and on 23 January 1521, *Decet Romanum Pontificem*. Secure in his alliance with Charles, Leo thought that Luther's arrival at Worms (April 1521) would have coincided with the burning of the heretic. But Worms became Luther's triumph and the imperial banns remained a piece of paper.

To Pope Leo, Luther had written: "... the Church of Rome, once the holiest, has become a nest of murderers ...", its sins were worse than the Turks', and "it is actually true that if once Rome was the door of Heaven now it is the gaping mouth of Hell ...". In November 1524, he wrote that whatever happened to him he would not marry, but six months later he had wedded Catherine de Bore.

Luther's wife belonged to the nobility, and from the age of ten had been locked up in a convent near Leipzig because her family was too poor to provide her with a dowry. But when Luther's ideas clandestinely reached the convent, Catherine learned that the link between a nun and God rested on "their" private deal and that forced vows were invalid. Together with another eight girls, Catherine ran away from the convent and asked for Luther's help. The nine former nuns reached Wittenberg where they found a refuge and where Luther laboured to find them husbands. But Catherine refused two suitors and let it be known that she would only marry Luther himself. He was irritated by her pretension but, as he himself wrote, a day arrived when "the Lord, suddenly, and at the time I least thought of it", threw him in the way of matrimony. He was forty-one and Catherine twenty. Theirs was a happy match. They lived in the convent which the Prince of Wittenberg had given Luther, and Catherine became the embodiment of what Luther had preached as the ideal wife: a companion, busy cooking for the many visitors, her mind on the economy of the household. (Luther had little money as he refused to be paid for his writings.) They had seven children and, in 1546, when Luther died, Catherine was left penniless. The prince was generous and gave her an estate, which she could never exploit because of the wars and the Black Death. She died at fifty-three, the embodiment of the perfect Protestant wife of the new urban middle stratum.

The aristocratic Protestant wife, on the other hand, abided by different rules. One such woman was a follower of Luther's, a relative of Renée of Ferrara, whom we have already encountered corresponding with Vittoria Colonna – Margaret of Navarre, the elder sister of King Francis of France. Although never formally

21. *Margaret of Navarre* by Robinet Testard from "Livres des Echecs Amoureaux" This charming and highly intelligent woman was the older sister of Francis of France. Her second husband was Henry d'Albret, King of Navarre and her daughter the amazing Jeanne d'Albret, mother of Henry IV Bourbon. She was the patroness of Clement Marot and Rabelais. Although she died a Roman Catholic, she was really a Reformist and her daughter fought in the Huguenot army.

converted, Margaret (1492–1549) supported the Reformation and interceded on behalf of reformist groups led by Bishops Briçonnet and Lefèvre d'Etaples; she protected Marot and Rabelais, two "heretics". In 1509 she married Duke Charles of Alençon and, after his death in 1525, Henri d'Albret, to whom she bore Jeanne, the Huguenot mother of the future King Henri IV, the man who was to unite France. Margaret of Navarre was an enlightened woman, full of charm and progressive ideas. "Marriage", she said, "must not aim at either pleasure or interest. It is not a perfect state; it is enough to take it with wisdom for what it is, a medium and honest state." She wrote poetry of religious devotion, and in her *Heptameron*, first published in 1558 under the title of *Histoire des Amants Fortunés* – seventy stories arranged in the manner of the *Decameron* – Margaret made an important point: woman was free to deny herself to men, in soul and body. Woman had a choice; she was not a thing, the property of her husband, her lover, of a man who could discard her after using her body. By her very choice of not giving herself, she obtained the status of "person", of human being. In her original stories Margaret of Navarre contributed to the fashionable subject of honest and profane love, with a difference: honest love was woman's contribution – not man's. The tenth novella of *Heptameron* is an interesting study on this theme. It tells the story of a grand widow (like herself) who lived to educate her two children. So noble was she that she received the visit of the viceroy, in whose train was the chevalier Amadour, not a valiant soldier, but an intelligent, sensitive man. That Amadour should be an attractive character because of intellectual and not military qualities is already an original departure and in this story man does not impose his mastery on his woman.

In Margaret's stories women could be detached from men because they were rather aloof from sexuality – probably like Margaret herself, whose conflict with the Church of Rome was mainly due to her championing the new status of women. She developed the theme of mutual respect between a man and woman achieved by intellectual curiosity; hers was not the medieval mystical concept of love, but of friendship. Mutual respect between men and women could only be achieved if women were educated, and girls began to be taught writing, reading and music. The elite used private tutors to teach girls French, Italian and a bit of Latin, besides music and arithmetic. The emerging intermediate class had money and time to educate themselves and to read. Leisure, which the middle class was conquering through wealth, is a friend of progress. The urban woman had a better chance of education than the country girl; a physician from Lyons taught his daughter, Louise Sarrasin, to speak Hebrew, Greek and Latin by the age of eight.

We know that the Reform, especially in its most benevolent and democratic Erasmian and Lutheran aspects, favoured education for women; Protestantism was based on reading the Scriptures; and in fact it never penetrated those strata that had not achieved literacy. Besides, Luther, and to some degree the young Calvin – before he became dictatorial and intoxicated by power – saw that an educated woman would raise a family better: she would content her husband, who would not look for other women; she would be better trained to keep her household in order, both morally and economically. And as medical science made notable progress, there appeared books which specialized in female diseases: childbirth was looked upon as a "medical" operation and no longer as the vengeance of God, and (according to Braudel), if there was a choice between the baby's and the mother's life, the latter was saved, principally out of economic and rational considerations. Around the mid-sixteenth century the first women doctors came out of French universities.

The Reformation seemed to appeal to the middle-class and aristocratic woman because it made her responsible, gave her a spiritual status, and it preached a matrimonial role that was no longer solely passive. All this was due not only to religious thought, but to the new fast-changing economic climate which pervaded France. The wives of lawyers, merchants and royal officers not only supervised their households but often helped in their husbands' businesses or started their own, in their own names. Tradesmen and craftsmen no longer had their workrooms within their houses which, therefore, were becoming larger and more comfortable, with rooms allotted to the different activities of cooking, sleeping, and eating. The richer women had baths in their houses; the rest went to public baths where they could meet other women – and these baths took the place of the church, in so far as they became meeting places.

Among the "*menu peuple*" (the poorer lot), many women worked in the textile, leather and provisioning trades; they ran inns; they made shoes and collars; in Lyons they prepared silk. A merchant shoemaker from Lyons who had become prosperous said that his money was due more to his wife's business as a linen merchant than to his. Some guilds welcomed women, but never gave them the same prominent role that men enjoyed.

While the Catholic hierarchy disapproved of women "knowing about the Bible", the author of *The Way to Arrive at the Knowledge of God* retorts that if Catholic priests called such women lewd it was because they did not consent to seduction: "You say it's enough for a woman's salvation to be in her house, to work, sew and spin? Of what use are Christ's promises to her? You'll put spiders in Paradise, for they know how to spin very well." Women began to accuse Catholic priests of spreading the message of evil; since the women themselves had read the Scriptures they knew what Christ had said, often better than the priest himself.

In spite of the drain on the country's resources caused by the many wars that France had fought in the 1550–60s, there was a progressive spread of wealth and education. Window panes were becoming so popular that, in a journey through France, Montaigne noticed that hardly a single house in any of the villages was not provided with them. Heating was still primitive, although the new idea of chimneys at least carried the smoke away from the room: one lady remembered a royal dinner when the water and wine in her goblets turned to ice. Until the middle of the sixteenth century, food was plentiful in France and elsewhere in Europe. A Breton peasant described how ham, lamb and chicken could be obtained cheaply, and vegetables even more so; and Chanon Lithem in 1560 looked back to the good old days when "we ate meat every day, dishes were abundant, we gulped down wine as if it were water."

Lyons was a privileged city, situated on the meeting point between the Saône and the Rhône, at the gateway to Italy, Savoy and Switzerland, much visited and loved by the Valois, a great centre of trade. In 1522, it contained about 60,000 inhabitants; its population depended heavily on immigration. "I never saw a more beautiful site for a city, nor a more noble or useful, nor did I ever see a finer city than this Lyons, contained within a circuit of walls, such a large city", wrote Gabriel Symeoni Fiorentino in his *Dialogo Pio et Speculativo* (Lyons, 1560).

Louise Labé, who was born in Lyons in 1522, was the daughter of an artisan who belonged to the "*menu peuple*". She was the true daughter of the French Renaissance. She may have been an exception in the sense that her talent was exceptional; but as for the fact that her father decided to give her an accomplished education, he was imitating others: Labé was advancing himself into the middle class and copying what other fathers were doing to promote their daughters, to give them a superior status.

A middle-class girl, the daughter of a ropemaker, Louise Labé developed into one of the finest poets of her time, in fact one could say of all time; her work was well known abroad even before 1555 when it was first published. But more interesting than her ardent and original style is the fact that because Louise Labé was a poet, she was well known; contemporaries – even Calvin himself – commented on her personality. She used learning as a launching pad for love, since she fell in love desperately and often and never hid it, elaborating on its pains and on its physical joys: something which few men had the courage to do. Trained in the Renaissance gospels, from Plato to Petrarch, and educated by some of the best teachers in Lyons, Louise never borrowed from anybody. In fact her openly sensual poetry goes against the contemporary fashion. She wrote a "debate on love", as so many – Tullia included – had done, and was original in arranging the debate between Love and Folly. Her prose in that text is littered with pronouncements such as: women should "bypass or equal men in science and accomplishments" and "lift their minds a little above their distaffs and spindles ... to apply themselves to science and learning ... and to let the world know that if we are not made to command, we must not for that be disdained as companions, both in domestic and public affairs, of those who govern and are obeyed." Women "cannot get rid of men as easily as men of women, not having the possibility of leaving and starting another liaison, chasing love with another love". And, once deserted by their lovers, women "curse all men for ever. They call mad those who love, they curse the day when they first loved. They protest saying they will never love again: but that does not last. If they have some objects which remind them of their lover, they kiss them, kiss them again, cover them with tears, make them into a pillow, and listen to themselves bewailing their miserable state."

Louise had lovers before she married and many others while she was another ropemaker's wife, but she seemed to have pleased her husband with her originality. Scandal she provided all the time, especially as Lyons grew more and more dominated by Huguenots, the Calvinist Protestant party which, although led by aristocrats, counted a majority within the urban middle class. Louise's stepmother could not bear her excessive freedom; nor could her father, who eventually disinherited her. But – for a time – she was surrounded by many good friends, most of whom were learned girls, all belonging to the middle class, or only slightly above Louise's station.

Louise's father, Pierre Charly – or Charlieu or Charliu – called Labé, had amassed considerable wealth at the time when he became a widower of Guillermette, in her turn widow of Jacques Humbert, and had been granted a few honorific privileges, such as "collector of charity for the hospital". He lived in a central district of Lyons with the three sons from his first marriage when he married another member of the middle class, Etienne Deschamps, who bore Louise and probably died in childbirth. Etienne brought to the family a small estate near Lyons, that of Parcieu en Dombes, which she left to her daughter: to have a place outside such a populous city was important, not only for social advancement but as a haven from wars and contagious diseases which took less of a toll of the richer inhabitants precisely because they could flee to their estates outside the infected urban agglomerations.

But Pierre, who was soon married again, this time to Antoinette Taillard, the much younger and probably penniless daughter of a butcher, had another country estate at a place called de la Gella, near the parish of St Vincent de Lyons. Wealthy, but of modest station, Pierre Labé had read the new bestseller *Pantagruel* by François Rabelais, with all its Renaissance pedagogical connotations; his bright daughter was to be educated "*à la mode d'Ytalie*", he decided.

In her childhood, Louise saw violence in the streets when Lyons revolted against new taxes and when "heretics" were burnt at the stake. She also experienced the silent hatred of her stepmother. Louise, who could not but feel superior to the illiterate Antoinette, was also a rival to Jeanne, Antoinette's only daughter by Pierre Labé. And Louise was growing into a beauty: with a perfect oval face, fair curly hair, languid brown eyes and a capriciously curled mouth. Her half-brothers, who loved her, trained Louise in masculine sports, because the girl was lively and loved to ride. Raised together with the three boys, Louise developed a sense of freedom, a love of arms, like a heroine from Ariosto, an author she knew well. She preferred riding to sewing seams or doing her *petit point*. But she loved music, for which she had a gift, and played the lute, sang and danced well. There, in Lyons, and in Louise's hands, the lute came to life once again.

Tradition has it that when she was sixteen she fell in love with the dauphin – and nothing could be easier to believe. To see the first prince of the land dressed in white and silver and, at times, to have the honour of being near to him, made her ecstatic. Royals were closer to commoners then, as we can see from Benvenuto Cellini's diaries. Since Louise was pretty and well educated, when the Valois were in Lyons she was often exposed to court life. She, but not the rest of her bourgeois family, was invited with other girls – no husbands or fathers were included – to the endless receptions and meals given by the nobility, where music was played, where she could dance and her gifts were appreciated. It is therefore quite likely that the dauphin's eye was caught by the girl who could dance and express herself well. Legends are never made of nothing, and although Louise's biographers deny this, it is possible that Louise shared a night or two with the enfant de France, to whose fair head, crowned with laurel, she dedicated many verses.

Louise's first love made her suffer: she was sixteen then and, as with any girlish love, it developed and took gigantic proportions in her memory. And whether her first lover was the dauphin or a noble courtier, he belonged to the aristocracy. Later Louise recollected the time when her lover first "took her": love was her element, and while the span in which she was happy was short, the memory of it lasted for years. Louise was furious at the time wasted far from the object of her love; her anger at having to wail alone instead of loving together is the anger of many women whose destiny is to wait. And yet, in her third elegy, she says that before discovering love she was happy playing with Mars, the god of war, and happy with learning:–

> Mais quoy? Amour ne peut longuement voir
> Mon coeur n'aymant que Mars et le savoir:
> Et me voulant donner autre souci,
> En souriant, il me disoit ainsi:
> Tu pense donq, ô Lyonnoise Dame,
> Pouvoir fuir par ce moyen ma flame?

> *But what? Love could not see for long*
> *My heart loving just Mars and culture:*
> *And wanting to give me more worry,*
> *Smiling he said like this:*
> *You then think, lady from Lyons,*
> *To be able to escape my flames in this way?*

And in her first elegy she gave vent to her violent passion, expressing a masochistic joy in remembering:-

> Au temps qu'Amour, d'hommes et Dieus vainqueur
> Faisoit brûler de sa flame mon Coeur.
> En embrassant dans sa cruelle rage

22. Louise Labé

A bourgeoise, Louise Labé was respected – and envied – for her learning. She could read Italian and admired the idea of the *cortesana honesta*, whom she imagined living in great luxury among celebrated men. She was an outstanding poet, writing erotic, vibrant sonnets and prose.

Mon sang, mes os, mon esprit et courage:
Encore lors je n'avois le puissance
De lamenter ma peine et ma souffrance.
Encore Phebus, ami des Lauriers vert
N'avoit permis que je fisse des vers.

At the time when love, conqueror of men and gods,
Made my heart burn with his flame,
Embracing in its cruel rage
My blood, my bones, my wit and courage:
Then I did not have the power
To lament my pain and suffering.
Phoebus, the friend of green laurel leaves,
Had not yet allowed me to write poetry.

In 1536, the king died and, as we saw earlier, Henri, the dauphin, husband of Catherine de' Medici, became King of France. Later, probably towards 1539, Louise fell in love with another courtier, a man who soon left Lyons and forgot her. Love's arrows were going to be a constant source of tears and erotic poetry.

Time quenched feelings and destroyed monuments, but after many years Louise still remembered her lover: "*... en moy il semble qu'il augmente avec le temps, et que plus me tourmente*" [... it seems to me that love in me grows with time and torments me more]. Maurice Scève, friend and follower of Clement Marot, took over Louise's education. Scève, who had a huge nose and bulging eyes, belonged to the lesser nobility and his sympathy – like Marot's – was with the Reformation, with the Huguenots. Together with Louise, he would read Virgil in the original, and Sannazzaro, the poet who was in Naples with Vittoria Colonna, and Castiglione. She also read the great writer and adapter of Aesop's tales, Charles Fontaine who, since his marriage to a Lyonnaise, lived in the same city.

In 1537 Marot was allowed to return to France. As we know, he had taken refuge with Duchess Renée of Ferrara; but then, taking advantage of the royal offer of pardon to Protestants who recanted, Marot abjured his faith, publicly, in Lyons. There he met Louise. Marot was the first poet to introduce the sonnet to France and, having translated psalms into the vernacular, he became the poet of the Reformation to which he was soon to return. He met Louise again, when he came back to Lyons in 1538 and 1541 and, at one stage or another, he not only fell for her but in a lovely alliterative poem he betrayed his admiration for her talents:–

Louise ha tant qu'en toutes on prise,
Que je ne puis que Louise ne loue
Et si ne puis assez louer Louise.

... Laissez-moi la et louez-moi Louise,
C'est le double fue don ma muse est eprise,
C'est de mes vers le droict but limité.

Louise has so much that all has to be praised
That I cannot but praise Louise
And so I cannot praise Louise enough.

… Leave her to me and praise her for me,
My muse is taken by a double fire,
This is the limited goal of these verses.

On his first visit to Lyons, Marot wrote a poem in honour of all the *"poètesses Lyon-naises"* – the women poets of Lyons – something which shows that Louise was no isolated case. It was with celebrities like Marot and Scève that Louise could find the company she yearned for: Rabelais, Fontaine, Etienne Dolet, a humanist of Protestant leanings who, in 1536, with the king's permission, established a printing press in Lyons.

The troubles of the Reformation did not seem to worry Louise much. She subscribed to the early philosophy of the Renaissance: live your life to the full; youth and beauty last but a season. She fell in love and gave herself; she accepted gifts. She loved fine clothes and jewels, which she wore only in private since, being a bourgeoise, the sumptuary laws (which in France expressed the aristocrats' resentment against the *bourgeoisie*) would not permit her to imitate the nobility. Her education and knowledge, on the other hand, were to be displayed. She mocked "That kind of learned gentleman who lived his wisdom in solitude … he will have all the time to plant cauliflowers" – instead of roses and lilies and thyme. Beauty, she advised women, should be sacrificed "neither to science nor even to virtue". And she took tremendous care of her body to please "the amorous curiosity of men". She certainly knew that women's lot had been transformed by knowledge, by the cult of the mind and she told them that "the honour that knowledge will give us will be entirely ours, and will not be taken from us … by the passage of time".

A Roman poet fell in love with her; she did not reciprocate his passion, though, and she made fun of his tight clothes which showed off "the movement of his well disposed body …". Together with her girlfriends Claudine and Sybille Scève, sisters of Maurice, and Fernette de Guillet, who was writing Petrarchan verses, Jeanne Gaillarde and Catherine de Vauzelles, she giggled and mocked the *"poète Rommain"*.

In 1542, when the French army put Perpignan under siege, Pierre Labé, supplier of ropes to the army under the command of the Dauphin Henri, took his daughter with him. The siege lasted three months, but Perpignan, which was defended by the Duke of Alba, resisted. Louise dressed up as a man, admiring the famous "viragos" of the Renaissance, and handled horses and arms as skilfully as the best soldiers. She took part in the siege and was nicknamed *"la Capitaine Loys"*.

The sight of this woman soldier inspired a poem from *Des Lovenges de Louise Labé Lionnaise*:–

> *Thus furious Louise*
> *leaving apart the soft clothes*
> *of women, and envious*
> *of war noise, against the Spaniards,*
> *often ran in great clatter*
> *and put them under siege*
> *when the French youth*
> *encircled Perpignan.*
> *There she showed her strength,*
> *with her lance she defeats*
> *the most valiant enemy:*
> *and brave on the saddle*
> *nothing showed in her*
> *but the guise of a valiant chevalier.*

It was rare, but not unknown, for a French girl to be taken in by the royal army to fight as a soldier, as a modern Joan of Arc, a Caterina Sforza. Many others dressed in armour and followed suit. A few years later, in Toulouse, a Huguenot woman bore arms against the Catholic army, and Jeanne d'Albret led the Bourbon army in her fierce crusades against the "Papists". Jeanne, the warring Huguenot princess, put her resentment in poetry:–

> *Those who say it is not for women*
> *To look at the Holy Writ*
> *Are evil men and infamous*
> *Seducers and antichrist.*
> *Alas, my ladies,*
> *Your poor souls*
> *Let them not be governed*
> *By such great devils.*

On her return, Lyons's tongues were busy. Louise's behaviour irritated the good old ladies of the more puritanical milieu; it certainly found no sympathy with her stepmother Antoinette and her circle. While affording more freedom in some spheres, since Protestantism was the religion of the middle class, it assumed intolerance towards anybody different, towards talent. Huguenot eyes were looking disapprovingly at Louise. Pierre Labé was growing old and wanted to marry off his vivacious daughter who, at the age of twenty, could be considered a spinster. But because of her notoriety, he could not choose the match he might have dreamt of for the girl he had so well – and so expensively – educated. Ennemond Perrin, a prosperous cordage manufacturer like his own father as well as Pierre Labé, was at least twenty years older than Louise. He owned a fine house in the rue de Confort with a garden behind it, which, through an alley, joined the one belonging to the Church of Notre Dame de Confort. The date of his marriage to Louise is unknown, but it certainly took place soon after 1542: Louise brought with her a good dowry, in money. She moved into her new house, which consisted of two floors with two windows on each and, on the ground floor, Ennemond's workshop. From then onwards, Louise became known as "La Belle Cordière."

Louise changed her new house, furnishing it with a taste that was foreign to her hard-working husband: she bought brocades and tapestries, panelling in leather. The floors, as was fashionable then, were strewn with scented herbs; the dressers, which showed off the household's wealth, were filled with pewter objects. She transformed the garden, which she shaped in the Italian fashion and then built a separate little house, a "drawing-room" where she would receive her friends, writers, poets and Italian visitors. Besides those whose names we have already encountered, there were Antoine du Moulin and Jean de Tournes, the fine Lyonnais printer, Clémence de Bourges, Luigi Alamani, Guillaume Paradin. Any literary celebrity who passed through Lyons was received by Louise. She bought beautiful clothes, which she wore at her *soirées*: she had one dress of yellow damask with a blue gown to be worn on top; the gown was embellished with gold embroidery, its sleeves with ermine. On her head she wore a cap sewn with pearls. During her evenings she would play the viola, the spinet, the lute, and sing, as Tullia and Imperia had done. Clement Marot praised her musical skill thus:–

> Louise has a voice, which enhances music,
> Louise has a hand, which so well plays the lute.

But, unlike Tullia and Imperia, Louise was no courtesan, in spite of the fact that her detractors, including Calvin himself (who, from Geneva, called her *"plebeia meretrix"*), said that she was. Why should she have been? She had money, both before and after marriage. She may have accepted presents – but she did not sleep with men for money, or presents. If she did sleep with Clement Marot, who was much older than her (and in no way could his brigand-like face have been described as handsome), she might have given herself for the pleasure of such a famous poet's company. It was quite obvious that those who wanted to condemn Louise's *mores*, especially in the climate of advancing Calvinism, would label her as a *putaine*, a courtesan. Rather, Louise threw herself into the turmoil of her passions. Besides, her elderly husband was amused by his wife, by her decorating his house and his life, but he would not have tolerated a wife selling her body. *Giving* her body, that was another question: infidelity was not uncommon for married women, and for some reason Louise could not have children, which would have reassured Ennemond that no bastard would inherit his wealth or his name.

Louise, like Elizabeth Tudor, knew she could not bear children. She could have been aware of it either because she had no menstrual flow (although that does not debar women from becoming pregnant) or from the fact that, by using crude methods of birth control in her early youth, she had damaged her body; that could have happened from introducing rings or coils, something that women did to prevent conception but which often caused internal infection. She does not seem to have minded; hers was not a domestic world. Nor were her girlfriends'.

When Fernette du Guillet, with whom Louise had shared much laughter and a taste for writing verses, died on 17 July 1545, her poetry was posthumously published. Another woman, Jeanne Flore, had also published her *Contes* three years earlier. Antoine du Moulin, who had been valet to Margaret of Navarre – what a small cultural world the Renaissance was – prompted Louise herself to publish; he knew her poetry well since Louise would recite her new poems during her evenings at which, at times, her husband was present; he was usually tired from his work and not literate enough to follow the sophisticated reasoning. But although he felt ill at ease with her friends, he was proud of Louise's talents. He was also proud of the fact that his house received famous and, in some cases, aristocratic visitors. But Louise's father was not, and, pressed by his wife Antoinette, in 1548 he changed his will and disinherited her.

At the end of the fifteenth century there were forty printing presses at Lyons; the city was the home of poets like Maurice Scève who claimed to have discovered the tomb of Laura, Petrarch's love, at Avignon. Scève, who was influenced by Clement Marot, brought to Lyons the Renaissance literary "mania" for Petrarch. Lyons, "the Florence of France", was a place where intellectual life flourished. When the new King of France visited Lyons in 1548, he was accompanied not only by his wife, but also by his famous mistress, the scholarly and fascinating Diane de Poitiers who, in her capacity as Duchess of Valentinois, owned large properties around Lyons.

The king was followed by the noble court, including the Cardinal de Guise, whose sister Mary had married the King of Scotland, and whose powerful house was staunchly Catholic. Lyons was the site of annual agricultural fairs and became the home of many Italian banks. Its silk industry made it prosperous; its printing presses (the first of which opened in 1473) were clattering, while those in Italy were slowing down; poets and writers were busy writing, while those on the other side of the Alps were frightened to jot down anything; in Lyons people bought and read books, while in Italy they were burning them.

The celebrations for the royal visit were superb: Maurice Scève was put in charge of them and he, in turn, asked some of his friends for help. The king, accompanied by Diane, was to arrive in the city the day before Catherine de' Medici, his queen, who was to make her entry from the opposite direction. Louise Labé was enthusiastic about her part in these celebrations. To honour Diane, a woman whose beauty, taste and fame could not but inspire, Louise Labé redesigned her garden with the lily of France entwined with the crescent moon of the goddess Diane, Artemis: everybody was going to see her garden, possibly even the beautiful Diane.

Diane de Poitiers, whose greatest glory was her taste and famous conversation, had become a symbol: that of intellect's victory. This woman, who had never been a real beauty, had been married to Louis de Bréze when she was sixteen and he fifty-six. Because of her intelligence, her husband's career flourished until his death in 1531; ever since then Diane, who was slender and tall, wore black and white only, to symbolize eternal mourning. In 1526, when she was twenty-seven, she had met Prince Henri, who was seven: the child was at Bayonne and about to be given to Charles V's court as hostage. In exchange, his father, Francis I who

23. Diane de Poitiers

Born to a noble family, Diane was the mistress of Henri II of France, who was twenty years her junior and who loved her all his life. Diane was well-read, a beauty and a great influence on the arts. The school of Fontainebleau is inspired by her and the goddess Diana became the symbol of Henri and the Court.

had been captured at the battle of Pavia by Vittoria Colonna's husband, was freed. Some years later, King Francis, who thought highly of the widow's fine conversation and her taste, gave her the delicate task of "initiating" Henri, who was silent, morose, and shy.

So Diane initiated the future king to physical love, but not only that. She made him aware of his own power; she gave him a dignity and a strength that the young prince – twenty years her junior – had never achieved before. She was to remain his greatest love and Henri hers. Strangely, but in a way typically, Diane became the intimate confidante of both her lover and of Catherine de' Medici, the wife he never loved; although the queen was jealous of Diane and spied on her and the king during their nights together. Catherine's world became filled with obsessions, with magicians, poisons, talismans, and where Catherine was obscurantist, Diane symbolized enlightenment, love of life, the very embodiment of the Renaissance. The Queen would often say, to her face, that France had been ruined by "*les femmes putaines*" meaning Diane de Poitiers.

During the prolonged visit of the royal couple in Lyons, Louise and her friend, Clémence de Bourges, were to take part in a kind of *tableau vivant* entertainment. Louise was to impersonate Immortality; Clémence, Virtue. For hours they stood, wrapped in white like two pagan goddesses, watching the long, elegant royal procession; at last six gentlemen dressed in white satin and six in crimson red preceded the king, wonderfully shrouded in shining gold. It was indeed fortunate that the queen was not present, because in one of the *tableaux vivants* a pretty maid from Lyons, dressed as the Goddess Diana, chased tame deer – a clear homage to Diane de Poitiers. Louise and Clémence then recited a poem written for the occasion by Maurice Scève: immortality and virtue promised to be with the king forever – a promise which was not kept.

On the following day, Queen Catherine arrived and everybody waited in order to repeat the festivities, but the queen, offended, entered the city at dusk, and it was impossible by then to display the *tableaux vivants* and the many decorations; hers was no way to conquer a city which had already succumbed to the royal mistress. The festivities went on for days; the entertainments involved the whole city of Lyons, and Louise had a wonderful time, since she met all the gentlemen of the king's court. Many noble courtiers had paid a visit to the famous salon of "La belle Cordière", a celebrity by now.

One of them, Antoine du Verdier, Lord of Vauprivas, wrote an account in which we see Louise receiving the nobility, at times from her bed, entertaining, singing and playing, reading Latin, Italian and Spanish poems, feeding the noble men with delicacies and asking them for money when "at last she revealed her most private charms". Louise is made to appear as a courtesan. Not to all, du Verdier recounted, would she give her body. But du Verdier might have been taking a delayed revenge on a woman who had refused him favours she accorded to other courtiers, because it is certain that Louise, taking advantage of the presence of the sophisticated aristocrats, did sleep with some of them at that time. She longed for their way of life, which she strove to imitate. She also loved physical love, although "the lubricity and ardour of the loins has nothing in common or little to do with love".

A woman like Louise was always going to be the target of malicious tongues, something that is not confined to Renaissance times. The new Protestant fervour grew as Europe was in social and religious turmoil which, as usual, was motivated by economics. In 1546 Scotland had rebelled against the Church of Rome, Geneva was getting strong international support; the minor nobility and the more assured middle class were attracted to Calvinism, whose revolutionary tendencies scared the Valois. In 1581 an edict was issued against the Protestants in France, the prelude to the religious civil wars. Lyons, whose middle class was predominantly Huguenot, trembled. So did the Italian exiles, like Tommaso Fortini, who had fled Spanish-dominated Italy and knew about religious persecution.

Louise had met Fortini, the Florentine lawyer, and would ask him for details on legal language and procedure to include in the tongue-in-cheek *Debat* that shows off her familiarity with the law. In her *Debat* (which she probably completed in 1552), Louise describes how Jupiter has organized a festival for all the gods. Cupid, who is blind, and Folly, who is mad, arrive at the gates of Jupiter's palace at the same moment; they are late and the gates are already closed. As Folly pushes forward, the two gods begin to quarrel: Folly should precede Love, she says, it always does. To settle the dispute, which had grown out of proportion, Jupiter calls for the council of gods and, electing himself as judge, appoints two barristers to put the cases of the litigants. Mercury will act for Folly, it is decided, and Apollo for Cupid.

This debate, which was later translated into English and passed off as his own work by Robert Greene, made an enormous impression for its feminist point of view. Apollo, the barrister for Cupid, says:–

> So you should hear me attentively. The injury which I claim has been inflicted upon Cupid is the following: he came to the festival late, and just as he wished to pass the gate, Folly pushed ahead of him and putting a hand upon his shoulder dragged him back, so forcing herself in first. Cupid, wishing to know who she was, asked her. She replied insultingly in such manner as does not become a well-spoken woman ... He wished to subject her to the power of love; she avoided the blow and, pretending not to be offended by what Cupid had said, began to argue with him, and then suddenly at a stroke destroyed the eyes in his head ... The wound is visible, the harm is manifest, of the authorship it is needless to enquire but she, who has dealt the blow, admits it, excuses it, and everywhere tells her story ...

So this is what Folly did to Love: she made him blind!

At the end of the debate, Jupiter concludes:–

On account of the difficulty and importance of your differences and diversity of opinions, we have postponed our decision three times seven times nine centuries [a dig against the slow pace of the law]. And meanwhile we command you to live in harmony, without injuring one another. Mad Folly will guide blind Cupid and will conduct him everywhere it seems good to her to go. As for the restoration of his eyes, after we have spoken of the matter with the Fates, a decision will be made.

On 13 August 1554, Louise was granted the privilege of printing her own works, consisting of the *Debat*, three elegies and twenty-four sonnets.

Just before Easter that same year, Olivier de Magny, a young man, a poet already known for having published a book of promising verse under the title of *Amours*, arrived in Lyons. He was twenty-three and had been engaged by Jean d'Avanson, who enjoyed the protection of Diane de Poitiers and had been sent as ambassador to the Holy See. On their way, they stopped in Lyons, the ambassador and his train, waiting for the king's instructions before proceeding to Rome. Naturally Olivier was received at the celebrated salon of La Belle Cordière.

In spite of her literary success, Louise was going through a troubled time; there had been a trial in Geneva in which a cousin of hers had been accused by her husband, Jean Varoz, a doctor, of having tried to poison him. Varoz, a Huguenot, had taken refuge in Geneva and the Calvinists did not miss the chance of advertising the wickedness of Catholic women like Louise and her cousin. Intolerance was even more ferocious on the Catholic front: after examining the case of Etienne Dolet, the judges of the Sorbonne in Paris had condemned him to be burnt at the stake (1546).

But in Lyons, Louise could think of nothing but love. Although she was older than him, the dashing Olivier de Magny saw in Louise a pleasant prey. Their idyll started, Louise resisted; Olivier unhappily commented:–

> Mais que sert toute la caresse
> Que je recoy de ma maitresse?
> Et que me vaut passer les jours
> En de telles esperances d'amours,
> Si les nuiz de mile ennuiz pleines
> Rendent mes esperances veines?

> *What is the use of the caresses*
> *Which I receive from my mistress?*
> *And is it worth spending the days*
> *In such hopes of love,*
> *If the nights full of a thousand sufferings*
> *Stress the vainness of my hope?*

On her side, in the *Debat* Louise described her state as a common feminine sickness: "... as they [women] become aware that they are loved ... they declare their weakness, they confess the fire that burns them: at times shame restrains them and they don't let themselves go if not when they are vanquished, and half-consumed ... The more they have resisted Love, the more they are taken." All women's activities, Louise goes on, seem to stop in order to see "him". "Women take the pen and the lute in their hands; they write and sing their passions; and in the end that rage grows so much that at times they abandon father, mother, husband ... and they withdraw where their heart is."

When she finally gave in to Olivier, she loved him passionately:–

> Baise m'encor rebaise moy et baise:
> Donne m'en un de tes plus savoureus,
> Donne m'en un de tes plus amoureus:
> Je t'en rendray quatre plus chaus que braise.
>
> Jouissons nous l'un de l'autre à notre aise
> Lors double vie à chacun en suivra.
> Permets m'Amour penser quelque folie:
> Toujours suis mal, vivant discrettement,
> Et ne me puis donner contentement,
> Si hors de moy ne fay quelque saillie.

> *Kiss me again, rekiss me and kiss:*
> *Give me one of your tastiest,*
> *Give me one of your most loving:*
> *I'll return four hotter than embers.*
>
> *Let us enjoy each other at leisure*
> *As our different lives will part us.*
> *Love allows me to conjure up some mad thought:*
> *I have always been unhappy when living discreetly,*
> *And cannot give my own self fulfilment,*
> *Unless I am up to something naughty.*

This is Louise's identity; no courtesan, but unhappy when she could not dash into a new love; not asking for payment, but intimately begging Love to send her some means to be involved in some *"folie"*. In much more conventional and less gifted verse, Olivier celebrated the fall of Louise's fortress.

She became obsessed with Olivier: nobody else existed, her salon closed down and received Olivier alone; another young suitor, Claude de Rubys, was sharply dismissed; he was later to take cruel revenge in writing. Her whole mind and body lived only for Olivier. She described being in love:–

> Je vis, je meurs: je brule et me noye.
> J'ay chaus estreme en endurant froidure:
> Le vie m'est et trop molle et trop dure.
> J'ay grans ennuis entremeslez de joye.
>
> ... Ainsi Amour inconstantamment me meine:
> Et quand je pense avoir plus de douleur,
> Sans y penser je me treuve hors de peine.

I live, I die: I burn and I drown.
I am boiling hot while freezing cold:
life is too sweet and too hard at the same time.
My suffering is mingled with joy.

… Thus Love leads me inconstantly:
And when I think I am in my worst pain
Without thinking, I am rid of sorrow.

But then Olivier had to leave Lyons and Louise. Olivier promised he would come back to her, and indeed from his journey he sent a poem dedicated to the brown eyes of his mistress, to her mouth and laughter, to those trees and rivers which had witnessed their love.

She wrote to him, long letters, and she wrote sonnets to ease her distress:–

O beaus yeus bruns, ô regars destournez,
O chaus soupirs, ô larmes espandues,
O noires nuits vainement atendues,
O jours luisans vainement retournez.

O beautiful brown eyes that will not deign
To look on me, o sights, o tears of yearning,
O blackest nights in vain, alas, returning,
O brightest days awaited now in vain.

He was away in Rome, and she was left at the rue de Confort with her old husband. In spite of the black clouds which were gathering over the sky of her country, of her city, nothing else but Olivier mattered. She could no longer tolerate her husband's coarse pretence and found little consolation in her friends. Anyway, owing to the raging religious persecutions, people avoided meeting.

Another gossipy book appeared in Paris (1555), *Le Fort Inexpugnable de l'Honneur du Sexe Feminin*, written by a François de Billon, in which the author said that although La Belle Cordière was often compared to Cleopatra, in her sexual behaviour she should have been called a man. In this sarcastic comment, the author was near the mark.

She had loved Olivier like a man, their intensely physical and blazing love had lasted a few months; on the other hand, Louise went on also tormenting herself with feminine masochistic recollections; every word, every instance became the source of enraged hours of miserable thoughts. In her way, she was a "pure" spiritual lover too, because the epicentre of her love was desperate recollection. She waited for Olivier forever.

She longed for his return, but Olivier, so much younger than herself, had other fish to fry. He often came back to France, as the personal envoy of the ambassador to Diane de Poitiers: in the presence of Diane, the living goddess, in that court where the best painters of France depicted her as Artemis, Olivier had no time for Louise. He wrote an *Ode to Sire Aymon*, a vulgar recitation in which he pictured

24. *Two Women Bathing*, Ecole de Fontainebleau

Because of Diane, Fontainebleau became the centre of the arts; the goddess Diana, chasing tame deer and the crescent moon were depicted everywhere, along the magnificent galleries painted by Primatice and Rosso Fiorentino, on objects chiselled by Benvenuto Cellini. At Fontainebleau life was easy, sex was a beloved pastime, hunting and dancing filled the day.

Ennemond Perrin as a typical dull tradesman in a greasy apron, preoccupied only with his business. Louise was referred to as "*la belle capitaine*", and everybody recognized in Magny's scurrilous description the husband of the poet. She must have felt betrayed by Olivier's vulgarity.

From Parcieu, where she went alone, Louise prepared for the publication of her *oeuvre* which, in her mood of fierce mistrust of men, of all men, she dedicated to Clémence de Bourges, her noble and chaste friend. Her dedication became a feminist statement:–

> *Since the time has come, Mademoiselle, that the severe laws of men do not any longer forbid women to apply to science and discipline, it seems to me that those who have the opportunity must apply that honest liberty to learn them, something that our sex has in other times so much desired: and thus to show men the wrong they did in depriving us from the good and honour which derives us from using them ... Having spent part of my youth in the study of music, and that time which remained, having myself found it short for refining my intellect, and not being able myself to satisfy the good will I feel for my sex of wanting to see women not only surpass men in beauty, but in science and knowledge.*

Louise's book was a great success, to be reprinted four times in two years. Jean de Tournes, her printer (one of the 200 who were now established in the city of Lyons), reprinted the book a few months after its first appearance and another clandestine reprint sold in the north of France.

At that time Olivier de Magny was the guest of Diane at her magnificent palace of Anêt and he dedicated an ode to her, and also published another book of poems, *Soupirs*. Most of his work, according to L. E. Kastner (*Modern Philosophy*), was sheer plagiarism, straight translations from Sannazzaro and Petrarch.

In 1556 Olivier was at Ferrara at the court of Duchess Renée, exactly twenty years after Vittoria Colonna's visit. By then, as we said, Renée was a virtual prisoner, the French ambassador and his secretary had come to see her in order to persuade her to abjure the Calvinism that embarrassed her husband the Duke of Este, a vassal of the pope, and the King of France.

Renée was not well treated by the Calvinists either, as she was accused of meddling in the affairs of the consistory. "She is turning everything upside down in our ecclesiastical assembly ... Our Consistory will be the laughing stock of Papists and Anabaptists. They'll say we're being ruled by women", a pastor wrote to Jean Calvin.

In Ferrara, Olivier Magny spent most of his time courting Marguerite de Gordon, Viscomtesse de Cardaillac, a lady of Renee's entourage. Then he returned to Lyons. We do not know whether Louise saw him again, whether he looked for her or not, but it is unlikely that her pride could forgive the young man's poetry that insulted her husband, or his long absence and his silence. But then Louise turned Olivier, as often happens with women, into a dream, a flight of her imagination. Perfection, the sublime, somebody who did not exist, could not exist and would have never existed but for her longing desire – and her sublime poetry. She created him.

In the more and more obsessive climate of Puritanism, Louise was again attacked by a scurrilous lampoon which alleged that Tommaso Fortini, the Florentine lawyer, was her lover and paid her money, and that hers was a body for sale. That Tommaso was her lover was certainly true but Louise did not have to sell her body and did not need money. Maybe the opposite was true, Louise might have helped her Tommaso financially. Envious of her fame and success, people loved to recite the obscene verses even if the name of the rue de Confort had been changed into rue Belle Cordière, honouring the fame of one of Lyons's most gifted daughters.

Life was becoming increasingly difficult at Lyons. Even Maurice Scève was suspected of heresy. It would have been unthinkable in such troubled times for Louise to reopen her salon, to entertain her friends, to converse, recite and play music. Any intellectual gathering was suspect: the equally intolerant Catholics and Huguenots spied on each other with hatred. The Catholics saw heresy in anybody; the Huguenots condemned anything that was not wholly sombre. France was becoming increasingly intolerant. In Lyons over 900 families were suspected of heresy; the tutor of Maurice Scève's children was burnt at the stake, and the same end was reserved for Pierre Bouchillon, a Huguenot jeweller. As intolerance advanced, 2,000 families left the city that was once so free, rich and fair.

Unable to unite his empire spiritually, in 1555 Charles V abdicated in favour of his son Philip who, four years later concluded a popular peace with Henri of France. One year earlier those kings had been caught by surprise: Mary, Queen of England, who had re-established Catholicism, died and was succeeded by her stepsister Elizabeth Tudor, whose sympathy lay with the Reformation and with the rebels in the Netherlands. Northern and southern Europe were divided by a religious movement which was taking the form of warfare. France for one was split between its two natures: its southern and northern souls. When Henri II died (1559), his son Francis II became king for a few months and, since he was married to Mary of Scotland, a Guise on her mother's side, France fell under the control of that powerful Catholic family. Religious intolerance grew, exacerbating social discontent: the Guise family controlled the army and the artillery, considered the best in Europe. Then Francis II was succeeded by the young Charles IX, and France became effectively ruled by Catherine de' Medici, the Queen Mother. In effect, Catherine secured the regency and that made her the dominant figure in French politics for over twenty years. She was "herself indifferent to the subtleties of theology, which she regarded as matters of baffling incomprehensibility, she found it hard to believe that others might see them in a different light", writes J. H. Elliott. Catherine had a point: especially amongst the nobility, religious tensions hid economic struggles. The queen was caught in the middle of multiple rivalries because France was controlled by three families, the Bourbons in the south and west; the Guise in the east, and the Montmorency in the centre. The Catholic Guise faction strove to enforce its supremacy against the Huguenot Condé and Coligny on the other side; the Huguenot and the Catholic causes were used by aristocratic factions for their own ends. A clash of spiritual and material interests finally erupted in civil war in 1561. "This war is not like other wars", the Protestant pastor Pierre Viret wrote, "for even the very poorest man has an interest in it, since we are fighting for the freedom of our conscience." But he was talking for the lower strata. The Venetian ambassador, on the other hand, explained to his doge that the war was motivated by the fact that the Guise wanted "no equal" and the Admiral Coligny "no superior".

War, massacres and looting swept France. The country, where there had been plenty to eat and houses with window panes experienced hunger and destruction. Lyons suffered tremendously. In 1562 Lyons was conquered by the Huguenots under the command of the cruel Baron des Andrets; the angered Huguenots – women, children and soldiers – smashed statues, broke baptismal fonts, destroyed holy images, while singing psalms in the vernacular, which shocked the Catholics but united the Huguenots, giving them a sense of defiance, of militancy. The cathedral was ravaged by the iconoclasts; the magnificent funeral monument of the Cardinal of Saluce destroyed. The once enlightened printers from Lyons now published dull religious pamphlets about Lucifer, the Antichrist, or psalms. Then the Maréchal de Vieilleville reconquered the city for the Guise and for the young Charles IX, who made his entry into Lyons, but not for long: the Reformed Church was set up again. One of Louise's aunts, a female barber, became a Calvinist. The bloody religious war was basically motivated by the reaction of the new French middle class against the aristocracy, that ever-boiling and unstable co-habitation which erupted again in 1789.

Then, in 1564, the Black Death struck Lyons. The king, who was in the city with his court, fled just in time. Louise and her husband took refuge at Parcieu, the estate which her mother had left her; in the summer two-thirds of Lyons's inhabitants died and grass grew over its once busy streets. In the winter of 1565 Parcieu was cold and the countryside infested with brigands and Huguenots. The epidemic had been quenched by the colder climate, and husband and wife decided to return to Lyons. When she came back to rue de Confort, Louise found that the Black Death had killed Maurice Scève and her own brother François.

Two great friends had gone and now her husband, the good Ennemond, was old and tired; trade, as one can see from the records of taxes he paid, diminished drastically with the civil war and the Black Death. A few weeks after their return from Parcieu, Ennemond died. They probably had some good last years together, the old husband and the disillusioned Louise, abandoned by her family and lover, sheltering together from war and fear: Ennemond made Louise his sole heiress. Louise was now alone, her friends dead or gone or too afraid to see anybody. The thought of death, which had never occurred to her before, preoccupied her.

But she had Tommaso Fortini, theirs became a marital relationship – Louise unable to live alone, Tommaso bound to her by a long friendship and admiration. In April 1565 Louise Labé was in Tommaso's house, ill and near death. She called for a notary and, at the age of forty-three, dictated her will: she had sizeable property to distribute.

Her will is the document of a generous nature; she remembered those relatives who had deserted her, and helped financially the girls who could not marry because they had no money. It is important to note that Louise left no donation to any institution for former "lost girls", which she would have been bound to do by law had she been a courtesan. Tommaso Fortini was to be the executor of her will and to him Louise left the estate of Parcieu where she was born.

After writing her will, a full year went by before Louise, ill at Parcieu, died and, fearing the Huguenots, her Catholic funeral was conducted very early in the morning so that no one should be seen mourning the great poet. Louise Labé's best epitaph is her own twenty-fourth sonnet, in which she urged other women to try and understand her weakness in having loved so much:–

> Ne reprenez, Dames, si j'ay aymé:
> Si j'ay senti mile torches ardentes,
> Mile travaus, mile douleurs mordantes:
> Si en pleurant j'ay mon tems consumé,
>
> Las que mon nom n'en soit par vous blamé;
> Si j'ay faille, les peines sont presentes,
> N'aigressez point leurs pointes violentes:
> Mais estimez qu'Amour, à point nommé.
>
> Sans votre ardeur d'un Vulcan excuser,
> Sans la beauté d'Adonis accuser,
> Pourra, s'il veut, plus vous render amoureuses:
>
> Et ayant moins que moy d'occasion,
> Et plus d'estrange et forte passion.
> Et gardez vous d'estre plus malheueuses.
>
> *Ladies, let not my love incur your blame.*
> *If I my time in fruitless weeping spent,*
> *A thousand toils and travails underwent,*
> *And if I burned with a too ardent flame,*
>
> *Yet let now your reproach put me to shame;*
> *If I have sinned, I bear the punishment.*
> *Make not my present pangs more violent*
> *But recollect that Love his prey can claim*
>
> *At any instant, nor does he require*
> *Adonis's beauty or swart Vulcan's fire,*
> *Ladies, you more than me to subjugate.*

And so with less good reason for your state
But ridden by more strange and hot desire,
Beware lest you be more fortunate.

But, although she asks forgiveness – from women, not men – for having loved so much, it is to her lute, the companion of her sighs and of her inspiration, that she talked in the most poetic vein:–

Lut, compagnon de ma calamité,
De mes soupirs temoin irreprochable ...

Lute, companion of my calamity,
Irreproachable witness of my sighs ...

rulers in adversity

During the late Renaissance most of Europe was ruled by women. The Regent of France, Catherine de' Medici, strove to find a balance between Catholics and Huguenots; less able, the Regent of Scotland, Mary of Guise, had been deposed by the lords of the congregations inspired by John Knox; her daughter, Mary Stuart, Queen of Scots, was unfortunately rather stupid; Margaret of Parma, the regent of the Netherlands, depended ultimately on her brother the king's deliberations. The daughter of Charles V, who later became Ottavio Farnese's wife, Margaret was a wise, tolerant and intelligent woman. Although she was not Spanish, the Dutch saw in her the foreigner, the governess of the Netherlands who hardly spoke Spanish. She was the mother of Alessandro Farnese, the most valiant captain of Philip II's army; but Philip never trusted his half-sister, judging her an appeaser and even a sympathizer of the rebels in the Low Countries.

Only Elizabeth of England ruled by her own fine mind, developing her brand of politics, using "feminine coyness" for political means, with a firm vision of her country's role as much as her own monarchical duty, as we shall see in the next chapter. Elizabeth had the advantage of ruling a country to which she belonged. Both on her father's and on her mother's side she was wholly English, unlike her half-sister Mary Tudor, who was half-Spanish, or Mary Stuart, who was more French than Scottish. Indeed, Mary Stuart, who was born in 1542, was sent to France at the age of six and was educated at the court of Fontainebleau. In 1558 she married the dauphin who, together with Mary, claimed the throne of England. Mary's claim stemmed from Henry VIII's eldest sister, Margaret, Queen of Scotland but, when she returned to Britain, she could hardly speak English. Queen of France for only seventeen months before she became a widow, Mary had to leave Fontainebleau and the Louvre Palace and go back to rule her native Scotland. Catherine, the Queen-regent of France, had been in a hurry to get rid of her after the death of her son: the removal of another Guise from court diminished the power of that family. Catherine also thwarted Mary's attempts to marry into the house of Spain, since Catherine wanted her own daughter, and not a Guise, in such a powerful alliance. In that, the queen mother, whose politics have so divided historians, was wise. In trying to keep a balance of power among the aristocracy that was threatening royal supremacy, a balance so fatiguingly built by the Valois, Catherine was acting as a good guardian of the throne of France.

25. *Margaret of Parma*, circle of Sebastiano del Piombo
Margaret married Ottavio Farnese, Duke of Parma, in 1542. She was Charles V's daughter by a Flemish woman. The bust behind her in this painting represents her father. Her half-brother Philip II made her regent of the Netherlands but the tide of protest against the Spaniards and their religious intolerance drove her away from Flanders.

One can only imagine Mary's horror at returning to the backwardness of Scotland after the luxury of Fontainebleau, where she had been the darling of the graceful court. The beautiful, spoilt girl, accustomed to objects by Benvenuto Cellini and galleries painted by Primatice and Rosso Fiorentino, back in the bare-walled Holyrood is an image that could haunt one. A visit to Mary's apartments in Edinburgh is enough to give one an idea of the Scottish queen's misery at returning from the position of Queen of France to that of miserable queen of her hostile, cold kingdom. Morever, "Mary Queen of Scots totally antagonized nobles and people by her personal behaviour and matrimonial proclivities – and was driven to abdication in 1567", writes J. H. Elliott.

The Calvinists were a threat to monarchical power. John Knox in Scotland was determined to carry out a religious revolution. Coligny, the leader of the Huguenot army in France, worked in tandem with the holy ministers while European royalty – even the Protestant Elizabeth – considered the Calvinists' radical tendencies as dangerous to her authority. Moreover, being a militant philosophy, Calvinism made common cause with discontent; not so much in Geneva as among the Huguenots, who were prepared to fight.

In March 1560 an ill-conceived plot of Huguenots at Amboise, aimed at the Guise-dominated government, resulted in failure. The Protestant Condé fled to the mildly Protestant kingdom of Navarre, ruled by his Bourbon brother. There a decision was taken to ally the Huguenots with other European Protestants: the Swiss cantons, Elizabethan England, and the Protestant German princes. The French civil war was thus turning into a European confrontation. In 1561 a large consignment of gunpowder from Geneva was sold at Lyons.

The queen-regent tried in vain to pacify the two factions: the Guise and the Bourbon–Condé. Without money to raise troops, and with the royal army under the control of the Guise, Catherine turned to the Bourbon–Condé faction. She secretly summoned their admiral, Coligny, asking him how many soldiers the Huguenots could put at her disposal. Coligny offered the 2,150 Huguenot communities on condition that they would be allowed to worship openly. With her edict of January 1562, which granted the Calvinists a certain degree of freedom of worship, Catherine became the supporter of the French Protestants.

As described earlier, Catherine de' Medici was the daughter of Lorenzo, Duke of Urbino, and Maddalena de la Tours d'Auvergne. She was born in 1519, the same year in which both her parents died. From the age of six months she was put in the care of her aunt, Clarice Strozzi, born a Medici, who was the wife of the ebullient gentleman who was close to Tullia and, as a prisoner, committed suicide. While Leo X was alive, Catherine was the heiress to the dukedom of Urbino, however, at his death, she became a landless duchess.

When she was six, she was sent to Florence to be educated by Cardinal Passarini together with her Medici cousins, Ippolito, aged sixteen, and Alessandro, who was fourteen. They lived between Florence and Poggio at Cajano, the wonderful country villa built by Lorenzo de' Medici. Ippolito, the womanizer who was soon to meet Tullia d'Aragona and then fall desperately in love with Giulia Gonzaga, liked his little cousin; many in Florence hoped that the two branches of the Medici family would join in a marriage between Ippolito and Catherine; Catherine being the last of the main Medici branch. But that was not what the pope aimed at; he wanted to ally his house with that of the Valois. Clarice Strozzi died when Catherine was nine, and the little girl was left alone to face the turbulence of the Florentine rebellion against the Medici rule and she was sheltered in a nunnery; in her triumphal days as Queen of France, she would write to the abbess and send donations to the convent.

When she was twelve, Clement VII, another Medici pope, called Catherine to Rome, where she found Ippolito distracted by his extravagant life and his many women. Then, Clement, in 1532, arranged two political marriages to bring about his design. Catherine was to be married to the son of the French king. The bastard but favourite daughter of Charles V, Margaret of Austria, was to marry Alessandro de' Medici. Magnificently clad, Catherine was sent to meet the nine-year-old Margaret of Austria, and rode alongside the young princess, her cousin Alessandro and Cardinal Cybo, the papal legate. On 23 October 1533 it was Catherine's turn to be married: in Marseilles, surrounded by a luxury rare even in those days, the fourteen-year-old *duchessina* married Henri of France. The pope gave her a dowry of 100,000 scudi, and the king a casket made of rock crystal, containing jewels worth 27,900 scudi. Catherine was asked to renounce her inheritance in favour of her uncle (see Appendix C), something for which Clement rewarded her with an added 30,000 scudi. She was married in the presence of the King of France and the pope, who blessed the couple. Her cousin Cardinal Ippolito de' Medici, who might have been her husband, came to witness Catherine's unexpectedly important marriage. The Queen of France accorded Catherine the honour of accompanying her to her nuptial chamber. But Catherine already knew that the dauphin had eyes only for Diane de Poitiers.

The Medici newcomer was to feel most unwelcome in France: in spite of her being half-French, in spite of her noble blood and vast dowry, she was nicknamed "the banker's daughter". The union between a Medici and a Valois did not mark any political rapprochement between Paris and Florence – in fact quite the opposite. Both Alessandro and Cosimo were subject to Spain; and France welcomed many Florentine rebels such as the Duke Alessandro's assassin, and the sons of Filippo and Clarice Strozzi, Piero and Leone, who were loved at the Valois court and given important jobs in the French army and navy.

Two years after her marriage, when Catherine was sixteen, Cardinal Ippolito de' Medici died in Giulia's arms. Many said that he had died of poison; indeed Catherine was thus informed, by letter and, when she received the news, she cried like a child, which, of course, she was. Many sad years had gone by. On 6 December 1558 she wrote to Duke Cosimo, insisting that he should lend her 100,000 scudi, reminding him that she – and not he – was the direct heiress of the main branch of the Medici family: "I am the first woman of your House, and I have been wife of a king, and am mother of a king, and have three sons, for which reason it can be hoped that the Crown will remain in this House ... and that, for the grace of God, never is nor ever was a greater queen than I."

Catherine had turned into an embittered widow. As France drifted into civil war, the Huguenots whom at first she protected, were told that they were now defending the "authority of the King, the government of the Queen, and the tranquillity of the realm". But Catherine was isolated, Spain being allied to the Guise faction, and Paris, her capital, opposed to Condé and his army. When the Duke of Guise took the capital, Condé fled and missed the opportunity, which was his duty, of going to Fontainebleau to defend the queen-regent and the king. Therefore, the queen reluctantly had to submit to Guise's demand and return to Paris: from then onwards the Catholics, and no longer Huguenots, were to be the guardians of the crown. She was not pretty, her very pale face was made heavier by too large a nose and somewhat masculine eyes. But she dressed magnificently and conducted her court with immense style, the style of a Medici. Her French was flawless of course – her mother being a French aristocrat – and she famously brought to France the greatest cooks from Venice who gave birth to French cuisine.

A mobile Protestant army was levied from Germany; Lyons, Basle and Strasbourg raised loans to finance the campaigns and, fearing the victory of the Guise, who would then have encircled England, Queen Elizabeth offered a loan to the Huguenots in exchange for the city of Le Havre.

For a time the governors of the French provinces watched developments as the Huguenots infiltrated and subverted: in the Dauphine, Languedoc, Guienne and Provence, the Huguenots gained control of public offices. At the beginning of the war, which erupted when a number of Protestants were killed while at church, Lyons was the first city seized by local Huguenot ministers. Apart from the works of art systematically stripped from churches – which distressed Calvin (it is unimaginable how much was destroyed) – the possession of such an important financial centre as Lyons was a great asset for the Bourbon–Condé faction. While the royal army was essentially made up of mercenaries, Condé's depended on enthusiastic troops who, in the name of Jesus Christ, fought "to enter the kingdom of Heaven", and marched into battle singing the psalms translated into the vernacular by Clement Marot. The first ferocious bout of war lasted one year after which, fortunately for Catherine, a "pacification" was effected mainly because the most troublesome leaders on both sides had been killed. Catherine reinforced her edict which, although it gave a limited freedom of worship to the Protestants, restricted their freedom territorially: a measure that has to be read in the light of the Huguenots' political structure and militancy.

The queen mother was desperate to maintain national unity until her son reached maturity: preaching the virtue of peace, in 1565 Catherine progressed through France together with the young Charles IX, whose majority had just been announced. Spectacular festivals were organized throughout the royal progress to dramatize the importance of kingship. The climax came at Bayonne where the queen met her daughter, the Queen of Spain, but, instead of accompanying his wife, Philip II sent the Duke of Alba to represent him.

Philip's third wife, Isabelle or Elisabette de Valois, was the figure that Schiller later put at the centre of his romantic drama *Don Carlos*, set to music by Verdi, one of the greatest musical creations of the nineteenth century. Although Verdi recreated the characters and the dark atmosphere of the Escurial – drawing an unforgettable portrait of Philip II – his son Don Carlos, a sadistic degenerate who suffered epileptic fits, was dead by the time Philip married the Valois Princess.

Not only did Philip send the Duke of Alba in his own stead but, from Bayonne, Alba proceeded towards the Netherlands at the head of a formidable army to stamp out the Protestant rebellion: the Huguenots became convinced that Catherine had abandoned them. Exactly one year later, Condé attempted a *coup d'état* by seizing Catherine and the king. Charles IX, surrounded with Guises, and his brother the Duke of Anjou, urged action against the Huguenots; the latter defeated them in a battle in which Condé was killed. The new and popular leader of the Huguenots was Admiral Gaspard de Coligny, who worked closely with Jeanne d'Albret, the protestant mother of Henri Bourbon. Both armies fought inconclusive battles and, exhausted, signed a further peace treaty in August 1569. Again Catherine preached moderation and, at the end of the terrible bloodshed, the Huguenots won some further liberties: the Guises left the court in furious protest.

The seventeen provinces of the Netherlands were governed by Margaret the regent, who, like Catherine, faced a divided aristocracy and an empty treasury. But Calvinism in the Netherlands was not well structured, and several forms of Protestantism, such as Lutheranism and Anabaptism, were widespread, in spite of the repressive measures of the Spanish government. Margaret appealed to her brother to adopt a tolerant formula similar to Catherine's edict, but Philip II told her that the Inquisition was to punish heretics as harshly as always.

Back in France it looked as if the marriage of Henri of Navarre, to Margaret of Valois, Catherine's youngest daughter, would pacify the two factions, and that Catherine's policy would be thus consolidated. All the Huguenot nobility gathered in Paris. The marriage took place on 18 August with great splendour. A few days later, on the night of 23–4 August 1572, Catherine allowed a horrible massacre of those men, women and children who had come to Paris for the marriage of her daughter. The night of St Bartholomew was followed by a butchering of Huguenots all over France. Why had Catherine abandoned her policy of toleration?

Coligny had gained the trust of the young king, but had found strong opposition from Catherine to his plan to invade the Netherlands to aid the Protestant rebellion. The three royal brothers – Charles IX, Anjou and Alençon – hated each other. While Anjou was on the Catholic side, the other two sympathized with Coligny. The admiral's belief that a war with Spain would be not only honourable but also a religious crusade was opposed by Catherine who was anxious to avoid yet more bloodshed; moreover, Coligny had succeeded in alienating Charles's affection from his mother, whom he called "*Madame la Serpente*", the lady snake. Catherine's progressive hatred of Coligny matured into the idea of eliminating him at the wedding of her daughter Margaret to Henri of Navarre; however, he was wounded, but not killed.

Catherine panicked. With great difficulty she convinced her son the king to prepare a list of Huguenot leaders who would have to be eliminated; but neither the king nor Catherine had foreseen the fury of the Parisian Catholics and the Guise desire for revenge which, on St Bartholomew's night, killed between two and three thousand Huguenots in Paris alone. Queen Elizabeth's court went into mourning: St Bartholomew's night was seen in England as part of a wider Catholic movement to extirpate Protestantism from Europe. "The massacre of the Huguenots in 1572 was thus a departure (and a fatal one) from a tenaciously pursued policy, and is best seen as an act of desperation by a clever woman who had momentarily lost her head", writes J. H. Elliott in *Europe Divided*.

For a month the French ambassador was banned from Elizabeth's presence although, at the time, the queen was being courted by Catherine's third son – a courtship which pleased the English queen. Elizabeth was in a sea of adversities, but she faced them with confidence. In her work of establishing her Reform – slow steps which, seen in the light of what was happening elsewhere in Europe, call for admiration – Elizabeth was disappointing many Protestants who had hoped to make the queen – a woman, after all – the puppet of their politics. No one expected to encounter such finesse and wisdom in her frail feminine body. Dr Jewel, who was to become Bishop of Salisbury, was keeping a Protestant theologian back in Zurich well informed of Elizabeth's religious progress. That theologian was none other than Peter Martyr, the man who had warned Bernardino Ochino and who had fled from Italy with him, causing scandal and consternation among the *spirituali*. On 14 April 1559, Dr Jewel was reporting to Peter Martyr that the Mass had already fallen into disuse in many places because of the unpopularity of the deceased Mary Tudor. "But this woman, excellent as she is", he wrote of Elizabeth, "and earnest in the cause of true religion, notwithstanding she desires a thorough change as early as possible, cannot however be induced to effect such change without the sanction of the law".

Instead of choosing Catherine de' Medici's option of balancing factions, and knowing the unpopularity of the Catholics with the lower strata, of the Calvinists with the upper classes, Elizabeth used her feminine faculty of adaptability and commonsense by inventing a religion *ex novo*.

Through the Reformation women achieved a degree of equality: for example, when celibacy for the priests was abolished, the ridiculed maid who spent her life with him, in the eyes of onlookers, turned into his worthy wife. Ministers' wives generally came from a middle-class background and looked after the pastors' households. Protestant men taught their wives and generally speaking the Protestant woman came from the literate new middle class and was able to answer the Inquisitors by citing Scripture. The many who died were honoured as martyrs. To ensure literacy in cities under Huguenot control, Protestants set up catechism classes in the vernacular, encouraging even the poor to learn to read.

On the other hand Marie Dentière, a former abbess from Lyons, who had been expelled from her convent as a heretic, married a pastor and fled to Geneva; there she "invaded" men's exclusive field of preaching, and this did not please the Calvinists. From the city of heresy, she addressed an epistle to Margaret of Navarre, whom she recognized as an ally in feminism. It was printed in Geneva in 1538 under the title of *Defence for Women*. It caused a scandal for its criticism and Calvinist Geneva did not print any other work by a woman. Women were abused by the Catholics, she said, but also by the Protestants: ultimately, religion was always a weapon in masculine hands. "If God has graced poor women to reveal to them through his Holy Scripture some good and holy thing", she wrote, "dare they not write about it, speak about it, and declare it, one to the other? ... Is it not foolish to hide the gifts that God has given us?"

Out of 650 women arrested in Lyons as heretics, we find that by no means all had been converted by their husbands but the other way round. (The conversion of the Prince of Condé was effected by his wife Eleonore de Roye in 1558.) Some women professed Calvinism while their men went on being "polluted in idolatry"; many were widows or women who had a trade of their own (dressmakers, merchants, midwives, inn-keepers). Frequenting preachers more often than men, in churches or squares, women were more approachable, more easily converted by good orators. Spiritual leaders like Beza and Calvin even went to visit powerful women, knowing full well that the conversion of an aristocrat meant that several would follow.

But although most trades required a degree of literacy and independence, the Huguenot feminist force did not include literate women who had already striven for and conquered a position. The best example is, of course, Louise Labé, who clearly had little sympathy with the Huguenots – or they for her. She might have sympathized with the teachings of Erasmus, of Valdés, or Luther; but Calvin was a misogynist, blind to intellectual research, ultimately reactionary. Women had been created subject to men, John Calvin said, and: "Let the woman be satisfied with her state of subjection, and not take it amiss that she is made inferior to the more distinguished sex." During their painful labour, "a horrible torment" as Calvin put it, women were to sigh and suffer in obedience to the Lord. They were not even left with the consolation, as the Catholic Marie Le Jars de Gournay pointed out, of praying to some holy women, like St Margaret, the protector of women in labour, or to the Virgin Mary. As Marie sharply suggested, by robbing women of a female deity, Calvin had peopled heaven with men alone: the Calvinist religion had become wholly male. Moreover, Calvin objected to women with a vocation for preaching; his concept of overthrowing the priestly class and substituting it with well-trained pastors was threatened by women who, having read and learnt the Scriptures, thought that they could repeat the word of God. Women were to be excluded once again, even from pleasure. Montaigne thought that procreation was hampered by the woman who enjoyed making love.

In the Reformed Churches women were second to men in partaking of the Holy Supper and the consistories punished women with prison if they shouted back at their husbands. Somebody like Louise Labé, who had found liberation, was anathema to Calvin, who said that she was a strumpet, while Guillaume Paradin, the Catholic deacon of Lyons, a humanist scholar, praised Louise for her virtue, for her angelic face and an understanding "superior to her sex". In fact the Catholics, especially if far from Rome, ultimately accorded more tolerance to the exceptional woman: if she sinned, Louise could always ask for the forgiveness of other women and of the Almighty God.

Sadly, the spread of learning among the middle class was resulting in a violent movement of censure towards the excesses of the Renaissance upper class, a movement which swept the whole of Europe. Loyola's army-like Society of Jesus was hardly religious, it was a mystical combat unit (the Communist Party later consciously imitated Loyola's pyramidal structure, its tight rule of obedience and its widely distributed cells answerable only to one man at the top): it was a weapon of power. Political repression needed such an organization. Former times had allowed the excessive development of the individual and the "dangerous" faculty of individual criticism. The Renaissance movement was one that, if not quenched either by the Counter-Reformation or by the Reformation, might have resulted in anarchy because it encouraged individuality and expression. That is possibly why the more attractive and tolerant branches of the Reformation – Luther, Valdés and Erasmus – did not fulfil the needs of the contemporary rulers and met with little success.

In a different way, but with a similar end in view, Calvin was unconsciously imitating Loyola: he shaped his militants into a tight organization of cells. The French Refomed Church – the Confessio Gallicana – was organized on well-defined militant lines, a network of disciplined bodies ideally suited to subversion and revolt. Each church had its own "consistory" of ministers and lay elders; a group of consistories formed a "colloquy", which supervised the affairs of the region. On a provincial level several colloquies formed the synods, and at the summit was the national synod. The organization represented the force of change, of a new class intolerant of the past, eager to destroy in order to rebuild.

Thus religion was but a disguise for a political–economic movement that swept through Europe. It was the first sign of a newly enriched class which wanted to keep those who were ahead in check and those who had stayed behind in subjection. Change meant revolt: civil war in France started in 1562. Earlier, in 1520, Sten Sture, the leader of the Swedish resistance against the Danish king, died, but his widow Christina defended Stockholm for eight months. In the Low Countries the population rebelled in 1566. In Scotland the queen was deposed in 1567. The northern English nobility rose in 1569. Italy – now a province of Spain – gave few signs of life.

In addition to the bloodshed caused by the Geneva–Rome confrontation, the Christians and the Moors were fighting each other in another war whose roots lay in economic rivalry. It was part of the confrontation that still sees the Western world and the Arabs opposed; by losing the battle of Lepanto (1571) the East lost its race to supremacy. The economies of Central and Northern Europe gained from being governed by women because of these women's tolerant attitude – with the exception of Mary Tudor who was herself governed by Spain (she was Philip's wife). Sometimes women ruled behind the throne, like Diane de Poitiers or Margaret Beaufort, the formidable mother of Henry VII, a great influence on him and a promoter of scholarship amongst women. Eventually, as the long shadow of Spain stretched northwards, in the guise of Philip II and of his commander-in-chief, the Duke of Alba, the north rebelled, something that Italy had failed to do.

The new religion, which had originally brought women and men together singing psalms, marching, learning and reading together, venturing into the male preserve of theology, ultimately left women unequal and frustrated. Religion was the basis of a well-ordered society and the preservation of religious unity was thought essential to the survival of the state and of the monarchy. "Un roi, une foi, une loi" (1560) expressed the French rule of one king, one faith and one law. The contrasts between Catholics and Protestants developed into a form of hysterics that provoked the most barbarous acts; Geneva and Rome left no room in the middle for tolerance.

the Englishwomen

It must be said that Elizabeth was fortunate to rule subjects who accepted her peculiarities because, though fundamentally wise, her behaviour must have appeared pretty eccentric to those on the outside. In order to maintain valuable alliances, she allowed herself to be courted by foreign princes whom she had no intention of marrying. She surrounded herself with favourites, to whom she permitted many indiscretions, and – even for an unmarried queen – to keep lovers as openly as she did must have seemed somewhat odd. In later years, her appearance must have been horrific: she wore huge wigs, her face was covered with layers of white powder and, in spite of the image in her portraits, she became portly.

Following the reign of her half-sister, Mary Tudor, Elizabeth inherited an explosive situation which could have resulted in civil war and carnage; there was a bigoted nobility and middle class, and the extremes of John Knox's Presbyterianism influenced many parts of England. On the other side, Catholicism had been dangerously strengthened by Mary's support; even Reginald Pole's nephew tried to scheme against Elizabeth, one of the many Catholics – and Calvinists – whom she had to keep in check.

Elizabeth was twenty-five years old when she acceded to the throne. She was tall, slender, and lovely, with tiny hands and long, white fingers, which she displayed with pride, and a complexion whitened with a lotion made from off-white poppy seeds and alum. Her hair was famously red, like her father's, and her nose was visibly hooked. A charmer like her mother, she was flirtatious and loved the company of men. Even when she was old and ugly, she was convinced that every man was in love with her.

But Elizabeth had made up her mind not to marry. "She will never subject herself to any man", the Count Guzman de Silva declared in one of his letters to Philip II. She might have been tempted to change her mind after her seduction by the charming Valois, whose courtship was elaborate and witty. Since she could not marry one of her subjects – a Leicester, or an Essex, or a Hatton, for example – it was thought that she might agree instead to marry the son of France. But the French prince belonged to the family that had promoted the slaughter of the Protestants on St Bartholomew's night, and Elizabeth finally decided to give him up, though she dedicated a poem to him, written in Petrarchian style, and entitled "On Monsieur's Departure":

I grieve; yet dare not show discontent;
I love, and yet am forced to seem to hate;
I dote, but dare not what I meant;
I seem stark mute, yet inwardly do prate.
I am, and am not – freeze, and yet I burn,
Since from myself my other self I turn.

In the same year that Michelangelo died in Italy, Shakespeare was born in Stratford-on-Avon. Shakespeare was by no means a unicum of the English Renaissance, although, with his very English talent for being able to speak to anyone, whether high- or low-born, rich or poor, his genius underlines a shift in the Renaissance movement. The women he describes in his plays cover the whole spectrum of types, and he never diminished womanhood per se. John Webster, the great playwright, could be described as a feminist *ante litteram*. Francis Bacon was the prophet of modern science: his inventions were only bona fide if they could be applied in a practical way. "Human knowledge and human power come to the same thing", wrote Bacon, "for where the cause is not known, the effect cannot be produced". Bacon always advocated thorough investigation and condemned the occult, for which there was a contemporary popular mania, as a "lazy art", not because he despised it, but because it could not be proven and, hence, in his eyes, was not valid.

The occult, astrology and magic were as popular in the Renaissance as they are today. John Dee (1527–1608), one of the leading mathematicians in Elizabethan England, "conducted geographical and hydrographical surveys of newly discovered lands for the Queen and did important work on trigonometry, navigation and the reform of the calendar", writes Anthony Gottlieb. Dee, who was admired and respected for talking to angels using mirrors and mystic numbers, "may well have been the model for Shakespeare's Prospero in *The Tempest*".

Elizabeth consulted Dee on all sorts of matters, from a political confrontation to the interpretation of a dream, from a toothache to a new comet. She was superstitious and believed what the fascinating doctor claimed to perceive in his astrological instruments. In 1577, Dee predicted the founding of "an incomparable British empire", and the queen followed his vision and advice. Dee, who belonged to the scientific mould of the Renaissance, believed in the exploration of new lands and encouraged the queen to support her pirates, Drake, Raleigh and Gilbert, in their voyages, which, because of Dee, became voyages of exploration.

Had it not been for Elizabeth's patronage, Dee might have been in danger, suspected as he was of forbidden practices. In 1564 he wrote of how she "in most heroical and princely wise did comfort me and encourage me in my studies philosophical and mathematical." Eleven years later, "the Queen's Majesty, with her most honourable Privy Council and other lords and nobility, visited my library." Elizabeth would have liked Dee to have apartments at court, but he turned down what so many others coveted, afraid that life at court might distract him from his scientific and esoteric studies.

The Elizabethans craved education. The claim that education made women immoral was "not borne out by the facts," wrote Ludovicus Vives, the scholar who had been Mary Tudor's tutor; in fact, he said, the contrary was often true. Richard Mulcaster, the master of a school in Pultney, preached that well-educated women raised good families. And a foreigner observed that in England "the rich cause their sons and daughters to learn Latin, Greek and Hebrew for, since this storm of heresy has invaded the land, they hold it useful to read the Scriptures in the original tongue." Intellectual education in England became fashionable. Since nunneries had been abolished, girls studied either at home or in elementary lay schools open to both sexes; during Elizabeth's reign, girls were admitted to grammar schools as well.

On 17 November 1558, the day of her accession, Elizabeth, dressed in black, summoned her councillors. She was at Hatfield when the not unwelcome news of Mary's death reached her. On 23 November, accompanied by over 1,000 splen-

26. *The Procession of Queen Elizabeth I*, attributed to Robert Peake the Elder
Elizabeth had the advantage of ruling a country to which she belonged: both on her father's and on her mother's side she was wholly British. Elizabeth invented her role of monarch. She was feminine and needy of affection; eager not to offend or go against a people with whom she created an empathy no other monarch enjoyed.

didly dressed courtiers, who transformed the gloom of the winter season into a festive summer, Elizabeth travelled to London to be received in the capital as queen. Everyone wanted to see the young woman as she was cheered along the streets. She was welcomed by the Lord Mayor who together with all the London representatives, kissed her famously white hand. But when the Bishop of London was about to pay her the same homage, she withdrew her hand. During Mary's reign, Bishop Bonner had burnt many Protestants, and the new monarch was publicly showing her disapproval of him and his religious inclinations. It was a spontaneous gesture, a strong and disdainful sign which gained Elizabeth a great deal of sympathy.

London was enthusiastic. The courtier Sir John Hayward wrote:–

If ever any person had the gift or the style to win the hearts of the people, it was this Queen. All her faculties were in motion, and every motion seemed a well-guided action; her eye was set upon one, her ear listened to another, her judgement ran upon a third, to a fourth she addressed her speech, her spirit seemed to be everywhere. Some she pitied, some she commanded, some she thanked, with others she pleasantly and wittily jested, condemning no person, neglecting no office, and distributing her smiles, looks and graces so artfully that thereupon the people again redoubled the testimony of their joys, and afterwards, raising everything to the highest strain, filled the ears of all men with immoderate extolling of their prince.

This is a wonderful description of a new monarch who artfully takes on a role that she has longed to have, one which she thought would probably never be hers. Hayward's description also shows a woman flirting with her people, enthusiastic to be amongst them, glad to be alive and able to display and make use of all her knowledge and talents.

Ultimately, the woman who came to the throne of England when the country was poor, weak, and dangerously divided, was an extraordinarily polished and multi-faceted person, perfect for the position she had never been destined to occupy. Her father having gone back on his decision to exclude her from inheriting the throne, her step-brother, Edward, having died of tuberculosis, and her half-sister, Mary, also having died, the realm of England was finally hers.

On her coronation day, to the sound of fifes, drums, portable organs and the peal of London's bells, Elizabeth walked on a blue carpet which stretched from Westminster Hall to the abbey. "She had wanted the ceremony to take place on a propitious date, and – at Robert Dudley's suggestion – had consulted Dr John Dee, who studied his astrological charts and told her that, if she were crowned on the 15th of January, her reign would be glorious and prosperous", writes Alison Weir.

Elizabeth had insisted that her coronation and its attendant celebrations be as magnificent as possible, so as to make an indelible impression upon those who had cast doubts on her legitimacy and her title to the throne. The appearance of splendour and majesty meant a great deal in an age that equated greatness with lavish outward show, and so the Queen meant to use her coronation to make a political statement.

Foreign observers were impressed, not only with the coronation and the festivities but with the queen herself and her speeches. They also noticed the enthusiasm with which both nobility and people had acclaimed a woman "to rule over men". The new queen was beautiful, they claimed, her body trim and her movements regal.

Upper class women eagerly followed Elizabeth's lead in fashion, sporting colourful, expensive materials, jewels, and ever-new shapes which idealized and personalized the individual. It was an approach which was financially ruinous. A sour Puritan, Philip Stubbs, looked back on the good old days when fashion never changed, and one could wear one's father's or mother's clothes. But now, he wrote, a new-fangled device had been introduced to England: "There is a certain liquid matter which they call starch, wherein the devil has taught them to wash and dive their ruffs; which, being dry, will then stand stiff and inflexible about their necks." But what fun it was for the critics to watch a grand procession being surprised by a rainstorm, "striking sail and fluttering like dish clouts" about those elegant women's necks!

Elizabethan Renaissance fashion was forever evolving and that is in itself a sign of wealth and of cultural growth; fashion is a great betrayer of the times it mirrors. When it stops still, it reflects a society which does not move. Women's hairstyles are subject to fashion and reflect turbulence when they became extremely elaborate, as in late Roman times or before the French Revolution. Braudel considers that frequently changing fashions denote societies in motion, civilizations which are expanding both culturally and economically, and which like to spend time and money on outward appearances. For centuries after the fall of the Roman Empire, the same shaped clothes had been worn: the "sack" sported by Franciscan friars, with two holes for the sleeves and one for the head. The same type of dress, he adds, is still to be found in stagnant societies, where it has been worn for thousands of years, and where there are no farthingales, no starch, no time to spend on "satanic" devices – and, most importantly, no money to purchase them, or leisure time to keep them clean and tidy. In Elizabethan times fashion took off.

Elizabeth was an aristocrat who had lived many lives. She was three when her mother, Anne Boleyn, was beheaded, and she was turned overnight from royal heiress into bastard. But, little by little, with her intelligence and wit, she managed to win over her father, who must have seen himself in the girl's features, which were Tudor, not Boleyn. After Henry's death, his widow, Queen Catherine Parr, remarried in haste, causing a scandal. But Catherine was a good woman and in 1548 asked her stepdaughter, Elizabeth, to come and live with her at Chelsea. Catherine knew how unhappy Elizabeth was at court; what she didn't know was that, during her own pregnancy, her stepdaughter was sleeping with her dashing husband, Thomas Seymoure. Catherine, who provided Elizabeth with an excellent education, was not bitter when she discovered that her husband had "seduced" Elizabeth – although, judging from her character, it is more likely that it was Elizabeth who seduced him.

She was the embodiment of the English Renaissance, moulding it to fit the English characteristics of good commonsense and pragmatism. Elizabeth made women central to politics. In spite of the fact that most of Northern and Central Europe were at that time ruled by women, outsiders marvelled at the wise way in which, in England, a woman was governing.

The English sacrificed idealism to social order. Even in their great explorations of the world, Elizabeth's men avoided confrontations with the natives, something that stained instead the Spanish and Portuguese colonial conquests. Richard Hakluyt's account of his travels, a contemporary bestseller, Richard Chancellor's explorations in northern Russia, Sir Jerome Bowes's patient embassies to Ivan the Terrible (when he used to be locked up for weeks at a time before being admitted to the tsar's presence), sprang from an almost divine mission, a duty. Theirs were adventures that had to be faced in the interests of knowledge.

Elizabeth clearly avoided confrontation with the Turks; on the first day of the moon of Rabie Livol, in the year of the prophet 1002 and of Iesu 1594, the Almighty and Most Powerful Empress Safiyyeh, favourite wife of Murad III, mother of the future sultan Mahomet III, wrote to Elizabeth:–

> *... Written from the mother, this letter is addressed to the Very Serene and very glorious amongst the wisest of Women, the elect amongst the triumphants under the standard of Iesu Christ, very powerful and very rich ruler, and unique in the world in the feminine sex, the very serene Queen of England, who follows the example of the Virgin Mary, whose aims may become true with worthy perfection and following her desires.*

Safiyyeh's letter, written in Italian, mixed the glory of Mahomet Mustaffa with that of the Virgin Mary, and Elizabeth's with the sultan's. This empress, who belonged to the Venetian family of the Baffos, had been captured in Corfu as a child; she had become Muslim and the favourite wife of the sultan. Her letter to Elizabeth reflects religious tolerance and admiration for the role of another woman.

Although concerned with commerce, the letters that the Sultan of Turkey sent Elizabeth occasionally dealt with their common Spanish enemy and the letter that follows throws light on the tantalizing question of translation. Addressing the queen, the sultan in fact expected Elizabeth to be "loyal and firm-footed in the path of vassalage and obedience and to manifest loyalty and subservience" to the Ottoman throne. Mercifully, the diplomatic translation into Italian, the lingua franca of this correspondence, rendered this tirade as *sincere amices*, a mistranslation which possibly saved the alliance.

With growing prosperity all over England, there was a gradual improvement in women's lives. The population was expanding and all strata of society enjoyed an increase of wealth. London was a crowded capital that had grown at random and was dirty and full of vermin, "a danger to the Queen's own life". It grew quickly as a result of the increasing prosperity: from 93,000 inhabitants in 1563 to 123,000 in 1580 and 152,000 in 1593. At that time Rome housed 100,000 people, Paris 180,000, and Naples an amazing 300,000. But, although in decline, Naples (and Paris) had expanded gradually over centuries, while London was a pandemonium built in a hurry. In 1580 there came the first restrictions on building, followed by stronger measures in 1593. But town planning was never going to be a strong point with the English: there were no Alberti, Piero della Francesca, or books by Vitruvius this side of the Channel. The intermediate and middle classes were growing in importance and that meant wealth. Morality changed to suit the new social strata. The image of woman as an obstacle to spiritual life was discarded in England as priests endowed her with an authority beyond the home.

Soon after Elizabeth's accession, King Philip II travelled to London to see her, but, much to his fury, he was unable to have access to her alone. She was too busy, she let him know politely, with plans for her coronation. To dismiss the mightiest king on earth in such a fashion was almost unbelievable, especially because he wanted to marry her, thus taking back the kingdom that had practically been his when he was married to Elizabeth's half-sister, Mary. But Elizabeth wanted to be crowned before she met with Philip, and she wanted to be single when she received the crown of England. Besides, she did not intend to be seen by the hopeful Protestants and the scheming Catholics conferring with Philip behind closed doors. She wanted to keep everyone guessing about her political decisions and religious choices.

Philip, the powerful king on whose land the sun never set, thought that the tiny kingdom of England could be conquered with a mere marriage. When Elizabeth turned down the offer of Philip, her former royal brother-in-law, as a husband, Spain considered her gesture an affront. It was, but it was also a statement of liberty, of personal and national independence.

England was not strong and France was bellicose. From Scotland, the Catholic Mary Stuart was claiming the English throne on the grounds that Elizabeth was a bastard because Henry's divorce from Catherine of Aragon was invalid. On the other hand, there had been many cases of divorce in England, especially after the end of Catholic rule.

One interesting case of divorce was that of Elizabeth and George Hulse who, in 1561, appeared before the officials at Chester. They had been married at Knotisford when she was three or four (she could not remember), and he seven. George would have been happy to go on living with Elizabeth, had she consented to. But she did not and refused to have sex with him: thus they had decided to separate, and a divorce was granted. Women, or rather girls, could be married at twelve and granted an easy divorce if the marriage was not consummated. But, of course, like elsewhere in Europe, English girls had to abide by their parents' choice of husband. The parents of John Andrews, aged ten, and Ellen Dampart, eight, had decided to marry them for economic reasons; they were put in the matrimonial bed together with John's two sisters. A divorce was granted. But women were under *potestate maritorum* and, in accordance with the marriage act, all their wealth became their husbands'. English marriage had become a contract under the thirty-ninth article in 1552: the businesslike, practical relationship of man and wife was thus legalized.

For the English middle classes, man and wife became an economic unit and was therefore of use to society as a whole. In the north, adultery was less acceptable than in France and Italy precisely because the family had become a business partnership. On the other hand the aristocracy went on producing bastards. Childbearing remained a dangerous and daunting obstacle, although it was the ultimate goal of the marriage contract. Alice Thornton the daughter of a merchant from Yorkshire confided to her diary that when her sister, aged thirty-two, had died giving birth to her sixth infant, she had been delivered from a hard life. Although she had married "a good party", she had known little joy because of so many pregnancies, "and I know that she was almost happy to die".

But women read and women wrote. Over fifty English women published manuscripts between 1524 and 1640, producing eighty-five books, but the large majority created religious works – not poetry in a Renaissance vein. Only Jane Anger used her gifts to answer men's attacks by writing *Protection of Women*. Other books written by men, but with women in mind as consumers, became very popular. There was the *Book of Good Manners* by Jacques Legrand, published in 1487 and reprinted six times in twenty-eight years; also Erasmus's *Booke of Good Manners for Children* came out in 1532 and was reprinted in 1540, 1554 and 1578. On the death of Margaret of Navarre, Jane Seymour honoured her with Latin poetry which was published in Paris (1551), but no one could claim that it was particularly inspired or original.

Twenty cookery books appeared before 1640, giving recipes and ideas for preserving. "In the begynnge of Marche, or a lytell afore," says *The Book of Husbandry*:−

is tyme for a wife to make her garden, and to gette as many good seeds and herbes as she canne and specially as to be good for the potten and to eate … This will fulfil her time in between spinning and weaving. Her husband will have his own sheep and she will sew clothes for herself and him … It is a wyves occupation to make malte, to wasshe and wrynge, to make heye, shere corne, and in tyme of need to helpe her husbande to fyll the muchewayne or dounge-carte, dryve the ploughe, to loode hey, corne and suche other. And to go or ride to the market, to sell butter, cheese, milke, egges, chekyns, capons, hennes, pygges, gese, and all manner of cornes.

But English women did not, and never would, belong to an international community of wit; in continental Europe, Margaret of Navarre corresponded with Vittoria Colonna who, in turn, was a friend of Renée of Ferrara, who had given hospitality to Clement Marot – the poet who had served Margaret as secretary and fallen in love with Louise Labé. The literate English noblewomen were guardians of law and order, eager to conform, while it is generally critical faculty which develops creativity. England was channelling her learning into social order; it was the English way to sacrifice creativity for reasons of state.

Indeed, for reason of state Elizabeth could not afford to offend Philip. Not for a moment did the Spanish king, with whom the young Elizabeth had already flirted, think that he would be turned down. He wanted England so as to be able to control the riotous Low Countries and the trade routes to Holland. But a confrontation with Spain was to become inevitable, not because Elizabeth eventually rejected the king as a husband, but because she started supporting the Dutch rebellion against Spain. Her determination to keep her country in the "wrong faith" could not be tolerated by Spain either, and Elizabeth's model of government, a modern way of ruling, disturbed monolithic and tyrannical Spain. But Elizabeth's England had a small navy, a weak army, and no money – all things that Philip thought he himself possessed.

The age witnessed the birth of capitalism, a phenomenon which concerned women as well as men. The English currency was getting stronger and, in 1562, as Roger Ascham, who was proud of his former pupil, Elizabeth, wrote in a letter, "… the coin that had been debased and entirely alloyed with copper, she has restored to the pure silver standard."

Almost all lower- and middle-class English women worked, in contrast to the Italian Renaissance woman, although they received lower wages than men. In 1604, those who hired themselves out to the small farmers and laboured the land received four pence with food, and nine without meals, against the five and ten pence respectively given to male labourers. Those women skilled in making malt, beer and bread in Yorkshire fetched thirteen shillings a year in 1593, and forty in Suffolk in 1630, in addition to clothes, food and lodging.

Contemporaries found money "a difficult cabale to understand", and were even more puzzled by what came with money, i.e. book-keeping. Those who made their living from the new job of "accountancy" were greatly resented. In a practical way the English middle classes began to drop Latin and taught their girls arithmetic instead: thus women became the home accountants for the English tradesmen. That practicality was what Bacon had called progress and, if taken literally, it was the antithesis of Renaissance ideals.

In the middle of the sixteenth century there was no longer metal enough in Europe to meet the demand in cash: when silver diminished, copper was introduced, salt taxes were levied in kind, and at times salt became money, as it had in Roman times (salary, from the Latin *salis*, meaning salt). Barter was still widely

used. Then came paper money, i.e. credit, and paper money gave birth to inflation. Credit created confusion, although it was by no means a new idea: cheques
had been exchanged in Babylon twenty centuries before Christ, bank notes in
China by the ninth century, and Islam had been using credit for several centuries.

As women were acquiring an enhanced economic status, the English law
began to recognize such changes: the widow who had helped her husband in his
trade for seven or more years was allowed to take it over. Helen Manning, a
widow from Devonshire, employed over 100 workers in manufacturing clothes
and continued to work after her husband's death.

"Next to birth, that which commends a woman is beauty, wherewith men are
much taken." The model of the age was Elizabeth: she was "the sky". Faces
should be "rounde and ruddie" with a smooth forehead. Under small eyebrows,
plucked and marked with a pencil, grey eyes, wide apart, marked the idealized
face. Cheeks should suggest roses and lilies "in combat", and be dimpled. Breasts
should be high and round, like fruits in May, spread with small blue veins. Ideal
hands were small and white, hips large and fruitful. Hair was perfect if fair and
curly. For Philip Sidney, the best feminine attributes were gold hair, alabaster
skin, cherry lips and eyes which were, as usual, described as stars or suns. Why
golden hair should have been an attribute of beauty throughout the Renaissance
is something that anthropology and social science should study. Perhaps black
hair suggested the deeper south, i.e. poverty. Or perhaps the lighter tone was a
symbol of femininity, in the way that dark-haired men were (and are) immediately understood as being more virile than blonde ones. The "cherry lips" are, on
the other hand, a clear sexual symbol, arousal in women being reflected by a
deepening of the colour of the lips. Clear eyes, of course, are a sign of youth and
health. Breasts were at times "displayed, naked" and painted in white: "It is sheer
common wonted use, with naked breasts to walke", Pyrrye writes. Jane Anger in
her *Protection for Women* (1589) says, "We have rowling eyes and they railing
tongues: our eyes cause them to look lasciviously, and why? Because they are
given to lecherie."

Political stability and good government produced wealth. A northern foreign
traveller was amazed by the wealth of some English homes: "In number of dishes
and changes of meat the nobility of England do most exceed. No day passes but
they have not only beef, mutton, veal, lamb, kid, pork, capon, pig, or so many of
them as the season yields, but also fish in variety, venison, wildfowl, and sweets."
Raisins, dates and spices were imported in vast amounts because the English,
whose black teeth shocked visitors, ate them in quantity. Sugar had also made its
appearance on the Englishman's table: "Whereas before, sugar was only obtaina-
ble in the shops of apothecaries who kept it exclusively for invalids", Ortelius
wrote in *Théâtre de l'Universe* (1572), "today people devour it out of gluttony ...
What used to be a medicine is nowadays eaten as a food." Jean Nicot who, in
1560, as French ambassador in Lisbon, sent Catherine de' Medici some tobacco

for her migraine, was to notice a similar kind of phenomenon taking place with tobacco and nicotine.

By the end of the seventeenth century, England had achieved international recognition and wealth as a result of foreign trade. Spain had neither defeated the England of Elizabeth nor the Dutch rebels. Add to this the exhaustion of Spain's American mines and the burden of taxation on its subjects, and one can see the initial crumbling of the mighty Spanish Empire. Elsewhere in southern Europe, tyranny, hunger and overpopulation drove the poorer sections of society to banditry. The territory of the papacy was under continuous threat from armed bandits, as much of the Mediterranean was swept by pirates and privateers, against whom not even the Venetian fleet was able to react. There was also agricultural change which led to starvation and economic upheavals: raising cattle became preferable to raising corn, as less labour was needed; much agricultural land was given over to pasture and, in some instances, other plots were abandoned due to the spread of malaria. Before the end of the century the populous city of Naples was hit by several years of famine. The south now needed the north: Baltic corn arrived aboard English, Dutch and Hanseatic League ships, a new development that changed European economics. Spain tried to ban the Dutch ships from its harbours, but the measure was self-defeating. Between a Protestant north and a Catholic south, a new line marked the division between an expanding economy and a waning one. The West flourished while the East of Europe became desolate. This period saw the birth of the Dutch Republic and the flowering of England.

The personality of Philip II cast the shadow of religious intolerance over his vast kingdom. But the eventual fall of Spain was symptomatic of a wider phenomenon: the north of Europe had defeated the Mediterranean countries. Conflicts of creeds narrowed the former cosmopolitan nature of culture: the University of Padua, for example, was no longer crowded with brilliant foreigners; everybody tended to study at their own national universities. Although still used in embassies and in churches, Latin was losing its connotation of *lingua franca*, thus leaving the European nations hopelessly misunderstanding each other.

As England became richer, more buildings sprang up; the more affluent ones were plastered on the inside walls and hung with tapestries. There was mead in abundance; the rich ate wheat, the poor barley bread. Beer was brewed at home. Wine was much appreciated in richer households. Windows, formerly in wickerwork, were now glass. Soap was a luxury; clothes were washed with dung, nettles and hemlock.

Meals became more consistent and orderly, especially in the lower and middle classes. A light early meal was followed by a heartier dinner, before and after which people washed their hands in basins. Tables were arranged around the hall, some holding tankards and dishes of food, others for the family to sit at. Women sat together with the men if there was a maid in the household. On one side of the room there was the dresser, the article of furniture on which the rich displayed vessels of precious metals, a form of investment which showed off the wealth of the family. For, while the richer farmer used the dresser for its intended purpose, i.e. the arrangement of vessels useful for the table, his woman considered it to be a personal testament of how well life had treated her. This new status was attributed to the good government of the monarch. Thus the safety of the queen became the prime concern of the nation. "The Queen herself, a desperately vulnerable figure in a world of treachery", writes J. H. Elliott, "represented the sole guarantee between the country and the perils of civil strife and Spanish and Catholic domination. Loyalty to the Queen therefore became charged with new emotional overtones at a time when English nationalism was being powerfully intensified by the swift growth of Protestant hatred of Rome, and patriotic hatred of the Spaniards." The queen's very person symbolized security for her subjects, both male and female.

When a French envoy asked for the council to be present at his audience with the queen, Her Majesty furiously replied, "The ambassador forgets himself in thinking us incapable of conceiving an answer to his message without the aid of our council. It might be appropriate in France, where the King is young, but we are governing our realm better than the French are theirs." Indeed, the new Valois king who was asking for her hand was young, too young. Via her able ambassador, his mother Catherine de' Medici had sent Elizabeth a proposal that her son, Charles IX should marry Elizabeth; encircled as she was by Spain, Catherine strove to prevent Elizabeth from marrying a Habsburg.

People would say that the king had married his mother, Elizabeth answered. And she later added that she would not enjoy everybody making fun of "an old woman and a child". At the time, she was thirty-one and Charles fourteen. For five months, Elizabeth allowed Charles to court her, exchanging portraits, but she eventually let the French ambassador know that all she wanted from a consort was an heir, and that she would never allow her husband to be in charge of her treasure and her kingdom. It is quite obvious that she never took this marriage seriously, but that she enjoyed the letters, the poems, and the courtship that came with it. In any case, her subjects would not have loved her for marrying a foreign monarch and thus delivering England, that fiercely nationalist island, into other, possibly Catholic, hands. At home, Catholic rule had, of course, been horribly tarnished by Elizabeth's half-sister, Mary and the slaughters in the Netherlands carried out by the Spanish army under the command of the Duke of Alba were well publicized.

Elizabeth never forgot the love of her subjects and always mentioned the fact that she was one of them, that she came from the same stock, and she knew how to deal with her people, as her godson, Sir John Harington, described:–

> Her speech did win all affections, and her subjects did try to show all love to her commands; for she would say her state required her to command what

27. Elizabeth I as Europa

she knew her people would willingly do from their own love to her. Herewith did she show her wisdom fully: for who did choose to lose her confidence, or who would withhold a show of love and obedience, when her sovereign said that it was their own choice, and not of her compulsion? Surely she did play her tables well to gain obedience thus, without constraint. Again, she could put forth such alterations, when obedience was lacking, as left no doubt whose daughter she was.

John Harington was a bright boy to whom Elizabeth wrote in a maternal and highly practical vein. He was the son of two of her father's courtiers, who had been loyal to her during Mary's reign, when she had been in the Tower of London; they had been imprisoned for her sake, and Elizabeth rewarded them well.

In 1576, while John was still at Eton, the queen wrote to him, hoping to turn the young man into a future councillor and politician. Witty and sharp as he was, her godson was just what Elizabeth wanted and needed. Together with her letter, he enclosed a copy of her speech to parliament.

"Boy Jack", she begins in a joking and intimate way,

I made a clerk write fair my poor words for thine use, as it cannot be such striplings have entrance into Parliament assembly as yet. Ponder them in thy hours of leisure, and play with them till they enter thy understanding; so shall thou hereafter, perchance, find some good fruits hereof when thy godmother is out of remembrance. And I do this because thy father was ready to serve and love us in trouble and thrall.

Indeed, Elizabeth blasted her parliament with wonderfully furious reprimands, shaming and scolding even her council, but at times also pleading with them. This was the feminine Elizabeth, using emotions and charm to get her way.

In a sense, Elizabeth might not have enjoyed such staunch support from her people had it not been for Mary Stuart's claim to the throne of England. Since 1558, the Catholic, almost French, queen had declined to acknowledge Elizabeth as the Queen of England, and she herself sported the English royal arms. This made the person of the monarch the more important, and Elizabeth the more carefully guarded.

Although officially the protector of marriage and of family, Elizabeth did not herself embrace domesticity. But she knew that the family was the strong base of the social structure on which Elizabethan society rested. Woman was a practical companion, and had a status similar to that of men. Although they always judged them to be inferior, English men assigned women a useful role: Petrarchian and chivalrous ideals were forgotten.

Servant women led a harsh life as an anonymous pamphlet specifies:–

A servaunt woman is ordeyned to lerne the
wyves rule and is put of office and werke
of traveyllye, toylynge and slubberynge.
And is fedde with grosse mete and symple,

and is clothed with clothes and kepte lave
under the yoeke of thraldom and of servage;
and, if she conceyve a chylde, it is thralle
or it be borne, and is taken to servage.
Also if a servynge woman be of bonde
condicion she is not suffred to take a
husbonde at her owne wylle; and he that
weddyth her, if he be free afore, he is made
bonde after the contracte. A bonde servaunt
woman is bought and solde lyke a beeste.
Also a bonde servaunt sufferith many wronges,
and is bete with roddes, and constreyned and
holde lowe with diverse and contrarye charges
and travayles among wretchydness and woo.

Servants ate in the same room as their masters while serving them at table but theirs was a miserable life. The young girls of the house were forbidden to talk to them unless in the presence of their own mothers.

Women (and children) spun at home; a man in Colchester employed 400 women who wove wool in their homes. In London and York, women barbers and surgeons were famous, and in Southampton those women who emballed wool formed their own guild. Silk was worked by women who were slightly better off, and even by the high-born, who also had the monopoly on the selling of silk; in the sixteenth century, most Englishwomen seemed to be busy spinning and weaving items for their men to export, thus enriching the country.

To Francis Bacon's practical eye, "wives are young men's mistresses, companions for middle age, and old men's nurses." Patrick Hannay (*Mulierium Pean*) said that a wife should look after man's possessions and be trusted, for she would look after the servants better than him because "the woman hathe a quycker wytte". And then he explained what his wife was to him, again in a thoroughly business-like concept of matrimony:—

My lady must recyve and paye
and every man in hys office controll
And to eche cause gyve ye and nay
bargayne and bye and set all sole
by indenture other by court roll
my lady must ordre thus all thynge
or small shall be the manners wynnynge.

Francis Bacon worked for Elizabeth during the latter part of her reign and understood her well. From being the Earl of Essex's friend, he became his accuser when the former favourite incurred Elizabeth's hatred. In her deep resentment of Essex and her need for revenge, there emerges the feeling of a former lover. Womanly, the queen always had a man beside her, either a husband-figure, like Leicester, or filial characters, like Essex or Anjou, and wanted their exclusive attention. She was often jealous of her men's mistresses and wives, and with them she behaved coyly and bossily at the same time. But she loved her women friends too, and there were many around her. When the Countess of Nottingham, Elizabeth's closest friend, died, the queen sank into a deep depression, withdrawing from life.

When she had lost her looks and needed hours to prepare her appearance, her wigs having become less and less credible, and her décolletage more and more embarrassing, she took terrible offence as Essex burst into her bedroom and saw her in total disarray. She never forgave him. She had certainly loved him, and had also been in love with Anjou – but not with his brother, King Henry III, to whom, at one time, she had been betrothed. (He was homosexual, anyway.) Furthermore, she almost certainly slept with all her men; she was sexy and knew she was barren. So why should she accept a foreign prince as her husband, who would have taken over her realm, or indeed one of her subjects, unless they could make her produce an heir, a Tudor?

In her highly practical way, she used her hand as her strongest card in the diplomatic game – to keep the French at bay, the Spaniards out of her way, to make alliances or to ward off invasions, but always in an attempt to avoid confrontation. Her feminine mind was disposed towards peace, unlike Mary Stuart, who was no true Renaissance woman, and who, of course, lacked the brains and the education which made Elizabeth so formidable.

When Elizabeth turned down a prospective husband, she would blame her council, even if, in reality, she had not even informed its members of her decision. For example, when she eventually decided she would never marry Charles of Anjou, she didn't even inform Cecil because she wanted to keep Catherine de' Medici waiting, thereby avoiding the possibility of the Valois family making an alliance, through marriage, with Spain.

Although her mind usually ruled her passions, she did not always manage to control them; however, she was well advised by the men she trusted. When she made a mistake, with her army as well as her heart, as she did in entrusting Essex with the Irish campaigns, she was furious not only with him but also with herself for having failed in her role as sovereign.

She knew the value of popular entertainment and she herself sponsored and patronized the theatre, which was so popular that it was used for political and propagandistic purposes, much as was the cinema during the last century. A Swiss traveller, Thomas Platter, visited London in 1599 and stayed for a month. He visited the newly built Globe Theatre where he saw Shakespeare's *Julius Caesar*. Besides the Globe, Platter visited many other theatres:–

On the 21st of September, after the midday meal, about two o'clock, I and my company went over the water and saw in the house with the thatched roof the tragedy of the first Emperor Julius Caesar quite aptly performed. At the end of the play according to their custom they danced quite exceedingly finely, two got up in men's clothing and two in women's. – The actors are dressed in a very expensive and splendid fashion, since it is the custom in England when notable lords or knights die, they bequeath and leave their servants almost the finest of their clothes which, because it is not fitting for them to wear such clothes, they offer them for purchase to the actors for a small sum of money.

Spectacle was also the people, the way they dressed, what they said and Elizabeth enjoyed looking at them, unseen. We can also observe her in some vignettes.

One day she was leaning out of her window at Whitehall Palace when she noticed Sir Edward Dyer. The poet had asked for a job at court, but had been unsuccessful.

"What do you think about when you think of nothing?" she asked him, in Italian.

"*Delle promesse delle donne*", he answered – of women's promises.

"Anger makes dull men witty", she retorted and, one likes to imagine, closed the window.

She was proud of the languages she spoke. She was fluent in Italian; we know of her singing Italian songs and reading Italian verse. In her later years, Venice finally sent an ambassador to her court. The *Serenissima* and her doges had ignored her for forty-five years, Elizabeth said, but, finally, they had sent their envoy. Having protested in Italian to the ambassador, she added, "I do not know if I have spoken Italian well; still, I think so, for I learnt it when a child and believe I have not forgotten it."

Of course, the unfortunate ambassador would have had to agree, but he must have been pleased to hear his language spoken so fluently, as indeed he wrote in his dispatch. Venice was no longer such a great maritime power and, to some extent, it could blame the English fleet for that. But Venice's new weakness was also due to Spain's war against the Ottomans, which had disrupted Mediterranean trade, as had the Holy See's insistence that Venice join the fight. Besides, the newly discovered trade routes, used by British and Dutch ships, were closed to Venice.

From 1580 onwards, Philip was planning a war against England. In that very same year, Pope Sixtus V – who was later to extol Elizabeth – sanctioned the assassination of the queen, whom he considered to be a heretic and enemy of the Church. Speaking like an Osama bin Laden, Sixtus said that it would not be a sin to strike at "that guilty woman, who is responsible for so much intriguing against the Catholic faith, and for the loss of so many millions of souls. There is no doubt that whoever dispatches her from this world with the pious intention of doing God service, not only does not sin, but gains merit. And so, if these English nobles", (here he was referring to Mary Stuart's coterie), "decide to undertake so glorious an action, they will not be committing any sin." Elizabeth's moment of glory came when she defeated the Spanish Armada in 1588, thanks to the "guerrilla" tactics by which she allowed Sir Francis Drake to plunder the Spanish silver which was vital in paying for Philip's many wars. This silver went instead to enrich the coffers of England.

The English knew that their continued independence depended on Elizabeth's remaining alive; her death would have plunged the country into civil war, and made her the prey of both Spain and Rome. A few months after the pope's sanction and in defiance of Philip II, the queen knighted Francis Drake at Greenwich. She did so in the presence of the French commissioners who had come to London to finalize both a defensive alliance with England and Elizabeth's marriage to Anjou. But, by then, Elizabeth had stopped thinking of the seductive and ineffectual Anjou as a possible husband. In order to get him out of England (where he was costing the treasury greatly), Anjou had to be bribed. Thinking that he was gaining another kind of crown, and in spite of being a Catholic, the duke finally landed at Flushing to take up arms on behalf of the Dutch Protestants. But he spent most of his time playing tennis, while the Spanish army destroyed city after city. After his departure, Elizabeth knew that the final chance of her marrying had disappeared: "I am an old woman", she said, "to whom paternosters will suffice in place of nuptials".

But in June 1584, when Anjou died of fever at Chateau-Thierry, Elizabeth was devastated and wept copiously, in public as well as in private; she did not care who saw her. Her "Frog", as she had referred to him in her passionate correspondence, had gone. The poor Queen Mother of France, Catherine de' Medici, once so proud of her many sons, could now only count on her eldest, Henri III, who had no issue, was unlikely to have any, and hated her anyway. There was still a daughter for whom a diplomatic marriage could be negotiated, and it soon became obvious that she was to marry Henri Bourbon, King of Navarre, the direct heir to the French throne and a Protestant.

To Catherine, Elizabeth wrote a moving letter on Anjou's death:–

Although you are his mother, your sorrow cannot exceed mine. You have several other children but, for my own part, I can find no consolation, unless it be death, in which I hope we shall be reunited. Madame, if you could see into my heart, you would find there the image of a body without a soul. But I will not trouble you with my sorrows, for you have too many of your own.

Almost at the same time as Elizabeth was writing this letter, a Jesuit was arrested in England, carrying documents detailing Philip's Enterprise of England, which, two years later, would be blessed by the pope. The war against England was on, and it was to be a very special crusade against the English queen, who symbolized religious tolerance and a new way of governing that had to be erased.

To have such a woman as Elizabeth as monarch led to a marked advance of the liberalization of women in England. "England is a paradise for women, a prison for servants, and a hell or purgatory for horses" – thus ran the saying, to which Robert Greene added perceptively that Italy, instead, was a paradise for horses and a hell for women.

Elizabeth was offered the crown of Holland but she turned it down: she had enough headaches already, she said, without additionally taking on the expense of having wholly to finance the Dutch rebellion. Besides, she was not after a larger empire. On the other hand, portraits of the queen began to express imperial power, they were icons of magnificence also proclaiming her right to rule. "The splendour of her appearance, her vision and her self-control are evidence of the majesty and the authority which inhere in the person of the Queen", write Andrew and Catherine Belsey. "The imperial theme, too, was a recurrent feature of royal portraiture in the 1580s and 1590s. The globe first appeared with the Queen in 1579 in the earliest of the 'Sieve' portraits by George Gower. This was two years after the publication of John Dee's *General and Rare Memorials Pertayning to the perfect Arte of Navigation,* a plea for the establishment of a British Empire." An empire, as Dee had predicted, there was going to be. Thanks to the exploratory voyages of Drake and others like him, the English were navigating the high seas. Philip's coffers, meanwhile, were much emptier than before, and many of his ships had been lost. Morever, Elizabeth's army was loyal to her, unlike that of Spain, which was made up of mercenary troops: Elizabeth could count on an army and a navy which were not only loyal to the crown but also to the Protestant faith. This, perhaps, is why she was confident that she could win; her calm presence amongst her soldiers at the moment of utmost danger, when the Spanish Armada was close to the English coast, confirmed her even strength.

But there was another side to the medal and since, under Elizabeth, women came to be accepted as part of the social structure, their newly elevated status turned them into targets. Robert Richardson wrote in 1530 that women were the worst of the human species; he must have meant all species, because he went on to explain that women were more ferocious than lions and more lascivious than monkeys, poisonous like aspids and more dishonest – and then he departed from both the human and animal species – than mermaids. In sermons, women represented an obstacle to piety and an end to spiritual peace. Another misogynist, John Knox wrote to Sir Robert Cecil saying that queenship and slavery were the same things – unavoidable evils brought to the world by the sin of Eve. John Aylmer answered Knox's anti-women tirade stating that, as Aristotle said, there was reason in women too, and that in women could be found the same virtues as men. Edward Gosymhill published a book, *The Schole House for Women,* ferociously attacking the "gentle" sex; but it was followed by another, *The Prayse of all Women* (1542), written by the same author. In this second book he stated that, at night, he had been disturbed by the vision of women who begged him to consider their sad state and protested against his previous book, which had insulted them. Men had always reproached women, he wrote, but it was women who take care of them in sickness; Ceres invented the sewing of grain, Minerva the spinning of wool, Sappho the harp. Women looked after children while men struck them. And the Bible showed that women at times were more commendable than men.

And so the debate went on; were women different, better, worse, or the same as men? Pages, volumes and, no doubt, speeches and sermons were dedicated to the matter at this time and in England. Why? Because of the queen's good rule.

But beside the gentle, educated, literate woman was the "bad" woman, the ignorant woman, the witch. A simple woman like Anne Askew (1521–46), from Lincolnshire, was investigated in 1545 for her heretical views, imprisoned, tortured and finally burnt at the stake. The Protestant Bishop of Ossory published an account of her examination.

> The summe of the condemnacyon of me Anne Askew.
>
> Anne
>
> ... After that they willed me to have a priest. And then I smiled. Then they asked me, if it were not good? I said I would confess my faultes to God, for I was sure that he would hear me with favour. And so we were condemned without a quest.
>
> ... Then they said that there were diverse gentlywoman that gave me money. But I knew not their names. Then they said that there were diverse ladies which had sent me money. I answered that there was a man in a blue coat which delivered me X shillings and said that my lady of Hertford sent it to me. And another in a violet coate did gave me VIII shyllyings and said that my lady Dennye sent it to me.

Prostitutes had no status in England, and there was no trace of the *cortegiana honesta*, probably because English women were generally more sociable than on the continent, where the courtesan offered company in addition to sex. During the time of Henry VIII, London prostitutes lived in a special district – the Stewes, on the River Thames. There, houses were organized as brothels and bore painted names such as "The Cardinal's Hat". Brothels were closed down at the end of Henry VIII's reign but there must have been hundreds of clandestine houses in Elizabethan times, and indeed Robert Greene recounts a story of a young girl seduced by a gentleman who then abandons her, and she ends up in one of these houses.

The hothouses, or "sweating baths", or "hammams" were rendezvous points where women could spend the day in each other's company and gossip; many hothouses served refreshments. The poorer sweating baths merely provided tables for the women to use for the picnics they had brought with them. Hammams were very popular but hothouses soon became synonymous with brothels. The hospice of Bridewell, where rescued prostitutes were supposed to repent by spinning and weaving, became one of the most notorious places of "sin".

As Elizabeth's reign brought more security, some women were forgetting manual tasks. "Let nobody lothe the name of the keychen", wrote Richard Mulcaster: women of every class should know how to cook. Spinning, weaving, milking, butter-making, and turning flax into thread were considered as important for a woman as playing upon the virginals, the lute or the citron. Dancing and music never came under censure in England because the queen loved dancing so; she was still enjoying it at the age of sixty-six, when the French ambassador was surprised to see her dancing *"gayement et de belle disposition"*. Elizabeth liked her court ladies to play "lutes, citherns, pricksong, and all kinds of music". But it must be added that in the late years of Elizabeth's reign, the economy was in serious trouble and her control was not as tight as the images of the queen want to project. A succession of bad harvests from 1594 onwards led to inflation. There were food riots and the government resorted to the sale of monopolies to raise funds (*plus ça change!*).

There were, of course, other women of note in Renaissance England besides Elizabeth, but no one as exemplary of the Renaissance and brilliant. Lady Jane Grey was executed so early in her life that it is difficult to assess her talent, although for Nicholas Rowe, who wrote *The Tragedy of Lady Jane Grey*, she was a heroine and a symbol:–

> ... The only love that warm'd her blooming youth
> was husband, England, liberty and truth.
> For those she fell; while, with too weak a hand,
> She strove to fare a blind ungrateful land.

A more homely and delightful description of Lady Jane was written by Roger Ascham – the coarse-looking, sympathetic scholar who subsequently taught Elizabeth Tudor – who tutored Lady Jane in Greek, Hebrew, Arabic, Italian, French and philosophy:–

> I found her in her Chamber readinge Phaedon by Plato in Greek, and that with as moch delite as Some gentlemen would read a merry take in Bocace. After salutation and dewtie done, with som other taulke, I asked hir, whie she wold leese soch pastime in the Parke? Smiling, she answered me: I wiss, all their sports in the Park is but a shadoe to that pleasure that I find in Plato. One of the greatest benefites that ever God gave me, is, that he sent me so sharpe and severe Parentes, and so jentle a scholemaster.

Mary of England had herself been educated by Ludovicus Vives, writer and lecturer (at Oxford) and had translated Erasmus's *Paragraphs of the Gospel of St John* into the vernacular; a strange choice on her part, considering her bigotry but maybe it was at Vives's suggestion. Vives was also a friend of Sir Thomas More, the minister of Henry VIII and author of *Utopia*, who lived in a large mansion by the Thames, a beautiful garden sloping down to the river. For More, his family – wife, sons, daughter-in-law and his three beloved daughters – was the centre of his life. He was proud of the Renaissance education he had given Margaret, Elizabeth and Cecilia: "One could have said that Plato's academy had been transported to that house." Erasmus, who was his friend, continued that he loved his eldest and brightest daughter Margaret best; she could speak Greek and Latin, was versed in physics, mathematics and logic, and she was a skilled musician. But Erasmus thought that Thomas More was wise with the wise and "jesting with the fools ... with women especially, and his wife among them". And that was Erasmus's way of saying that Lady More was no genius.

But although one finds women of great education, intelligent, original women, the really outstanding individual of the English century was Elizabeth. Had she not been queen (although, if one were to considering this hypothesis seriously, it is almost certain that she would have been beheaded), she would have developed her creative faculties, one feels, in other ways. Once again it must be stressed that her talents were magnified by education. "I was present one day", the admiring pen of Roger Ascham recalls in a letter dated 11 April 1562, "when she replied at the same time to three ambassadors – the Imperial, the French, and the Swedish – in three languages – Italian to the one, French to the other, Latin to the third – easily and clearly, without hesitation, and without being confused." There were not four men in the whole kingdom who could speak Greek better than she, he added.

One cannot imagine that the poor lived well under Elizabeth, but we find that farmers recollected the "bad old days" in which they were lucky if they slept on a straw mattress and had a sheet under them to prevent the straw pricking their "hardened hides", while now they slept well and ate with tin, or even silver spoons, and off pewter. Previously, they had eaten with wooden spoons, and off beech-wood platters. Harrison, that critic of the new-fangled "soft times" of the Elizabethan era, laments the fact that yeomen's wives no longer clothed the whole family with homemade, English cloth: instead, they had started adopting the French fashion, and bought foreign silks, damasks and taffeta.

Elizabeth adapted the role of monarch to herself, frequently using her sense of humour, as when she told Francis Drake that she should have used her golden sword to cut off his head for piracy, rather than knighting him. She was girlish and in need of affection when nicknaming her friends, and tiresome when she misled her council and ambassadors by delaying marriage negotiations. Power never went to her head and she was able to follow the advice of good men; she delegated and, at the same time, she was eager not to offend her subjects with whom she had created an idyll. In spite of her bad temper and capriciousness, she enjoyed a popularity which no other monarch ever matched; people were ready, for example, to forgive her for deserting her post when she disappeared with her lover, Lord Leicester, for a whole week. Her ability was most in evidence, however, when, in negotiating between the intolerant trends of the age, she managed to produce, like a conjurer, a brand of religion which the entire country accepted. It was a pragmatic religion that left ample manoeuvres for the soul in private, but maintaining a theological order cut down the power of the clergy; and this was the crux of the whole European storm, the overbearing and greedy hand of Rome, and of Spain.

Hers was not a cult dictated by cynicism because Elizabeth was herself religious and convinced of her role of supreme governor of the Church; but she must have taken religion with a pinch of salt for, even if she was a monarch, no scripture allows as much liberty with sex as she took. At the end of the century England had achieved great prominence. She enjoyed wealth as a result of foreign trade, as well as international recognition. Her great rival, Spain, had neither defeated the England of Elizabeth nor the Dutch rebels.

At the end of the century England had achieved great prominence. She enjoyed wealth as a result of foreign trade, as well as international recognition. Elizabeth gave the English a sense of pride in nationhood and provided the institution of the British monarchy with an identity that became the envy of the rest of the world, only to be severely damaged later by a German dynasty.

The Latin inscription on her tomb in Westminster Abbey would have pleased her; maybe she wrote it herself.

> *The mother of this country of hers,*
> *the nurse of religion and learning,*
> *for perfect skill of many languages*
> *for glorious endowments as well of mind as of body,*
> *a prince incomparable.*

✍ CHAPTER THIRTEEN ✍

Women in the North

The Spanish Netherlands was governed by very capable women for seventy-seven years, between 1506 and 1583 and this is a factor to consider when writing about the Low Countries and about the special position of women in that society. What makes things confusing is that two regents were both called Margaret, one being the Emperor Charles V's aunt and the other his daughter. The three women, all Habsburg princesses, believed in tolerance and had been given the role of regent because they were forceful and intelligent politicians, not in the belief that they would be ineffectual as is often written. The two Margarets with Mary of Hungary, the in-between regent, brought with them talent and political know-how but, thwarted by a divided and suspicious nobility, a decline in the authority of the crown and religious warfare, they found themselves isolated.

Margaret of Austria (1480–1530), Duchess of Savoy and Regent of the Netherlands from 1507 to 1530, was the daughter of the Emperor Maximilian and his first wife, Duchess Mary of Burgundy, and was born in Brussels. Her nephew Charles, who inherited Brabant – today part of Belgium – from his grandmother Mary of Burgundy, was also a "local", being born in Ghent on 24 February 1500. Charles's father, Philip the Handsome, had died leaving him prey to his dangerous maternal grandfather, Ferdinand of Aragona. Not only did Ferdinand dislike Charles but he had locked up his own daughter Joanna spreading the rumour that she was a lunatic. To keep Brabant and Charles out of Ferdinand's rapacious hands, the regency of the province and the guardianship of Charles went to Margaret.

She was a highly sophisticated woman, loved dancing and was a fine musician; she wrote poetry and music, played various instruments and sang beautifully. Her court at Mechelen (Malines) in northern Belgium, became a meeting place for musicians and her library was famous for being rich with musical manuscripts as well as classical texts. When she was portrayed by the Master of Moulins she was only ten but the Flemish painter caught the glow of her alabaster skin and the playful curve of her lips, the Habsburg genetic feature which was to become more and more pronounced, as each generation tended to intermarry. In this portrait Margaret of Austria looks regal, wearing red velvet, her back to the Louvre, the castle she would have inhabited had her betrothal with the dauphin not been broken. In fact, aged three (!) Margaret had been formally married to Charles of France, who succeeded to the throne of France in that same summer. This marriage was, of course, part of her father's elaborate negotiations; Margaret was accorded all the honours due to her rank as Queen of France and was educated at Amboise with other members of the French royal family. This is important to note since the fine education that she received was passed on to her ward Charles, the future emperor. But in 1491, she found herself repudiated so that her husband might marry instead the young Duchess Anne of Brittany. Hostilities broke out between Charles of France and Maximilian of Austria and Margaret was held in France until 1493 when she was allowed to return to Flanders by then a thoroughly French-speaking and sophisticated princess. In early spring 1497, after a stormy sea-journey, she arrived in Spain where her marriage to the Infante John, heir to the throne of Castile and Aragon, was solemnized at Burgos on 3 April, Palm Sunday. Margaret was however destined to enjoy only six months of marriage before John, Isabella and Ferdinand's only son, fell victim to a fever and died at Salamanca on 4 October. Shortly afterwards Margaret gave birth to a stillborn child, ending all hopes of securing the succession in the line of los Reyes Catholics, the title that Alexander VI, the Borgia pope, had conferred to the royal couple. However, Margaret had so endeared herself to the king and queen and also to the people during her short time as Infanta of Spain that she stayed on for two years, treated as a daughter. She taught Catherine, her twelve-year-old sister-in-law (who was to be Arthur's and then Henry Tudor's wife) to speak perfect French.

Four years later Margaret became the wife of Hilbert II, Duke of Savoy, who only survived until 1504 and whom she truly loved. After her two husbands' deaths, her brother Philip, who was perhaps the person she loved most of all, also died (25 September 1506). She decided to wear black all throughout her life, indeed from then on she was perpetually in mourning, looking like a nun and wearing the widow's bonnet.

In a later portrait by Conrad Meet, Margaret is indeed wearing black but at the same time displays her fine almond-shaped eyes and her long pale hands. An enlightened patron of the figurative arts she had the intelligence to employ one of the greatest masters of all time, Albrecht Durer and she commissioned a magnificent tomb at Bru, Bourg-en-Bresse, for herself and her husband Philip of Savoy. Durer who, in Venice was to befriend another protagonist of the times, the banker Jakob Fugger, was committed to Luther's cause, as he recorded in his diary.

In the Low Countries Margaret sponsored the development of a new architectural style described by Hugh Honour and John Fleming as "a more robust but equally rich version of Gothic was evolved in the Low Countries. The Town Hall of Ghent is a notable example, one of which the opulence of a great trading centre found expression in 1518, one year after the regent of Flanders, Margaret of Austria, had an addition to her palace of Mechlin, built in pure Renaissance style."

Margaret started looking after Charles when he was a few months old and became regent when the boy was seven. Her ward was due to inherit Spain, southern Italy, Sicily, the Low Countries and Austria and, although she was not to know this, he was to become also Holy Roman Emperor, with the name of Charles V. His three sisters, Eleanor, Isabella and Mary grew up together with him and were also brought up by Margaret in the humanistic Renaissance spirit. Little Mary, who was to be a fine art collector herself, could recite whole passages from Erasmus, and Charles famously spoke so many languages that he would later boast of using Italian with women, Spanish with God, French with politicians and German with his horse. Margaret took good care of Charles and prepared him for the great offices he would inherit. He saw her as his only parent, Charles having hardly known either his father or mother. When Charles left Brabant to claim his Spanish inheritance in 1517, the area known as the Spanish Netherlands was placed under Margaret's regency. She grew weary of the nobles for their selfishness and divisive politics.

The coolness that developed between Margaret and the nobles reached such a peak that in 1524 Charles who, for all his faults (especially the financial burdens he imposed on the region) was loved by the people because he was a Burgundian, received a petition in Spain. The Dutch nobles complained that when they needed to see the regent, they were kept waiting, and at times she even refused to discuss major matters with them. Charles then wrote to his aunt from Valladolid, urging her to show more regard for the nobles and begged her to consult the counts of Nassau and Lalaing.

When Margaret died the emperor was distraught and spent most of the year in Brussels. In 1531 he made his sister Mary, widow of King Louis of Hungary, regent and moved the capital from Malines to Brussels *"nel paese del basso"*, the low land. The Regent Mary was skilled in finance and was trusted by her brother although, in order to avoid the clash between the local nobility and the regent, he set up three new institutions: a body called the council of state, another council for finances and a third secret council. Besides, just like Charles, Mary had been born and educated in the Netherlands, which was important in the eyes of the people.

She was also a patron of the arts and wanted to promote local artisans; she commissioned an amazingly expensive series of twelve tapestries to extol her brother's deeds. This was after Charles's expedition to Tunis where he wanted to appear as the crusading Holy Roman Emperor attacking the infidels. It was important to show him as the saviour of Catholic Europe in a moment when the Christian forces were split in fratricidal battles. It was politically important also to establish the magnificence of the Habsburgs so Mary first commissioned the painter Jan Vermeyen to join the Tunisian campaign and draw the locations where the fighting had taken place and also make sketches of the characters involved. In June 1546 Mary signed a very elaborate contract with Vermeyen, in

Brussels, and then approached the leading tapestry makers to agree a contract, which was signed in February 1548, for twelve tapestries. Mary provided the gold and silver threads that were to be used in profusion. The tapestries were completed in April 1554 and sent to England to be shown at the wedding of Philip to Mary Tudor (25 July 1554). Not only were these tapestries impressive pieces of propaganda but they could easily be carried and shown to the people. Jan Vermeyen had also etched some of his drawings for the new technology of the printing press, which not only made them cheaply marketable all over Europe but also became a vehicle of propaganda.

Mary herself had a copy of the tapestries made in a reduced scale; another was ordered by the Duke of Alba, one of the commanding generals of the Tunis expedition. In this way, the regent had launched the great tapestry factory and from then onwards the Brussels makers received commissions from all over Europe, including from the Habsburg's arch-enemy, the King of France.

Before leaving Brussels, Charles had instructed his sister to sponsor a policy of unification amongst the states which he had inherited. Under her rule, which lasted twenty-two years, two more provinces, Gheldria and Zutphen, were added to Charles's *paesi di qua* (1548) but this came to mean the Spanification of the Netherlands. The feeling was magnified with the visit of the prince who was to inherit Charles's mantle. In 1548, Philip joined his father in Brussels but, in spite of Mary trying to curb the arrogant attitude of the infante, Philip was judged *"poco simpatico"* by the Italians, a Venetian ambassador wrote; *"very antipatico"* by the Flemish and "odious" by the Germans. He was seen as being cold and proud.

After 1559 he never returned to the Spanish Netherlands and Mary was left to rule over an increasingly difficult situation. Around this time she asked the Habsburg official sculptor, Leone Leoni, to potray her in bronze; her large eyes sheltered by her widow's headdress seem severe and knowing. But there was a soft side to her character, although she had the power of keeping the nobles under pressure. But Mary, whose regency was to last until 1553, found that Philip was completely Spanish in his "language and behaviour". Then Charles decided to abdicate in favour of his son, beginning with his realm in the Low Countries. Religious divisions had wrecked his dream of unity and he could not reconcile his hatred of the Holy See with his faith. Charles thought, and probably Mary agreed with him, that the policy of successive popes had destroyed any possibility of reforming the Catholic Church from within. He was tired and frustrated. He summoned the local nobility and establishment to Brussels, which he still regarded his home, and, accompanied by Mary, the emperor introduced his son to the Flemish assembly and declared that he had abdicated in Philip's favour.

The whole assembly was in tears listening to Charles reminiscing in Flemish and sometimes in French. The emperor also cried recounting details of his erring and tempestuous life as soldier and king; but when Philip took his turn, the assembly was disappointed because the new king spoke only Spanish. The emperor also abdicated as King of Spain in a document that was signed later in Brussels, on 16 January 1556. He also dictated a memorandum to guide his son to which, it appears, Philip paid scant attention:–

Always aim for peace. Go to war only when it's forced on you. ... In the north-east I have strengthened Flanders against France by my annexation of Guelders, Utrecht and Frisia. Still you must keep money on hand there in case there is need for a sudden mobilization; the inhabitants are reasonably loyal to us, but do not relax your watchfulness ...

The third and most outstanding regent of the Netherlands was Margaret of Parma (1522–86), the natural daughter of Charles V and his mistress Johanna van der Gheynst, a Flemish woman. Earlier in this book we caught a glimpse of Margaret when, alongside Catherine de' Medici, she arrived in Florence for her marriage to Alessandro de' Medici. Margaret was an able woman who had been educated in Flanders by her mother. She was rather coarse looking, but had an intelligent face surmounted by a high forehead; brown eyes and sensuous full lips. Her father honoured her with all the official titles due to a princess of the blood and she was known by the titles of Archduchess of Austria, Infanta of Spain, Princess of Burgundy, Milan, Naples and Sicily. In Italy she was Madama, in Spain Margarita de Austria.

Alessandro, her first husband, (1510–37), the son of the black servant Simonetta da Collavechio and Cardinal Giulio de' Medici (the later Pope Clement VII) was assassinated a few months after their wedding, in 1536. Two years later Margaret was married again to Ottavio Farnese (1525–86), the son of another pope, Paul III, with whom she had twins. Like her aunt, who had trained her, she was very sharp but also cautious. She spoke several languages including Latin and, like Mary, was a fine letter writer. For example she wanted to be kept informed on the minutiae of Elizabeth of England's movements, details which were provided by the gossipy Spanish ambassador in whom, strangely, Elizabeth had great confidence. On the other hand, shrewd as the Queen of England was, it is possible that she would have informed the Spanish ambassador of what she wanted Margaret to know. The regent was worried by the fact that in the Channel and the Bay of Biscay, Spain's communication with the Netherlands was being disrupted by the activities of Protestant Englishmen like Drake and Hawkins who had – everybody knew – the blessing of the Queen of England.

Philip II appointed Margaret his regent in the Spanish Netherlands but left her only nominal authority and she had to face the rising storm of local discontent with Spanish despotism; Margaret did not feel Spanish, she was a Burgundian and her loyalties were with the Habsburgs. Advised by a council of state headed by the Cardinal of Granvelle, her authority was restricted, but she was charged with the task of carrying out the religious policy of her half-brother, with whom relations were tense. Moreover, the cardinal was himself seen by the people to be merely the mouthpiece of Philip.

Because there was general unrest throughout the region due to the rigid position taken by the king and by the Cardinal of Granvelle, Margaret called an assembly in June 1562 and sent its representatives to see Philip II in Spain. In the following year William of Orange, one of the leading nobles, demanded that Philip should dismiss Granvelle and, when this did not happen, he resigned from the council of state, along with other representatives.

Margaret was powerless to maintain law and order and, when in 1564, Granvelle was finally dismissed, William of Orange and Count Egmont, Governor of Flanders and Artois (1522–68), rejoined the council of state. In the following year, 1565, during the festivities in Brussels for the marriage of Margaret's son, a group of nobles, both Catholics and Protestants, formed a league and demanded a change of religious policy. This compromise, with which Orange and Egmont became associated, was intended to stop the persecution of heretics and dissenters.

All European eyes were on this compromise; in France the truce between Catholics and Protestants imposed by Catherine could be reversed by any outside event. Elizabeth, from England, not only encouraged a tolerant type of Protestantism but also supported the budding Dutch rebellion. Margaret of Parma decided to abolish the Inquisition but her policy was undermined by Philip's religious fanaticism. He made it quite clear that he would wage war on the heretics and the dissenters "I would rather lose the Low Countries than reign over them if they ceased to be Catholic", he wrote.

In 1566, Calvinism within the region was based in Antwerp, but in other areas the less bellicose Lutheranism spread rapidly. However, persecution, the Inquisition and executions inflamed people to seek alternatives; the better organized Calvinists made more and more inroads everywhere. Philip appointed provincial governors responsible to Madrid; they represented seventeen provinces, fourteen of which, in the north, spoke Dutch dialects while the three southern ones spoke Walloon. The nobles and Margaret herself spoke French, which was more prevalent in the south than in the north.

Margaret felt that her policies of non-confrontation were being pushed aside by the provincial governors and the Catholics. She believed in a conciliatory policy between Catholics and "heretics" (the latter representing the middle and lower classes, in other words, the majority) but Philip was persuaded by the Duke of Alba to dispatch an army to crush the growing rebellion in the Netherlands.

As the duke entered Brussels in 1568 he immediately paid homage to the regent who was embarrassed by his presence and disapproved of his crusade. She wrote letters to the king in which she foresaw that Alba's heavy hand would be counterproductive and would turn religious militancy into patriotism. But her voice went unheard and Alba pressed on to subdue the Netherlands. His aim was to substitute the tolerant Catholicism of the Low Countries with the intolerant brand of Counter-Reformation Catholicism, to punish the rebel leaders and to centralize the government under the Spanish crown. He set up his "Council of Blood" imposing severe penalties including the arrest for treason (1568) of the counts of Egmont and Horn. The event that distraught the regent was not just the arrest of men who had assisted her for years, but their execution in the Grande Place in Brussels – in spite of her veto.

Onlookers who crowded every corner of the market square cried openly when the two young leaders were beheaded; Margaret realized that her policies had been reversed. Saddened, humiliated and desperate, she resigned her regency. The public execution of Count Egmont and Count Horn shocked the whole of Europe; tremors were even felt as late as the nineteenth century when Goethe wrote his drama based on Egmont, Beethoven composed his (unfinished) opera *Egmont* and Donizetti showed his hatred of despotism in his magnificent opera *Il Duca d'Alba*.

The regency of the Netherlands passed to the unpopular hands of the Duke of Alba who, during the six years of his rule was responsible for continuous executions and massacres; 60,000 people left the Netherlands. It was the start of the Eighty Years War against Spain. The Calvinists started "breaking images" in an orgy of iconoclasm that swept the Low Countries, France and England. Thousands of holy images, statues and textiles were burnt: in Bruges Cathedral one can still see a thick black line of soot, almost three meters high, running around the gothic walls.

While remaining friendly with Philip, whom she liked personally, Elizabeth I of England was sending money to the rebels who pressed her to form a Protestant army. The queen had no intention of fully supporting such an army nor did she want to accept the crown of the Netherlands, which was offered to her. She gave the rebels a large loan of £106,000, having already given them £20,000. Holland and Zeeland fell to the rebels and Brussels was threatened by William of Orange and Louis de Nassau, another Protestant prince.

In 1578 Alessandro Farnese, Duke of Parma and Margaret's son, became regent and returned the southern provinces to the crown of Spain. On the other hand the "Union of Utrecht", which included all the northern provinces (Holland, Zeeland, Utrecht, Gelderland, Overijsel, Friesland, Groningen, Brabant and Flanders) created a new state, called United Provinces of the Netherlands or the Dutch Republic (1579). Margaret left Brussels in September 1583 and retired to the Palazzo Farnese in Parma, a magnificent building started by her husband Ottavio Farnese and never completed. It still dominates the beautiful city and houses part of the Farnese collection of paintings.

The achievements of the three female regents were almost erased in people's memories by the violence of what happened during the civil wars. But if nothing else, the presence of women in the highest position of power produced a change of judgement concerning women in Dutch society. Men needed women not just to run their homes but to help build the wealth of their country; as a result in the

Netherlands the institution of marriage became a business partnership. This came about for economic reasons and was central to Dutch society; not only was the Dutch woman trusted but she was given the keys of both the home and the shop.

The Declaration of Independence by the Low Countries was finally signed in 1581; the struggle for religious and territorial independence had generated the central role that women enjoyed in Dutch society. This society amazed foreign travellers. People who saw women as heads of state for almost a century developed an attitude which differed from others' and travellers had a point when remarking on the "liberated" Dutch woman. Nevertheless they criticized the fact that men and women treated each other as equals.

For example, outsiders commented that it was odd that in Harlem and Leiden men and women worked side-by-side spinning and weaving, and that in the same city women formed one-third of the labour force and held official posts in charitable institutions, hospitals, houses of correction and orphanages.

There were as many instances of young women who showed their independence by marrying the men of their own choice rather than that of their fathers as there were Dutch widows who successfully took over the family business. Unmarried pregnant women could sue the putative fathers of their offspring; separation, divorce and remarriage were not solely a male preserve. The husband's adultery (or venereal disease) was justifiable grounds for a fair divorce. Women were even advised to be chaste after marriage but not before, possibly because Dutch women married around twenty-three or twenty-five, late in comparison with their southern sisters.

Young Flemish women, it was written, should be instructed on how to make sex more enjoyable for their men and for themselves. Several manuals on sex were published with guidance, not only on how to obtain pleasure by prolonging the sexual act, but also on how to avoid venereal disease. There were frank details on the anatomy of the woman's body and the clitoris was recommended to both sexes as the organ that gave pleasure to women, suggesting that masturbation was tolerated and even recommended. Despite all this, illegitimacy was low, which demonstrates that Dutch women practised contraception (as indeed did Ancient Greek and Roman women).

Visitors to the Low Countries were astounded by the parity between man and woman. And travellers flocked to the Netherlands from all over the civilized world; Antwerp became the most cosmopolitan city in the world. It was there that the Venetian and Genoese ships unloaded their cargos, metal ware, silks and spices. A new trade route had been opened up so silver and gold reached Antwerp, where the market offered the best deals for most textiles, in defiance of Spanish injunctions.

Throughout the upheavals of the rebellion against the Spaniards and the religious persecution, the Dutch had to battle against natural disasters; the sea gave them wealth but regularly threatened their land. So, while men were at war, or sailing the high seas, it was up to women to protect the land from the incursions of the waves. A contemporary Dutch writer described how "those women who had no barrows carried clay in their aprons; others carried it in sacks on their shoulders, others still made bundles of sticks …"

The new phenomenon of colonial economics was having a profound influence on the wealth of the Low Countries. Raw materials, including wool, tobacco, precious metals, etc., were imported, worked and then exported as manufactured goods, a process that required the employment of all able-bodied people of either sex. Consequently, women worked so hard that, on the 31 May 1531 a rebellion of female workers exploded in a "wool house" in Amsterdam. As the market for woollen cloth shifted to the Netherlands, northern Europe became the focus of international commerce. It was the birth of capitalism and enormous fortunes were made – and lost. But the powerful bankers were no longer the Medicis, but the Fuggers.

Goods arrived on barges via rivers and canals, or on ships sailing the high seas; travel by road having become dangerous. The number of road-side gallows outside towns, depicted in Brueghel's paintings (with putrefying corpses and crows picking semi-empty eye sockets), did not comfort the travellers either. There were deserters everywhere who robbed whoever could not defend himself – or herself. Usually, women only travelled locally and the dangers of the high road dissuaded them from crossing borders. Those who travelled further afield were women who followed their husbands to war, or they were laundresses, nurses, actresses, singers or prostitutes (which was often the real definition of the previous two). Pilgrimage, which had flourished and had been a kind of Thomas Cook venture of its day, became too dangerous. Therefore the sea was the preferred way of travelling in spite of the many other dangers it presented.

Antwerp was also the centre from which the bullion from the New World was distributed so Charles and Philip had more than one reason to hold on to the Netherlands. Not only was the countryside agriculturally rich, so that the revenue it brought into Spanish coffers was important but Dutch maritime power provided new goods and new discoveries. The Dutch also had their own Drake-like heroes, and privateering was turning out to be the major thorn in the side of the Spaniards – but a great business for the Dutch. Huge quantities of silver from the Americas which should have paid for Philip's wars were stolen by Dutch – and English – pirates who could claim that they were patriots *ante litteram* because they damaged Philip's coffers; like Ulysses, they ridiculed the might of the Cyclops Poliphemus.

These Flemish ships were manned by adventurers, superb seamen, under the protection of the Protestant monarchs and above all of Elizabeth of England. In the meantime, the pope was insisting on military intervention against Elizabeth. Elizabeth herself was scandalized by Henri IV's "great apostasy" when, as the Protestant King of Navarre, he succeeded Henri III, and abjured his faith at

Saint-Denis. On 25 July 1593, this most famous piece of pragmatism was put into words by the new King of France, "Paris is worth a Mass". In the face of the Spanish threat, England, France and, for the first time as a political entity, as a nation, the Dutch United Provinces, signed a peace treaty, on 24 May 1596.

The spread of wealth and the new capitalist economy (to which the notion of time contributed: clocks, which had been rare, huge and the posession of few, became almost a commodity) created a broad middle class; and because the menfolk were engaged in war, trading and sailing, it fell to the women to make it all work. Already being accustomed to see women manage the land and the home, men entrusted them with the social tasks of this new expanding class so much so that one can confidently come to the conclusion that the women of the Netherlands created a middle class. The home was the microcosm of a well-governed city, it was said, and within its walls was found the focus of social life, a natural occurrence in the cold north where squares and streets could not attract crowds. Dutch art depicts interiors of houses in which women sit and chat and almost invariably incorporated the shop or the trading counter; the houses which we see in Flemish paintings belonged to a middle class which was beginning to enjoy the trappings of wealth and which women "prettified" in a process that marks the birth of interior decoration. Rooms were small so that they could retain the heat and walls were lined with wooden panelling on which tapestries or oil paintings often hung (mixing powders with oil was first invented by the Flemish).

Wooden panels needed decoration and their limited size required small pictures: a new genre, decorative painting, was born. What had been a detail in an Italian Renaissance composition became the sole subject of Flemish painting. Almost every Dutch woman was a patron of the arts when she commissioned paintings for her house. While some were purely for decoration, others were intended to tell the visitors about the trade and the status of the owner.

Because the Flemish woman was the catalyst of her house, she appears in portraits either alongside her husband or often on her own. When the burgher's wife became richer she wanted her features to be remembered and so the art of portraiture reached the houses of the middle-class. Because the Flemish sitter was neither a Colonna nor a Medici who needed no introduction, it was essential for her to be flanked by objects which could demonstrate her background. So a new set of symbols came to life. The Persian carpet over the table (one type of rug is still referred to as the Holbein) highlighted the wealth of the family. Jan Steen wanted to indicate that the attractive young woman with hands full of flowers, in the *Girl with Oysters* (1658–60) is a courtesan. He used the symbol of the oysters and the flowers to suggest an offer, a promise, while in the background, he also portrays her encounter with a man. She is a geisha rather than a prostitute, and so this painting which she had commissioned from Steen would have hung in her front room, a sort of advertisement.

If we examine a painting by Vermeer we can tell quite a lot about the mood of his women and from the languid atmosphere that surrounds their loneliness, but nothing about who they were, and that is the novelty. Vermeer paints melancholy,

28. *The Lacemaker* by Vermeer

Although Vermeer looked for the mystery in the woman's soul, in her eternal waiting, combining this melancholic aspect of womanhood with languor, the idealization of woman in the Low Countries had to do with virtue rather than beauty. Associating needlework with Dutch feminine virtue was not new. Lace was wealth; as early as 1529 poor girls in Amsterdam could earn a living by making lace.

depicts these girls' thoughts, their souls – not their status. He is not a painter of the middle class, that is why we like him so much now and why he was totally forgotten in the nineteenth century. When he depicts a young lady seen from behind, or a *profile perdu,* Vermeer initiates another school, leaving much to the imagination, in fact, almost compelling the viewer to fantasize over the girl's mood, her thoughts and her melancholy. His are paintings without a story and this propels the observer to enter into the mystery of conjecture. Vermeer depicted needlework in his very fine painting *The Lacemaker*; associating needle-work with Dutch feminine virtue was not new, in fact the lace industry was a source of wealth; as early as 1529 poor girls in Amsterdam could earn a good living by making lace.

Whenever couples were portrayed together, paintings show how wealth has made them both elegant and happy. Even an Italian couple, like the Arnolfini, famously painted by Jan van Eyk (1434, now at the National Gallery in London) are shown as equals. Giovanni Arnolfini, a small banker in Bruges and his wife Giovanna, displayed surrounded by symbols (including the dog, emblem of fidelity; the bed, of physical love; the mirror, of truth and wealth) tell us the story of a couple facing life in partnership. Another example, which can be seen in Antwerp Museum, depicts a money-lender with his wife. Marinus van Reymerswael, its painter, shows a couple richly dressed sitting at a table covered with the straight-forward symbol of their trade, money and papers, on which they lay their hands. The son of the house stands behind his mother. And Pieter Coecke portrayed himself next to his wife Maaike, who was herself a fine painter, in their house in Antwerp. They had a daughter who was to marry his pupil Pieter Bruegel.

Because Dutch women enjoyed a considerable liberty in their choice of profession, the craft of painting was widespread amongst them. The paintings they produced were small and could be manufactured in a limited space and the style of these women painters was often that of a miniaturist. Theirs were accurate depictions, closer to a piece of lace than to the large canvases of, for example, an Artemisia Gentileschi and they do not seem to have been tormented by the philosophies that preoccupied their southern counterparts.

The sheer number of women painters who traded their art in the Low Countries and also travelled and sold their work abroad, is of interest to us today. They delivered their products in a totally matter-of-fact way which could be compared to selling eggs at the local market. Painters like Judith Leyster, Rachel Ruysch or Maria van Oosterwyk depicted objects, a vase or a basket on its own or groups of these items. Since illumination of manuscripts made more modest demands than painting, it was considered a lady-like occupation; it could be done at home, sitting by the window sill, alone or in the company of other women. Illumination was usually the result of team-work, in any case.

The daughter of Simon Bening, who was himself a famous illuminator and painter, Levinia Teerlinc, travelled to England to paint miniature portraits of the queen during the early years of Elizabeth's reign. One of them, showing her wearing her coronation robes, was copied by Nicholas Hilliard around 1600, but the original is now lost. Although there were many Flemish women painters, a woman was not allowed to be an apprentice in the painters' guilds but could only be trained at home which is why so many of them learnt their trade from their fathers. Katharina van Hemessen (1527–79?) was also trained by her father and worked at Mary of Austria's court, consequently she was very well known and received commissions from outside; mainly for smaller paintings, still lifes and ornamental drawings. Illuminating books became a big business at which the Flemish were the best exponents. The text was often in the vernacular but Latin came back into fashion when the world became more cosmopolitan – after Gutenberg, for example – or when rulers had to travel and meet one another. Women learnt languages; it gave them status, and Latin, Italian and French had to be learnt by any woman who aspired to learning. The menfolk, meanwhile, had little time to study.

From around 1480 the Flemish painted on canvas – rather than wood – another innovation; Italian painters who travelled to the Low Countries brought these novelties back with them. Then still life painting evolved; a woman painter would add the reflection of her face to a glass or some insects buzzing around a bunch of flowers, suggesting or disclosing the secrets of the household. When the tulip was brought from Turkey to the Elizabethan court, a huge industry made and destroyed fortunes in a matter of weeks – not in England but in the Low Countries. Judith Leyster made good money by selling her watercolours of tulips, costing less than the actual flowers. There were other women who specialized in flower painting and botanical illustrations, something that required a particular accuracy, but no great inspiration; Maria van Oosterwyck and Rachel Ruysch were successful in this genre but Judith Leyster could be a more inspired painter. For example her *The Proposition* (1631) is an elaborate painting, it represents a woman quietly embroidering in the dusk while behind her, we can see a man leaning on her shoulder with one hand and, with the other, offering her some coins, which she ignores. This painting embodies the desirability of a woman for her domestic virtue. "… the lack of a strong Neoplatonism movement in the North prevented the identification of female forms with the ideal beauty in painting", the writer Whitney Chadwick observes. This is an important point in the iconography of the Dutch woman to which I will return.

The landscape too became a novel form of decoration; until then it had been used as a background, often to please the person who had commissioned the picture. That is why, for instance, one finds behind the flight to Egypt, a landscape with Dolomite peaks or Gothic churches that have nothing to do with the Old Testament.

Women were essential to the economy and a new type of hard-working and almost sexless woman was at the forefront. The idealization of beauty was not a

29. *The Proposition* by Judith Leyster

The Proposition represents a woman quietly embroidering in the dusk. Actually, not so quietly because, behind her, we can see a man who is leaning on her shoulder with one hand and, with the other, is offering her some coins.

30. *Yellow-Red Tulip* by Judith Leyster
A product of the seventeenth-century tulipomania are the 'tulip books': albums
with water colours of different varieties of tulip. Both bulb lovers and professional
growers commissioned artists to produce these books.

preoccupation of the Dutch middle class, which was perhaps a liberating and economically sound philosophy of life. The lack of care for physical looks and the absence of the Neo-Platonism prevalent in southern Europe made the Dutch woman concentrate her desirability on her earning power. It is interesting to note the scarcity of those "how-to" manuals dedicated to beauty which were instead so successful in Italy, France and England. The Dutch preferred to print manuals on financial and agricultural affairs. No Botticelli shapes or Mantegna oval faces in this part of the world, and no Platonic elements; women were expected to be healthy and numerate. Therefore the idealization of women in the Low Countries had little to do with aesthetics. A domestic and hard-working woman, not a face idealized by Raphael, was the essential virtue of the Dutch woman.

"Plato had taught that the soul owes this idea" – the idea of beauty, of the beauty of the soul – writes E. H. Gombrich, "to its former existence; before it entered the body and was wedded to the matter, the soul was granted the sight of the Idea of Beauty undimmed by matter, and thus our knowledge of the ideal is really based on memory."

One thing for which Flemish women were not much praised was their cooking. They ate all the time, it was remarked. "Dutch men and women ... almost always eating as they travel, whether by boat, coach ...", wrote John Ray, an Englishman. Another traveller, this time in the Spanish army, wrote home complaining about the food. "This is the land where there grows neither thyme, nor lavender, figs, olives, melons or almonds; where parsley, onions and lettuces have neither juice nor taste; where dishes are prepared, strange to relate, with butter from cows instead of oil." They ate boiled spinach, stewed meat and plenty of fish like cod, oysters and pickled herring, which were for the "common people". Indeed the poor could count on an infinite amount of salmon, sole, dabs, flounders, haddock and turbot as well as mussels, which were the cheapest and also the most despised food. But, to capture the attitude of the south, an Italian visitor admitted that in Brussels he was "among foreign barbarians".

Several English travellers observed with horror the variety of cheeses that the Dutch made out of their abundance of milk; green cheese was said to be coloured with the juice of sheep's dung and made women's skin coarse. On the other hand, women considered milk too heavy to drink on its own and watered it down; judging by the obesity of those who drink it in adulthood today, they were right.

One may generalize that the Dutch women's desire for a change in religion was more motivated by economic and patriotic reasons than by their tormented souls. On the other hand, in Rome spirituality was sold for money, in Spain families were impoverished by exorbitant taxes and both Catholic powers repressed women, so it was natural that women of the Low Countries turned to the Protestant cause. Besides, the Lutheran and Calvinist preachers offered free entertainment and women were allowed to raise their voices and sing hymns, read the sacred scriptures and also interpret them, to express themselves directly

31. Work within the Home, anon. woodcut, Rotterdam
Gutenberg's invention changed Europe and more profoundly the status of
women, who could then have access to knowledge.

to God; all this may not sound so revolutionary today but it was a great conquest for women to be allowed to speak to God without the intervention of a priest.

As I have already said to be Protestant at that moment coincided with being patriotic and middle class. In a sense it also meant opting out of the great cosmopolitan world of Roman Catholicism and to become more inward-looking, more nationalistic – the nation being an invention of the middle class and, in embryo, a creation of those times. That is why high-born Dutch women tended to remain Catholic: a humanistic education could not be reconciled with Calvinistic ideas which were often mean and "John-Knoxian", resentful of new ideas, of anything that was different.

Some Flemish women, though, converted back to Catholicism because they could not stand the suppression of aesthetic spiritualism and the exaltation of conventional "bourgeois" life. In fact, although the Calvinist Reform brought advantages to middle-class women, it also robbed them of pleasure. Food, if enjoyed, was sinful; crabs were a pictorial symbol for an un-Christian upbringing; oysters for lust, onions for lies and naughtiness, overripe cheese for decay. Moralists condemned exotic spices, and preachers considered luxury goods, such as cinnamon and sauces reprehensible. But the main enemy was sugar, which poured in from Brazil in such quantities as to be affordable by almost everybody. Teeth became black from chewing tobacco, which the Dutch imported in huge quantities and then exported with enormous economic advantage after blending cuts, a form of commerce that has endured. Tobacco in the hands of women was thundered against (the pipe is synonymous with a phallus in all Dutch painting) and women drinking spirits were considered licentious. But, because it was so disparaged, the Puritan soul found it all the more attractive; as we all know, disobedience makes sin more exciting.

Before unification, the Dutch woman had much to occupy her. Literacy was encouraged but had more to do with being numerate than reading Petrarch; women were looking after the business accounts of their often absentee husbands. On the other hand, according to Jacob Cats, who wrote about contemporary life, the sisters Maria and Anna Visscher of Utrecht were two blue-stockings who wrote poetry. But as Cats observes, they were the exception which confirms the rule. The sisters kept a salon "for painters and actors, for singers and poets to meet." Anna, who lived 1583–1651 had a proper "intellectual" circle, almost an *accademia* in the Medicean sense and it is no surprise that both, whose verses were Italianate and Neo-Platonic, converted to Catholicism (in 1641).

The Renaissance took a new turn in the Netherlands, that of capitalism, that of growing better, acquiring knowledge and vision by making money. In their hunger for conquering new trade routes, for devising a technology which could make their travels and commerce swifter and easier, the Dutch were true children of the Renaissance. In their fight for independence, for religious freedom, for parity of the sexes, they were also the children of the Modern Age.

CHAPTER FOURTEEN

Epilogue

The double face of Janus; on the one side, the arts and on the other the sciences — that is the Renaissance. Or, on one side, the face of a woman and on the other, the face of a man. One side of Janus's face shows sacred, Platonic love. While on the other is profane love, freedom of the senses, enthusiasm and curiosity. The ambivalence of a movement which is a philosophy of life might be summarized in these ways.

The scientific-masculine side melted into the feminine artistic component through a spiritual need that created the Renaissance; and women were at the vanguard. Like all great eras, the Renaissance thrived at the expense of some. The early Renaissance exploited the lower strata of society while the late Renaissance sucked the vitals of the New World. But this growth of awareness and well-being did not happen as a result of the exploitation of women. During this period some women achieved the equality with men which had previously eluded them, their status was improved and their talent was recognized. Women began to attain the right to education and were socially recognized as valuable partners, especially in those countries where the Reformation had allowed them to become the official companions of God's ministers. "To understand the higher forms of social intercourse in this period," writes Jacob Burkhart, the leading scholar of the Renaissance, "we must understand the fact that women stood on an equal footing of perfect equality with men."

I have demonstrated that women promoted the Renaissance by choosing some protagonists; editors and critics will say that my evidence is scant but, short of staging a world in which the Renaissance took place without women, they cannot prove me wrong nor can I disprove them. On the other hand, when they select a cover for their books, publishers choose the female figure to explain the Renaissance at a glance. Raphael too explained to the pope that his search for perfection in Renaissance ideals was epitomized by the face of a woman "in order to paint one beautiful woman, I had to see several .... I make use of a certain idea which comes into my mind. Whether it carries any excellence of art, I do not know, but I work hard to achieve it." Of course this movement varied through the decades and evolved differently; women were more central in some societies and social orders than in others; besides, the movement spanned a wide period and matured early in some minds and not at all in others. The middle class expanded, as women were able to work beyond the home. As a result, in those European regions that were influenced by the Renaissance, modern woman was born.

A modern woman is able to manage her time; she has the ability and the opportunity to make her own life. In discovering that she is no longer a chattel, that a father, brother or husband no longer has control over her life, she has a will of her own and can make her own choices and decisions. That is the conquest of the Renaissance woman. In these pages we have seen her move inside rooms, travel and work; we watched her arguing her case on behalf of her man, for her family or for her people. We saw Renaissance women eat, dress, making their faces up with creams and colours. We saw them entertaining or being entertained, loving or being loved. Here she was playing instruments, there she was ill and suffering. We saw the Renaissance woman live and play, love and die.

"Civilizations acquire different characteristics, first at the top and then among the mass of the people, according to their way of redistributing wealth and according to the social and economic machinery which takes from the circulation of wealth whatever is destined for luxury, art or culture", explains Fernand Braudel. Yet the sparkle which, as always, came from the top, became arson in the hands of the reformist woman or the poet. In writing about women, the "other half" of the Renaissance, I am conscious of having only selected a few examples, and to have ignored several nations. But the Renaissance as a current of thought was embodied by a few: although its wealth spread, the poor women of the Auvergne, Calabria, the Swiss mountains or the highlands of Scotland were not even touched by the wings of the new movement.

Just as Margaret of Navarre wrote in her *Heptameron*, women fulfilled their freedom, by proving to themselves and others that their bodies and minds were no longer a commodity for males to possess. This is also exemplified by Louise Labé, whose lack of conventionality is even more astonishing in a woman of her middle-class background. She talked to all women when she wrote: "Having spent part of my youth in the study of music, and that time which remained, hav-

(facing page) 32. *Divine Inspiration of Music,* c. 1640 by Nicolas Regnier
The ability to play any instrument was a sign of an educated mind, wrote Castiglione in *The Courtesan.* Indeed Harmony and Music were also symbols of harmony between man and woman, especially in the Flemish world, and Music was depicted as a fair female together with Harmony.

ing myself found it short for refining my intellect, and not being able myself to satisfy the good will I feel for my sex of wanting to see women not only surpass men in beauty, but in science and knowledge."

Much abused by history, we cannot believe that she did not write anything from 1555 till the end of her life, sixteen years later. These were years in which the city of Lyons was the prey of iconoclasts, a time of turmoil and destruction. Besides, Louise was going through the phase which often comes with maturity: of being abandoned by family and friends alike. It is therefore unthinkable that her fertile pen would not give vent to her sorrows. But maybe the papers of a Catholic and "immoral" woman fell into Huguenot hands and were burnt. Louise Labé, the epitome of the Renaissance woman, admonished those women who did not know how "to elevate their spirits a bit higher than the level of cooking pots and the spinning-wheel", to look forward and fight for equality.

The female friends who appear in her story might have not fought in man's armour nor written such fine verses, but they conversed in Louise's drawing-room/academy and took part in the theatricals for the king's arrival. These women were on the same level as celebrated literary men and kept their company; yet, as always in the case of woman, they have been tainted with the "sexual" slur of being courtesans, prostitutes. Having risen intellectually, they were diminished by the little people, by the ever-present envy.

Labé's poetry shines for its inspired quality and musicality not only in French literature but also in the literature of all times. When she lamented her lost love, in a surrealistic way, Labé talked directly to her lute, the companion of her calamity:—

> Tant que ma main pourra les cords tendre
> Du mignart Lut, pour tes graces chanter
> Je ne souhaitte encore point mourir …
>
> Lut, compagnon de ma calamité,
> De mes soupirs temoin irreprochable,
> De mes ennuis controlleur veritable
> Tu as souvent avec moy lamenté …

> *As long as my hand will be able to pull the strings*
> *of my sweet small lute to sing your praise*
> *I do not yet wish to die …*
>
> *Lute, companion of my calamity,*
> *Irreproachable witness of my sighs,*
> *Truthful controller of my suffering*
> *You have often lamented with me …*

Tullia's sonnets and those by Veronica Gambara (1485–1550), Gaspara Stampa (1523–54) and, above all, Vittoria Colonna have survived the centuries. Today

Veronica Franco (1546–91) is well known for her poetry, in her lifetime she was the most beautiful of all Venetian courtesans; in the same way as others advertised their charms by displaying their portraits, Veronica describes her sexual gifts in poetry. First of all she tells a certain Marco, in so many words, that she wants to make love to him and then she goes on:–

> Cosi' dolce e gustevole divento,
> Quando mi trovo in letto,
> Da cui amata e gradita mi sento
> Che quel mio piacer vince ogni diletto …
> Febo che serve a l'amorosa dea,
> E in dolce guideron de lei ottiene
> Quel che via piu', che l'esser dio, il bea,
> A rivelar nel mio pensier ne viene
> Quei modi, che con lui Venere adopra,
> Mentre in soavi abbracciamenti il tiene;
> Ond'io istrutta a questi so dar opra
> Si ben nel letto, che d'Apollo a arte
> Questa ne va d'assai spazio sopra,
> E'l mio cantar e'l mio scrivar in carte
> S'oblia da che mi prova in quella guisa
> Ch'a' suoi seguaci Venere comparte.

So sweet and appetizing do I become when I find myself in bed with he who loves and welcomes me, that our pleasure surpasses all delight … Apollo, who served the goddess of love, received from her recompense so sweet that it meant more to him than to be a god, his bliss, to make my meaning clear, were those pleasures that Venus afforded him when she held him in her embrace: I too am versed in those same arts, and am so practised in the pleasures of the bed, that there I surpass by far Apollo's mastery of the arts. My singing and my writing are forgotten by those who have tried me in this other guise, that Venus shares with her followers.

It is typical of the Renaissance to extol the attraction of a handsome body entwined around another, inside another and in a bed.

Although it may be invidious to say so, no illiterate Inquisition victim, no slave or peasant, could have exchanged letters with Michelangelo Buonarroti or Charles V as Vittoria Colonna did; only a remarkable woman like Giulia Gonzaga would have been loved by a cardinal and portrayed by Sebastiano del Piombo. No ordinary female kept salons like those of Tullia d'Aragona and Imperia in which the intellectual and artistic flower of the age gathered. These women were symbols of the Renaissance and their lives were entwined with the political dramas and achievements of the era.

In spite of the fact that Catherine de' Medici accused Diane de Poitiers of being a prostitute to her face, even when the latter was no longer her husband's *maîtresse-en-titre*, the elderly Diane was respected for her knowledge and taste. When she retired to her palace of Anêt, the French Renaissance vein became a torrent. But Catherine de' Medici was also a great feminine presence in the Renaissance world. She made the great mistake of listening to her enemies, the Guise family, because her friends had abandoned her. The massacre of St Bartholomew's Night has stained her reputation in spite of the fact that she tried to prevent the violence from expanding all over France.

England was a totally different case from France, education and healthier social conditions allowed women to hold a more established position in society than in other parts of Europe, apart from the Netherlands. Also England was ruled by a woman and an exceptional woman at that. Elizabeth's British blood was reflected in her qualities of prudence and "hypocrisy".

Only a woman like Elizabeth could have provoked a pope to declare:–

She certainly is a great Queen, and were she only a Catholic, she would be our own dearly beloved daughter. Just look how well she governs! She is only a woman, only mistress of half an island, and yet she makes herself feared by Spain, by France, by the Empire, by all!

Sixtus V, whose predecessors had excommunicated her twice, went on saying that, were he free to marry, he would have made Elizabeth his wife: "What a wife she would make! What children we would have! They would rule the whole world."

The victory of the English fleet over the Spanish Armada is truly the triumph of femininity over machismo. Elizabeth of England was the central political presence of the late Renaissance period. Had she not been a highly cultivated woman who spoke several languages and understood "abroad", she would have been unable to occupy a role that made England great. Cunning and being a woman were Elizabeth's most disarmingly effective weapons. And how clever it was of her to turn down the crown of the Netherlands – a man, a king would have never resisted the offer; she, instead thought that for practical reasons it had to be avoided.

In demonstrating that Dutch women created a broad middle class that greatly enriched the Low Countries, I highlighted the fact that three women rulers paved the way for the individual women to become respected members of their communities. The three Habsburg regents were all Flemish by birth and hostile to the Inquisition and to Spanish occupation; they also understood that persecution would only lead to more conversions and bloodshed. Responsibilities of trade and family fell to the Dutch and Flemish women because their menfolk were so often absent in those times of warfare and long sea voyages. Women in the Netherlands, described by de Hooghe, a seventeenth-century Dutch writer, as industrious, house-proud and chaste, emerged as central in the building of a new

33. The Rose

Symbols change: in Renaissance Italy the rose was one of the many logos for sex in both painting and literature. Lorenzo de' Medici, for example, exhorted young girls not to wait but to gather their roses when in bud. What was easily understandable in Italy was not necessarily so in the Low Countries; for example the wife of a burgher would require to be painted surrounded by objects depicting her wealth, so roses suggested wealth – not sex.

class. In every sense they were the true partners of their merchant husbands and also, he added, the true mistresses of their houses.

While women painters were rare in southern Europe, the Netherlands bred them; it was easier to pursue such a career in the Low Countries and the market for landscapes and flower paintings, vignettes and interiors was almost inexhaustible. Middle-class women furnished their houses, chose and commissioned paintings, a factor that was essential in introducing the element of "decoration" into the world of painting. A picture as an ornament for a house is a modern concept and every household which had attained a degree of economic freedom wanted to show its newly acquired wealth by its decoration.

The Reformation favoured women and accepted them as valued members of the community, to be trusted on various accounts, at the same time as women of the Italian nobility achieved a prominent position in politics and literature, ordinary women, as they became better off and achieved the "intermediate" state, emulated their sisters of the upper class by realizing that, although their sex was treated as a minority, they were not members of a minority at all. Reformist women of the upper strata were in the majority, but those who had the courage to voice their ideas were few and quickly silenced by the Inquisition. Vittoria Colonna's mystical but energetic nature had been attracted by the irresistible energy sweep of the Reformation, but she never left the Church of Rome. Her devotion to an absentee husband made her accustomed to loneliness, which turned into the solitude of the poets. Among those who understood her mind was that most amazing man of any age, Michelangelo Buonarroti, whom she loved and who loved her.

By its very definition a Renaissance nature was multi-faceted; it was a personality versed and interested in the diversification of culture. An all-embracing personality like Vittoria Colonna changed throughout her life, whether using her poetry to express her ideas or struggling for greater religious tolerance. In befriending, counselling and corresponding with the brightest minds of her age, she was the quintessential expression of the Renaissance. Although her younger relative Giulia Gonzaga became a Protestant, causing Pius V to regret that she had died before he could burn her alive, Vittoria never formally did convert, but her worth was blotted by the many trials which the Inquisition mounted against her and the Viterbo circle; so much so that what is left of her poetry has re-emerged only in the last two centuries.

Giulia was stern and distant, bewitching men with her beautiful remoteness, inspiring poetry and tormenting her soul with spiritual doubts. Her "romantic" flight from the clutches of Suleiman the Magnificent made her legendary. Lost in the tempest of the early phases of the Counter-Reformation, she emerges as a brave woman, not frightened to try and find herself, her role, her love, and to fight for others. She had been a victim of an early marriage but then she found love with two cultivated men, Ippolito de' Medici and Carnesecchi who, from personal assistant to the pope, ended up a bloody sight on the bridge of Castel Sant'Angelo, one of the many innocent victims of the Inquisition.

Some of those whom we can truly call Renaissance women kept intellectual academies not unlike Proustian salons except that theirs were devoid of snobbery: the middle class was yet to invent it. The leading performers in such salons conversed beautifully, and there was a growing freedom in the choice of subjects. As food and drink became prominent in social intercourse, new rules were invented on how to handle them. Wits mixed freely with the nobility, and it was often a woman who presided over the gathering and suggested themes for discussion.

In trying to conform, Tullia d'Aragona lost; but she shone for her appetite for life, because she never yielded to unrelenting personal attacks and because, in her moments of passionate despair, she produced poetry that has given her a place in the history of literature; no good anthology of Italian literature fails to include her verses.

Imperia's short appearance was symbolic of the Renaissance ideal; her beauty and youth commanded honour and respect in spite of her being a *cortegiana*. She was the friend (and probably occasional mistress) of Raphael, of Sadoleto and of the mighty Agostino Chigi; she was granted forgiveness by the pope himself for her great disobedience to the law of God when she committed suicide. Although sex was a habit, Tullia and Imperia seem to have encountered passion only once in their lives but possibly that is typical of a woman for whom sex is a profession.

Women were still considered something different, like Jews, sodomites or blacks; a woman was a species on her own. Since she scarcely represented a minority the reason for this is to be found in the root of the question; she was a minority because she had been unrepresented, history was not recorded by her. There are historians who think that the male's vengeful attitude towards women goes back to the dawn of history when a matriarchy ruled. Indeed, today we can just perceive a time when women, the creators of life, were dominant and maybe that state lasted for far longer than we suspect. But those times were pre-historic, before writing allowed records to survive. In some surviving but "prehistoric" societies (for example, the Tuareg) matriarchy still rules. We can see from this how Ishtar, Inanna, Astarte, Aphrodite or Venus, who were all originally dominant goddesses, were gradually downgraded into temptresses and sinners; even at the very dawn of history the saga of Gilgamesh shows how the goddess is overcome by this superhero who resists Ishtar's dangerous charms, her sexual desire.

That sex should be equated with sin and should be entirely woman's responsibility is the inheritance of the intolerant Eastern monotheisms, Judaism, Christianity and Islam. The Renaissance broke many of these credos by the sheer force of necessity; women were needed in order to create a balanced society — something that might happen to Islam in the future although overpopulation will deter men from handing over responsibilities, jobs and education. With the Counter-Reformation women were demoted from public life, and even in the very core of the home. On the other hand, France, which did not have an all-powerful curia in its midst, was able to flourish; the history of thought was soon to be theirs.

Women, with their idealized beauty in both body and soul removed the Renaissance from that persistent labyrinth of hypocrisy. We can see how Jeanne d'Albret put it into words when she accused "dirty priests" who abused and exploited women. And the young beautiful and great poet Gaspara Stampa, their friends called her Gasparina, was never ashamed to proclaim her joy in physical love – *vivere ardendo e non sentire il male* – (living burning and never feeling its pain) and also the fact that she had desperately fallen in love:–

> Oime, le notti mie colme di gioia
> Io non v' invidio punto, angeli santi
> rimandatemi il cor, empio tiranno …

> *Alas! my nights filled with joy*
> *I do not envy you, holy angels,*
> *but you, tyrant, send me back my heart …*

and also when she addresses the night that gave her such joys and made the days more splendid:–

> O notte, a me piu' chiara e piu' beata
> Che i piu beati giorni ed i piuí chiari
> Notte degna da primi e da piu' rari
> Ingegni esser, non pur da me lodata;
> Tu delle gioie mie sola sei stata
> Fida ministra; tu tutti gli amari
> Della mia vita hai fatto dolci e cari
> Resomi in braccio lui che m'ha legata. …

> *Oh night to me brighter and happier*
> *Than the finest and clearest of my days,*
> *A night's worth of being praised by the greatest intellegence,*
> *You alone have been the faithful minister*
> *Of my days; of my life all bitterness*
> *You turned sweet and dear*
> *By returning to my arms he who bound me so. …*

Gasparina was the daughter of a jeweller from Padua who educated her in the art of music; but she became a poet instead, recognized and respected by her contemporaries; her *Rime* were printed in 1554, the year of her death, when she was thirty. She lived most of her short life in Venice, the victim of Cupid:–

> Che vuol dir che, da poi
> Che voi partiste, io son sempre con voi?

What does it mean that from the time you left,
I have always been with you?

Women fell in love, an all-enveloping love maybe unknown to men. Men's minds needed a simple explanation for falling desperately in love, and sometimes they blamed witchcraft, as we can see from the trials of the Siena Inquisition. Caterina Gerina (January 1534) confessed to knowing how to make a *fattura amorosa*, a love potion, and of giving the formula to Bartolomea Tornai:—

> mettendovi acqua di tre fiumi, pietre di tre incrociate di vie, acqua bene-detta di tre pile di tre chiese, sogna con oglio di una lampada di una chiesa, uno chiovo, uno mocholo di quelli che sonno stati a le messe et, per riem-pire, acqua di tre lavatoi.

> *pouring water from three rivers, stones from three roads which cross, holy water from three fonts in three churches, a wick with oil from a church lamp, a nail, the butt of a candle used up during Mass and, to fill it all up, water from public fountains.*

A certain Agnolo Palmieri had gone to Maffia da Cinigaiano and asked her to concoct a potion to make the object of his desires fall in love with him. (March 1508). As for Lucia da Pienza, she had been copulating with the devil for six years! (June 1540).

History has been written by men or at least was written exclusively by men often distrustful of women's achievements, not only because the subjection of women seems to have come to an end, but also for sound economic reasons. Women were – and are – taking over men's jobs and expected them to share unrewarding tasks within the home; in fact, women's advance in the field of labour was smoother in those societies that needed their contribution. Braudel warns us: "So civilization has at least two levels. Hence the temptation felt by many authors to separate the two worlds, culture and civilization, one assuming the dignity of spiritual concern, the other the triviality of material affairs."

Educated women were mistrusted and even became objects of hatred because their sexuality was not merely limited to procreation, to sensual pleasure but sex could express love, a spiritual partnership. Sex, food and the feminine is a difficult theme to develop but it belongs here, to the Renaissance, when quality of life was developed and food became cuisine. The elaboration of food, brought to Italy by the sophisticated Byzantines who, in the shining silks, contrasting leggings and exaggerated hats we see in Piero della Francesca's paintings, inspired and changed the fantasy of the Renaissance table. Why should physical sex be a trap? Why does man fear to be judged in his most intimate act? Of course it is a question of pride, women have the advantage of not having to perform. Copulation may or may not be a pleasure for both man and woman. Like food which can be superb, indifferent or revolting, sex can be sparse or absent – but we still need it.

Fear of contamination from women transformed the sex act into a source of disease for which the woman was blamed.

Let's imagine that, instead of the sexual mechanism, which eventually leads to procreation, man's anathema concentrated on another dominion of pleasure, the act of eating. The consumption of food is pleasurable and, for some, more so than the sexual act; it is equally physical and not aesthetic at all and might substitute sex. The idea is not so quaint. In the Bible we find that abstinence from food is compared to celibacy, a good dish is tempting, dangerously tempting. Later on in history, hermits and anchorites refused food as an act of penance. Digestion, like sex, can be difficult, even dangerous if food is rotten or, as could happen in Renaissance times, poisoned. Like sex, it can be expensive and, just like sex, the most expensive is not necessarily the best. The process of digestion can be noisy and embarrassing. If sex could transmit diseases like syphilis and gonorrhoea – the AIDS of the time – food can damage the stomach and intestines also carrying its victims to the cemetery. The risks of sex struck women particularly during childbirth, but this mortality also affected the male in economic terms, breaking the family. Therefore perhaps man's distrust of women as a sex trap hides a fear of disease, which, although prevalent on other areas of life, has not caused such cultural catastrophes. Also it may have been perceived subconsciously that the act of eating is even more essential than the act of copulation.

But persistent refusal of food causes illness to women, especially young women. Today we call these conditions bulimia and anorexia both of which can cause death, particularly prevalent in those social strata which have access to an over-abundance of food. In the same way, sex becomes less attractive when it is too easily available and when society is overcrowded. Bulimia and anorexia are more common amongst women in Northern Europe and in young women who refuse the "consistency" of their female bodies and in particular among the richer strata of society.

If the Renaissance, which admired the slender form of the female body, had been followed by a Counter-Reformation that fought the temptations of the table rather than the flesh, disapproving of food and of the digestion process, we might today look at paintings of sinful cakes and hams in place of naked Magdalenes, Venuses, Tullia or Imperia. Escoffiers of the Renaissance would have been tried by the courts of the Inquisition instead of Vittoria Colonna or Giulia Gonzaga. Maybe today we would whisper the words 'soufflé' and 'mousse' conspiratorially and there would be places called restaurants where the police would occasionally break in and arrest footballers, politicians and businessmen consuming an illegal banquet. Contemporary culture glanced at this possibility, notably with films by Luis Buñuel and with Marco Ferreri's *La Grande Bouffe*. In times of famine, when food was needed, a fat body was a sign of wealth. Obesity and extreme fatness, which were considered attractive (cf. Rubens) are now regarded as ugly, but in countries where food is scarce, fat women are still often desirable. In contemporary Western aesthetics where obesity is almost commonplace amongst the less rich, the idealized beauty is that of a thin, pale, almost diseased and androgynous female – a model of this is Simonetta Vespucci as portrayed by Botticelli, an almost annorexic shape, and that's why her image is so fashionable also today. (Simonetta died of TB at the age of twenty-three). Historically, the rich woman was fat and the poor thin; now the opposite is true. Architecture has followed suit by creating punitive Le-Corbusier-like shapes. Translucent-Gothic, cf. the Louvre's Pyramid, is preferred to Richard Roger's flabby fat Dome.

In one of his *Ballate*, Lorenzo de' Medici couples food with sex. Six women have lost their husbands and they find themselves alone, and quite happy, it is carnival time; they are peasants and grow fruit. They speak in the first person, in a bawdy and popular language that Ted Hughes caught beautifully. It is called "Carneval" (in Italian, "*Canzone delle Foreste*", Song of the Forest):–

> ....
> We have huge cucumbers
> Their skins seem to be studded,
> Just like warts, all rough and odd,
> But they are hearty and wholesome.
> You can take them in your both hands
> Peel aside a bit of rind
> Open your mouth and then suck hard
> You'll soon find, it does not hurt.
>
> A watermelon too, as fat
> As a pumpkin, among others.
> We keep these for the seed
> So more can be born....
> ....
>
> These fruits that are so good
> If you'll point out our husbands
> They're yours, and free for all.
> You see we are fresh and young.
> If you have no gratitude
> We'll find some other ready hand
> To help us plough our bit of land
> Here at the carnival.

Food would not have created a division between the sexes, only amongst gluttons, and there would have been less scope for that preoccupation so dear to humans – difference. It was not exclusively the clergy and small-minded males who excluded and perceived danger in the emancipated woman. In the past when food was served at banquets, it was presented like sex, with music and dance, everybody pretending to be young and looking as handsome as possible. One such banquet was given by Duke Ercole of Ferrara on Sunday 24 January 1529, in honour of his father, Duke Alfonso, and his aunt, Isabella Gonzaga of Mantua. There were 104 guests in all and it lasted fourteen hours. The entertainment opened with a new play, *La Cassaria*, by the court's chief poet, Ludovico Ariosto; oysters, oranges and pears, pastry with oysters, honey, milk and egg cakes were offered while instrumental music was played so that the guests could chat and servants could again clear the table for the next round of dishes. The guests washed their hands and confectionaries were brought in: pears, candied lemons, candied lettuce, melons and 300 scented toothpicks. Then a small orchestra played and five voices sang. A cake was brought in, and out of it came the printed name of each individual guest, and also necklaces, earrings, different jewels; the duke then organized a tombola. The guests went back to the rooms where they had been before the lavish meal, accompanied by the sound of trumpets, so that the hall could be cleaned – and the guests too. At half past eight in the evening, they came back to dance the pavan, the galliard, the almain. Only the Duke Alfonso and Isabella Gonzaga had eaten at a separate table, like monarchs; Ercole, his wife Renée, and Lucrezia had mixed with their guests. At three in the morning, a breakfast was served, with fresh grapes, cooked fruit, cherries, several jellies, dried grapes and apples. Fifty servants offered sweet water to drink, after which the guests went back to their dancing.

Not all women were so fortunate as to attend these events. Exclusion and ignorance, poverty and old age exiled some women from the Renaissance, and envy – as it is always the case – took revenge on those who were more privileged, and who possessed more talent, more learning, more courage, and more means to enjoy life. In short, the Renaissance flames burnt, but not for all, and envy was at times motivated by those flames.

England caught the Renaissance fire; it is enough to imagine that, had Francis Bacon or Christopher Marlowe been born in Italy, they would probably have been put on trial by the Inquisition and perhaps burnt at the stake. The great English universities were able to teach liberally and formed a tolerant nation prone to scientific research, keen to enquire and to learn from others: all those things that made England great and which, alas, it throws away today. Women in England continued to enjoy respectability and a status that their Latin sisters had lost. But it must be observed that England was lucky because the Reformation was imposed from above. Instead of preachers like Savonarola, Ochino, Peter Martyr or Calvin, there was a capricious king to will it through. On a whim, history turned round; Henry VIII could not obtain a divorce, something which the papacy had otherwise distributed liberally to any monarch who was prepared to pay.

Although geographically isolated, England had joined the Renaissance frenzy for learning, and the printing presses were busy. But because of its seclusion, England developed an original brand of culture, especially outside the aristocracy for whom an Italian lifestyle was the model. In *De Republica Anglorum*, Sir Thomas Smith, an academic lawyer, observed the importance of learning as a basis for civilized behaviour and, borrowing much from the nearly contemporaneous *The*

Booke of the Courtyer (Castiglione's masterpiece had been translated into many languages, the first English edition in 1561, was constantly reprinted) recommended an ideal of verbal and physical grace. Its codes of behaviour include table manners and washing often, before and after meals.

Women fully participated in the great controversies of the age and were at the forefront of the Reformation. Jeanne d'Albret and Renée of Ferrara were fanatical Calvinists, while Margaret of Navarre had been a feminist and a lukewarm Lutheran. In France and England women in particular clung to the newly reformed religion, which did not ban them as the source of "animal life", in spite of what Calvin said. Small conquests achieved great importance, such as the ability to sing psalms in church together and alongside men, which gave women a feeling of participation, of "sameness" in the eyes of God. Huguenot women were more militant than their husbands, like the one who, as the flames were reaching her face, once again turned down her consort who was begging her to recant. Protestant women had more reason to be militant than men because Catholic priests had exploited their ignorance, robbed and raped them for centuries. After a period of tolerance the growing intermediate class expressed three fanatical creeds: Counter-Reformation, Catholicism and Calvinist Protestantism. It is, alas, symptomatic that the more tolerant Lutheran and Erasmus reformists met with little success. "Within a matter of twenty years two types of Protestantism – two waves – followed each other", Braudel writes.

> One was dominated by the passionate activity of Martin Luther (1483–1546); the other was led by the thoughtful and authoritarian John Calvin (1509–69). The two men were almost totally different. Luther was a peasant from the frontier regions of Eastern Germany. There was something direct, strong and natural in his rustic spiritual rebellion, what Nietzsche called a "peasantry of the spirit" .... he remained in the opposite pole to Calvin, the city-dweller, the cool intellectual, the politician, tireless organiser, the lawyer who would always follow his logic to the end. For Luther Protestantism was a revealed truth; Calvin treated it as a mathematical formula and deduced the results.

The religious wars, dictated more by politics than spiritual needs, obviously involved women. On the other hand, women lived the religious upheavals of the century in a mystical way, needing a spirituality which, together with education and knowledge, had become a necessity. But intolerance, in its various aspects, religious and economic, once again tried to debase what had been gained: the Renaissance, with its enthusiasm for education, had given women parity with men. The two victorious lines of the reform, the northern Reformation and the southern Counter-Reformation, were a consequence of the fact that women had understood that they were to some extent human beings, not a subordinate, inferior species.

The masses were untouched by Renaissance philosophy; they were intolerant of each other and suspicious of critical wits. The great religious wars, the burning at the stake, tortures or the Inquisition, had nothing to do with the acceptance or non-acceptance of such items as "justification by faith", they were the result of ignorant human suspicion of those who are different. While freedom brought economic growth and well-being to the Low Countries, the south of Europe withered. This, as we said, was due to many factors, not only to the corruption of the church and the stifling of learning; the fact was that the Mediterranean was no longer the centre of the world, trade used other routes and the oceans were controlled by the English and the Dutch. The roads that the Romans had laid all over southern Europe were infested with bandits and had not been maintained so that the large rivers of the north provided the best network for trade and communication. Famine and epidemics swept Italy. The south now needed the north: Baltic corn reached the Catholic world carried by English, Dutch and Hanseatic ships, a new development which overturned European economics. The finances of Europe were turned upside-down when Spain tried to ban Dutch ships from its harbours but the measure was self-defeating because the nation needed corn trade and Dutch money.

Northern European success and wealth derived from the fact that women were industrious, which deprived them of time to waste in *Accademie* and *Dialoghi*, in salons and playing madrigals – occupations which were anyway despised by the Calvinists. But England, with which the Low Countries had a cultural tie, was fascinated by Neo-Platonism, especially in its literary aspect. This was in spite of the fact that Shakespeare and Webster, to take two examples, moved women back to an area of realism (but not always; Ophelia and Gertrude represent the two opposite poles, idealized virginity and realistic womanhood).

You might at this stage care to go back to the very beginning of this book where I quote Aristotle's declaration that history is a lesser vehicle for truth for history itself than poetry: "Poetry is more Philosophical and more weighty than history, for poetry speaks rather of the universal, the history of the particular." Of course Aristotle, a philosopher revered and loved by the Renaissance – and by us – meant epic poetry, Homer, Pindar – but in this case, my case, my story of women in the Renaissance can become history because it is carried by women's poetic voice. The women poets I have quoted sing of their love, their losses, their times, through their verses, they recount their story and the history of their times.

The Renaissance was too revolutionary not to be feared and the emancipation of women was contrary to a social order as wanted by autocratic rulers or by the petty middle class when it came to rule. Education and its spread turned into the spring of an intermediate class which became a middle class and can be observed in embryo not only in Northern Europe but in France and Italy.

But nothing is one-sided in this story, because everything is blurred in the history of mankind; if it seems that the great enemy of womanhood is the Roman Church, this is not entirely so, as we can see from Louise Labé's brand of Catholicism and the conversion of two Dutch women poetesses. In the end, Calvinism took on the characteristics of Knoxian meanness, something that Queen Elizabeth kept at bay beyond the borders of Scotland until New Labour brought it into England with the added "gift" of political correctness.

Women are more dedicated to men than men are to women, that is a physical fact but a generalization which cannot be proved. Women love more, they fall in love more often, more intensely than men, and they bask in love and live for it. They might be in love with their child – motherhood being a carnal experience – with a spiritual invention, with a god, passion runs in their blood stream. This is nothing that they should be ashamed of, they are different from men, and Nature was clever in swamping the woman's soul with love, otherwise she would have never consented to go through the exhausting and painful saga of giving birth. That is as true today as it was during the Renaissance.

Women were essential to the development of the new philosophies of the Renaissance, the quality of life, to spiritual enhancement and pride in the harmony of man that became the driving force of the whole philosophy. They were at the centre of the Renaissance and the initiators of what was to be the start of the Modern Age.

❦ ❦

Sources

CHAPTER ONE

The subject of this chapter has been treated in many books; publication dates given below are those of the editions I have used. I've used J. Burckhardt, *The Civilization of the Renaissance in Italy* (New York, 1958); F. Guicciardini, *Ricordi, Diari, Memorie* (Rome, 1981); J. Hale, *Renaissance Europe 1480–1520* (London, 1971); and also H. Thomas, *An Unfinished History of the World* (London, 1981). In this and other chapters I've drawn from F. Braudel's *The Mediterranean and the Mediterranean World in the Age of Philip II*, Vols I and II (London, 1973), and by the same author *The Structure of Everyday Life* (London, 1981). L. Vives's *The Instruction of a Christian Woman* (London, 1529) and *The Lawes Resolutions of Women Rights or The Lawes Provisions for Women* (London?, 1632) are full of interesting details. Other books I use in this and other chapters are the learned *Rievocazioni del Rinascimento* (Bari, 1924) by Marchetti Ferrante; N. Machiavelli *I Discorsi* (Florence, 1929); C. Muscetta and M. R. Massei (eds), *Poesie del Quattrocento e del Cinquecento – il Parnaso* (Turin, 1959); M. Ashton, *The Fifteenth Century* (London, 1968); and C. Camden, *The Elizabethan Woman* (London, 1952). For details on syphilis see *Libellus de Epidemia, quam vulgo morbum gallicum vocant* (Venice, 1542), and Franco's *Le Pistole Vulgari* (Venice, 1542). Also Bernard Lewis's *The Middle East* (London, 1995) and *What Went Wrong?* (London, 2002). I thank Carol Hughes for allowing me to use some lines from Ted Hughes's translation of the sonnets by Lorenzo il Magnifico, never published before.

CHAPTER TWO

Here we are in Ferrara. A. Reumont's *Vittoria Colonna, Vita, Fede e Poesia* (1883) was invaluable throughout my story of the poet's life. The same can be said for *Louise Labé, sa vie* by D. O'Connor (1926), in which I found details of Marot's time at Ferrara. Filonico Alicarnasseo (a pen-name for Costantino Castriota) was a contemporary author who wrote several biographies, such as the ones of Vittoria's husband (*Vita di Don Ferrando Francesco d'Avalos*) and Vittoria's cousin, *Vita di Pompeo Colonna* (MS Coll Ferrajoli). In the appendix of the *Supplemento al Carteggio di Vittoria Colonna*, beautifully annotated by D. Tordi (Turin, 1892), one finds

Alicarnasseo's *Vita di Vittoria Colonna*, not a very extensive work, but full of delicious contemporary gossip. In this and other chapters I've used *Il Carteggio di Vittoria Colonna* gathered by G. Müller and E. Ferrero (Torino, 1882); P. Giovio's life of Ferrante, *La Vita del Pescara*, which was translated *in vulgaris*, i.e. in Italian, by Domenichi (1550), and Mrs H. Roscoe's *Vittoria Colonna: Her Life and Poems* (London, 1868). Tullia d'Aragona's poem on Bernardino Ochino comes from *Parnaso*; her story from G. Masson's *Courtesans of the Italian Renaissance* (London, 1975) and from G. Portigliotti, *Donne del Rinascimento* (Milan, 1927) and A. del Vita, *Rievocazioni del Rinascimento* (Bari, 1924). Some details from Ferrara in this and in the fourth chapter come from Maria Bellonci's *Lucrezia Borgia* (Milan, 1979). G. Muzio's poetry is from *Egloge* (Venice, 1551); Ludovico Ariosto's poem comes from *Orlando Furioso* (37th canto). The spiritual trends are from Hauser and Renaudet's *Rinascimento e Riforma* (Turin, 1957), G. R. Elton's *Reformation Europe* (London, 1963) and A. A. Bernardy's *La Vita e l'Opera di Vittoria Colonna* (Milan, 1927).

Vittoria's meeting with Tullia comes from the Prince d'Avalos manuscript *Donne di Casa d'Avalos;* from the d'Avalos Archives in Naples, which I have also used in other chapters. Also useful was *The Rise and Fall of the House of Medici*, by Christopher Hibbert (London, 1979), a beautiful book.

CHAPTER THREE

For this chapter I've used the already mentioned books by J. Hale, G. Masson, Portigliotti and Marchetti Ferrante. Also F. Lane's *Storia di Venezia* (Turin, 1973), V. Cian's *Galanterie Italiane del Secolo XVI* (Turin, 1887) and R. Parker and G. Pollack, *Old Mistresses, Women, Art and Ideology* (London, 1981). For Il Pasquino I consulted the already-mentioned *Parnaso*; for Imperia, G. Masson's book and Marchetti Ferrante on Agostino Chigi; C. Gallico's *Storia della Musica* (Turin, 1978), which also reprints manuscripts, is used here and in other chapters, G. Procacci's *Storia degli Italiani* (Bari, 1975) and *I Dialoghi di Zoppino e Ludovico* (Arezzo, n.d.). For Rome's Renaissance topography, *Le citta nella storia d'Italia: Roma* by I. Insolera (Bari, 1981). Martin Luther's judgements on Rome came from *Discorsi a tavola* n 3478 (27 October– 4 December 1536). Thomas Coyat described Venetian courtesans in *Crudities* (1608). Other help is from *Key Dates in Art History* (Oxford, 1979). For this and future chapters, it might be useful to consult Appendix D – a list of popes and the dates of their papacies.

CHAPTER FOUR

This chapter goes back to Vittoria's life; the works I have used are by two celebrated historians, G. Müller and E. Ferrero. Also Tafuri's *Istoria degli scrittori nati nel regno di Napoli* (Naples, 1750); I have also drawn from F. Alicarnasseo's *Vita del*

Marchese del Vasto and *Vita della Principessa di Francavilla*, both from the work by Tafuri cited above. *The Canzoniere* by G. Tarsia was published in Naples in 1758. The correspondence of Charles V with his generals – and others – can be found in W. Bradford's *Correspondence of Charles V* (London, 1859). His letter to Vittoria is in Reumont's book and in the *Carteggio*. A booklet published in 1896, *La Tomba di Vittoria Colonna*, has interesting information about her and Ferrante's burials. On Vittoria's features, from M. Hirst's *Sebastiano del Piombo* (Cambridge, 1982), and Giovio's description of her breasts from his *Dialogo sulle donne illustri del Rinascimento* – published in part – by C. Volpati (1860). For the historical background, I went back to Procacci, Hale, and to H. A. L. Fisher's *A History of Europe* (London, 1979). More details on Vittoria Colonna come from E. Visconti's *Vita di Vittoria Colonna* (Rome, 1840) and *Lettere inedite di Vittoria Colonna* annotated by Piccioni (Rome, 1875). Giuliano Passeri's contemporary description of the marriage of Bona Sforza in Naples is reprinted in both Roscoe and Reumont. Vittoria Colonna's poems come from *Rime della Divina Vittoria Colonna* (1538).

CHAPTERS FIVE AND SIX

In these chapter we look at Vittoria's, Guilia's and Tullia's life through eleven important years. Giulia's conversation with Valdés comes from Portigliotti's *Donne del Rinascimento*, another book which I used extensively, and *Il Cortegiano* by B. Castiglione (reprint, Florence, 1840).

For Vittoria, besides the already mentioned books by A. Reumont, Mrs H. Roscoe, Müller and Ferrero, the *Carteggio* and *Supplemento al Carteggio*, I used E. Rodacanacchi's *Vittoria Colonna et la reforme en Italie* (Paris, 1892) and A. A. Bernardy's *La Vita e l'opera di Vittoria Colonna* (Milan, 1927); and *Delle cose di Napoli sotto l'impero di Carlo V* by Gregorio Rosso (1780). From R. Galluzzi's *Storia del Granducato di Toscana*, Vol. III (1820–1), I took the acts of the trial against Pietro Carnesecchi (more in Chapter Nine). The extract of Carnesecchi's trial was sent to Catherine de' Medici, Queen of France, who had met him at Cosimo's court. Vittoria's poems from her *Rime* and the other books which I have already mentioned. Her *Rime* were published at intervals from 1536 to 1546, then together with the poems by Gaspare Stampa and Veronica Gambara.

For Giulia, I went back to my main two sources; background information is from P. Grimal's *Histoire Mondiale de la Femme* (Vol. II, Paris, 1966). For Sebastiano del Piombo's letter, I went to M. Hirst, *Sebastiano del Piombo* (Oxford, 1982); details on Valdés and Ochino from Elton's *Reformation Europe* and *Reform and Revolt* edited by N. Williams (London, 1974). Giulia's adventure is described by many contemporary writers (first of all by Paolo Giovio, who was a witness to it all), and in detail in the already-mentioned *Donne del Rinascimento* and E. Rodacanacchi's *La Femme Italienne à l'Epoque de la Renaissance* (Paris, 1907). For Tullia's life, G. Masson's book was again of great assistance. S. Rosati also wrote a book on

Tullia d'Aragona (Milan, 1936), and there is more information on the famous courtesan in U. Gnoli's *Cortigiane Romane* (Arezzo, 1941) and E. Rodacanacchi's *Courtesans et Bouffons* (Paris, 1894). The translation of the poems is mine. *Venice Observed* and *The Stones of Florence* (London, 1980) by Mary McCarthy are beautiful books by a fine writer.

CHAPTER SEVEN

There is a vast literature about the subject of this chapter if one considers Michelangelo alone, many of these have looked into Michelangelo's love for Vittoria, such as E. Grimm in *Michelangelo*, Vol. II (1925). The account of Francesco de Hollanda's social calls is from A. Raczynski, *Les Arts en Portugal* (Paris, 1846) and P. E. Visconti's *Nuove ricerche sulla vita di Vittoria Colonna* (Rome, 1851); most authors who describe Vittoria's life use only part of de Hollanda's account of his days in Rome. F. de Hollanda or De Hollandia, *I dialoghi Michelangeleschi di Francesco de Hollanda* (translated by A. M. Bessone Aurely, Rome, 1926) prints the full text of the Portuguese's Roman diary. San Silvestro in Capite (see P. Giovio's *Vita di Pompeo Colonna*) was built in the eighth century and in 1285 became the home of the Franciscan nuns who had left their convent at Palestrina (a Colonna fief) founded by the Beata Margherita Colonna (from Coppi, *Memorie Colonnesi* (1929)). The church was always – and still is – linked to the Colonna house. Ascanio Condivi was a contemporary of Michelangelo, and his disciple; his *Vita di Michelangelo* (reprinted Florence, 1852) therefore is the best testimonial we have. For Michelangelo's poetry, back to my *Parnaso* and to the *Penguin Book of Italian Verses* (London, 1958) from which I took two translations, and Mrs Roscoe's book and *Le Rime di Michelangelo cavate dagli autografi* (Florence, 1863). I used again *Il Carteggio di Vittoria Colonna* and the *Supplemento al Carteggio* – both books being also an important source of news.

For the war of the salt see Reumont, Elton, Fisher and L. Salvatorelli, *Sommario della Storia d'Italia* (Turin, 1955).

CHAPTER EIGHT

For this chapter, as for others, I've used *Vittoria Colonna: her Life and Poems* by Mrs H. Roscoe. Also *Vittoria Colonna – Vita fede e poesia* by A. Reumont in the excellent version by G. Müller and E. Ferrero. These last two scholars edited *Carteggio di Vittoria Colonna* (Turin, 1889), from which I took all the letters from and to Vittoria Colonna. Other letters come from the *Supplemento al Carteggio di Vittoria Colonna*, beautifully annotated by D. Tordi (Turin, 1892). Vittoria's poetry is from these sources and also from *Tutte le rime della Illma ed Eccma Vittoria Colonna con la vita della medesima* by G. Rota (Bergamo, 1760).

For Michelangelo in this chapter I used A. Condivi's *Vita di Michelangelo*. From G. Manzoni, *Estratto del processo di Mons Pietro Carnesecchi* (1870) – also used in the following and previous chapters.

For Reginald Pole and the history of the Viterbo circle I consulted *Heresy and Obedience in Tridentine Italy* by Dermot Fenlon (Cambridge, 1972); *R. Pole, Cardinal of England* by W. Schenk (London, 1950); the excellent *L'eta del Rinascimento e della Riforma* by H. Hauser and A. Renaudet (Turin, 1957); and specific volumes from *Examinis Concilii Tridentis opus integra* (1609). For more details on Vittoria's life: B. Amante, *La Tomba di Vittoria Colonna e i testamenti fin'ora inediti* (Bologna, 1896).

For Tullia, and Giulia Gonzaga: the already mentioned *Donne del Rinascimento* by G. Portigliotti and F. Mauzoni, *Ritzatto del Processo di Mons. Pietro Carnesecchi* (Milan, 1830), G. Masson's *Courtesans of the Italian Renaissance* (London, 1975) and in G. Marchetti-Ferrante's learned and enjoyable *Rievocazioni del Rinascimento* (Bari, 1924).

CHAPTER NINE

In this chapter I summarized the vast subject of the movement which led to the Counter-Reformation. For Reginald Pole and the history of the Viterbo circle, I have consulted *Heresy and Obedience in Tridentine Italy* by D. Fenlon (Cambridge, 1972), again W. Schenk's *Reginald Pole, Cardinal of England* (London, 1950), and *Carteggio Epistolarium Reginaldi Poli S R E Cardinalis* (Brixiae, 1748). The entire text of Ochino's letter to Vittoria, sent to her from the convent of Montuoghi, near Florence, can be read in Cantú's *Eretici d'Italia* (1880). Her letter to Cardinal Cervini in A. Reumont, other letters and information from C. Tolomei's *Lettere* (Venice, 1578).

I went back to A. Condivi's *Vita di Michelangelo* (reprinted in Florence, 1852), which also contains the master's poetry; to M. Hirst's *Sebastiano del Piombo*; to the beautifully annotated and already mentioned *Supplemento al Carteggio*, edited by D. Tordi and to *Tutte le rime della Illma ed Excellma Vittoria Colonna con la vita della medesima* by G. Rota (Bergamo, 1760). For symbols I used M. Battistini, *Simboli* (Milan, 1991) and G. de Champeaux and D. S. Sterck, *Le monde des symbols* (Paris, 1989).

The Cesarinis were related to the Colonnas through several marriages. Their palazzo was to be inherited by the Sforza Santa Fiore and still belongs to the family; while the d'Avalos in Naples remains the only palace left in the area (with a different architecture and no more gardens, alas). Most of the characters described in this chapter can be seen at the palazzo della Cancelleria in a fresco illustrating the life of Paul III by Giorgio Vasari (1544): Sadoleto, Pole, Bembo, Contarini, Giovio, Michelangelo (it was painted in only 100 days and Michelangelo's comment was that one could see that).

Notar A. Castaldo's *Historia* (Naples, 1769) was also very useful as were P. Giovio, *Historiani sui temporis* (Florence, 1551) and *Elogia virorum bellica virtute illustrissima* (Basilea, 1575). For Tullia and Giulia, I went back to *Donne del Rinascimento, Rievocazioni del Rinascimento* and *Courtesans of the Italian Renaissance*. And to N. Martelli's *Lettere* (Florence, 1863) and T. F. Crane's *Italian Social Customs in the Sixteenth Century* (Yale, 1920). For Pietro Carnesecchi I used G. Manzoni's *Estratto del processo di Mons Pietro Carnesecchi*, and documents reproduced in the catalogue of the Medicean exhibition, *La corte il mare i mercanti la rinascita la scienza, Editoria e Societá, Astrologia, magia e alchimia* (Milan, 1980), such as Carteggio Mediceo F 3593 cc 144–5 aperto a c 144 r. From this extremely interesting volume I took many details which I used in later chapters.

I took Tullia's *Dialogo dell'Infinitá dell'Amore* (reprint, Milan, 1864), her poems from *Parnaso*, Vol. IV (Turin, 1958). The end of her story from *Donne del Rinascimento, Rievocazioni del Rinascimento* and *Courtesans of the Italian Renaissance*, and from B. Varchi, *Storia Fiorentina*, Vol. II (Florence, 1843–4). The voluminous veil which Tullia eventually was made to wear can be seen in C. Vecellio's *Habiti antichi et modelli di tutto il mondo* (Venice, 1598); Robert Greene sees the lady playing in a garden in his *Never Too Late* (London, 1881); P. Brantôme, *La Vie des Femmes Galantes* and *Memoires*, Vol. III (Paris, 1807) is an important document on contemporary man's view of women.

For more details on the trial of Pietro Carnesecchi and Serristori's letter, R. Gibbins, *Report of the Trial and Martyrdom of Pietro Carnesecchi* (Dublin, 1856), and A. Cockram's *The Romance of Woman's Influence* (London, 1906). I used Anthony Gottlieb's work on the Renaissance, *The Dream of Reason* (London, 2000).

CHAPTER TEN

For this chapter, which deals mainly with Louise Labé and with the Renaissance having moved on to France, for Luther's wife and Queen Margaret of Navarre I used *Histoire Mondiale de la Femme*, Vol. II, section "La Française au XVI siècle" by C. Mettra (Paris, 1966). Background facts and quotes from L. Febvre's *Autour de L'Heptameron: amour sacré, amour profane* (Paris, 1944); "City Women and Religious Changes" from *Society and Culture in Early Modern France* by Natalie Zemon-Davies (London, 1975); the inexhaustible F. Braudel in *Civilization of Capitalism – 15th–18th c*, Vols I and II (London, 1981–2); E. Picot, *Les Italiens en France au XVI Siècle* (Bordeaux, 1902); and the already-mentioned works by H. A. L. Fisher. Luther's quote comes from *Delle Libertá del Cristiano con una Lettera a Papa Leone* (1520). I have used the invaluable work by C. Boy, *Oeuvres de Louise Labé* Vols I and II (Paris, 1887), and the biographies by D. O'Connor and L. Larnac, *Louise Labé, la Belle Cordière*. There are many doubts about Labé's dates, but I mainly used O'Connor's – her most rigorous modern scholar (Paris, 1926). I have also used C. Boy in *La Belle Cordière de Lyon* (Lyon, 1929), and E. Giudici's *Louise Labé et l'Ecole Lyonnaise* (Paris, 1964).

The *Oeuvres* of C. Marot were re-published in Paris in 1901 and the edition I used of Louise's works in Lyons in 1762. The most modern English translation of the *Debate Between Folly and Cupid*, which I used only in part, is by E. M. Fox (London, 1925); that of the three sonnets, which I used in full, is by F. Lobb (London, 1950); there is also a translation by A. L. Cook (London, 1950); other translations are mine. *Europe Divided 1559-1598* by J. H. Elliott (London, 1968) is a splendid work. From Galluzzi's *Storia del Granducato di Toscana*, Vol. III, I took the acts of the trial against Pietro Carnesecchi.

For this and the following chapter, you could conuslt the family tree of the Valois–Bourbon (see Appendix A); I list my sources for Catherine de' Medici and the Guise rule in the sources of the following chapter.

CHAPTER ELEVEN

This chapter, which deals with women in power and leads us to Queen Elizabeth, derives its sources from L. Romier, *Le Royaume de Catherine de' Medicis* (Paris, 1922); A. J. Grant, *The Huguenots* (London, 1934); L. Fevre, *Philip II et la Franche-Comté* (Paris, 1912); and N. W. Sutherland, *Catherine de' Medici and the Ancient Regime* (London, 1966). As in other chapters, I am also indebted to F. Braudel's *Le Mediterranée et le Monde Mediterranéen à l'époque de Philip II*, which, in its second edition, (Paris, 1966, Vol. I and II) was thoroughly revised. And I used *La corte il mare e i mercanti*, the catalogue of the Medici exhibition (Milan, 1980) and Carteggio Medicio F. 3593 cc.144–5 aperto a c.144r, a great source of documents, letters and unexpected portraits.

Marie Dentière's quotes from her *Defence for Women* and other quotes on Calvinist anti-feminism come from previously quoted *Society and Culture in Early Modern France*. J. H. Elliott's *Europe Divided, 1559–1598* (London, 1968) continued providing me with a solid historical backbone. I also used H. R. Trevor-Roper's *Religion, the Reformation and Social Change* (London, 1969). Benvenuto Cellini's, *La mia vita* (Florence, 1870) was thought of being the fruit of his imagination as so many diaries are until John Pope-Hennessy demonstrated that Cellini's amazing adventurous life as described in his highly entertaining pages corresponded to the truth.

I also consulted J. R. Heale's *The Age of Catherine de Medici* (London, 1963). The letter of the Empress Safiyyeh comes from *I viaggi inglesi 1494–1600*, Vol. I, which also includes Richard Hakluyt's accounts, translated and edited by M. Arenco (Milan, 1966) and the mistranslation of the Sultan's letter is from B. Lewis's *The Middle East, 200 years of History from the Rise of Christianity to the Present Day* (London, 2002). *The Six Wives of Henry VIII* by Alison Weir (London, 1991) is wonderfully told and beautifully recorded.

For Elizabeth, I used *The Life and times of Elizabeth* by N. Williams (London, 1972); *The Letters of Queen Elizabeth*, beautifully edited by G. B. Harrison (London, 1935). And for the Elizabethan customs, C. Camden, *The Elizabethan Woman* (London, 1952).

Others' opinions: W. B. Rye, *England as seen by foreigners in the days of Elizabeth and James I* (London?, 1865)

CHAPTER TWELVE

For this and other chapters I have read *The Renaissance in Europe*, an anthology, edited by Peter Elmer, Nick Webb and Roberta Wood (New Haven and London, 2000). I have used M. Phillips and W. S. Tomkinson's *Two Centuries of English Women* (Oxford, 1926) and *La Femme dans le monde* by R. Marienstras (Paris, 1907). I have also quoted from R. Burton's *The Anatomy of Melancholy* in a reprint of 1924 (New York) and Ben Jonson's *Epicoene*. I have also used quotes from B. Burleigh James's *Woman in All Ages and All Countries* (Philadelphia, 1907), D. M. Stanton's *The English Woman in History* (London, 1957) and J. Knox's *The First Blast of the Trumpet Against the Monstrous Regiment of Women* (Glasgow, 1558).

I went back to *The Lawes Resolutions of Women Rights or The Lawes Provision for Women* by T. E. (London, 1652) and R. Burton's *The Anatomy of Melancholy*, Vol. III (Montana, 1964). The quotations on the portraiture of Queen Elizabeth come from *Icons of Divinity:Portrais of Elizabeth I* by Andrew Belsey and Catherine Belsey (London, 1995).

I have taken a few quotes from Erasmus's *Colloquia Familiaria* (London, 1510) and read H. R. Trevor-Roper's *Religion, the Reformation and Social Change* (London, 1967).

The instances of priests misbehaving in Venice comes from the *Archivio Storico Lombardo*, Book II, Vol. X (1893). *Elizabeth the Queen* (London, 1998) and, again, *The Six Wives of Henry VIII* by Alison Weir are wonderfully readable books, full of information.

CHAPTER THIRTEEN

I have read and used *The Embarassment of Riches* by Simon Schama (London, 1990), Anthony Gottlieb's *The Dream of Reason* (London, 2000) and *The Renaissance in Europe*, edited by Peter Elmer, Nick Webb and Roberta Wood. Also *A History of Civilizations*, Fernand Braudel, trans. Richard Mayne (London, 1994) and *The Dutch Republic, Its Rise, Greatness and Fall 1477–1807* by Jonathan I. Israel (Oxford, 1998). Other sources were Daniel Defoe, *An Inquiry into the Danger and Consequences of a War with the Dutch* (London, 1712) and *Renaissance Bodies. The Human Figure in English Culture*, edited by Lucy Gent and Nigel Llewellyn (London, 1995). *Pittura Olandese del Seicento* by Attilio Podesta' (Bergamo, 1960) and

Dipingere la musica, strumenti in posa nell'arte del Cinque e Seicento, edited by Sylvia Ferino-Pagden (Milan, 2000, exhibitions in Cremona and Vienna) were important for this chapter. *Illuminating the Renaissance*, the catalogue from the Royal Academy Exhibition (London, 2004) was a useful work for me besides, the exhibition was a joy. *The Prospect Before Her, Vol. I (A History of Women in Western Europe)* by Olwen Hutton (London, 1997) and, again, *Europe Divided 1559–1598* by J. H. Elliott, as well as Alison Weir's *Elizabeth*.

L'eta' del Rinascimento e della Riforma (fourth edition, Turin, 1954) and *Les debuts de l'age moderne* by H. Hauser and A. Renaudet (Paris, 1998) are sensationally fine books. I also used the catalogue of the Ghent exibition dedicated to Charles V: *Charles 1500–1558* (Brussels, 1999) as well as *A World History of Art* by Hugh Honour and John Fleming (London, 1984) and the excellent *Wordly Goods* by Lisa Jardine (London, 1996). One quotation comes from *New Light on Old Masters* by Ernst Gombrich (London, 1986).

It may be useful to have an idea of the Spanish–Austrian Habsburgs – see Appendix B.

CHAPTER FOURTEEN

I read *The Renaissance in Europe*, edited by Peter Elmer, Nick Webb and Roberta Wood, *Renaissance Bodies*, edited by Lucy Gent and Nigel Llewellyn, the great *Histoire de la pudeur* by Jean Claude Bologne (Paris, 1986), also *The Dream of Reason* by Anthony Gottlieb and *Maghi, streghe e alchimisti a Siena e nel suo territorio (1458–1571)* by Maria Assunta Ceppari Ridolfi (Monteriggioni, 1999). The banquet at Ferrara comes from *Banchetti Compositioni di vivande et apparecchio generale* (Ferrara, 1549). Again I thank Carol Hughes and Faber & Faber for allowing me to use some lines from Ted Hughes's translation of "Carneval", by Lorenzo il Magnifico, never published before.

For Gaspara Stampa's poetry, that comes from *Rime di Gaspara Stampa* (Milan, 1990) I use my own translation, and for Vittoria Franco's poem, Georgina Masson's – although I changed a few words – in her already mentioned *Courtesans of the Renaissance* (London, 1975); once again I availed myself of *A History of Civilizations* by Fernand Braudel, trans. Richard Mayne; otherwise, for this epilogue, which is not a conclusion, I drew from my own mind.

Chronology

1456	Johannes Gutenberg's invention of the press
1474	Birth of Isabella d'Este
1481	Birth of Imperia
1487	Birth of Bernadino Ochino
1486	Henry VII marries Elizabeth of York
1490	Birth of Vittoria Colonna
1492	Columbus discovers San Salvador
	The Spaniards take Granada
	Lorenzo il Magnifico dies
1498	Savonarola is burnt at the stake
1499	Birth of Diane de Poitiers
1500	Cardinal Pole born
1501–4	*David* by Michelangelo
1502	France and Spain at war
	Cesare Borgia takes Urbino
1503	Pope Julius II elected pope
1505	(?) Birth of Tullia d'Aragona,
1506	Erasmus, *In Praise of Folly*
	Excavation and identification of the Lacoon in Rome
1509	Francesco d'Avalos and Vittoria Colonna marry
	Henry VIII succeeds Henry VII
1510	Birth of Renée of France
1513	Birth of Giulia Gonzaga
1516	*Utopia* by Thomas More printed
	Orlando Furioso by Ariosto
	Macchiavelli dedicated *The Prince* to the younger Lorenzo de' Medici
1519	Isenheim altarpiece by Grunewald
	Birth of Catherine de' Medici
	Charles V elected emperor
	Cortes conquers Mexico
1522	(?) Louise Labé born
1525	Francis I captured at the Battle of Pavia
1527	Sack of Rome

1529	The siege of Florence
	The Medici restored
	Altdorfer paints the *Battle of Alexander the Great*
1530	Rosso Fiorentino arrives at Fontainebleau
1531	Henry VIII recognized as head of the Church of England
1534	Loyola founds the Jesuit Order
	Michelangelo returns to Rome
1535	Death of Cardinal Ippolito de' Medici
	Michelangelo starts painting *The Last Judgement*
1541	Calvin organizes church in Geneva
1542	Imperial expedition against the Turks
1545	Council of Trent starts
1547	Vittoria Colonna dies
	Francis I dies, accession of Henri II
1552	End of Mongol domination of Russia
1553	Queen Mary succeeds Edward VI
1555	Charles V abdicates, Paul III elected
1556	Tullia d'Aragona dies
	Philip II succeeds to the throne of Spain
1557	Carnesecchi is executed
1558	Death of Mary of England, Elizabeth I succeeds
	Cardinal Pole dies
1559	Peace of Cateau-Cambresis between Henri II and Philip II
1561	Mary Queen of Scots arrives in Edinburgh
1562–98	Religious wars in France
1564	Death of Michelangelo
	Birth of Shakespeare
1566	Louise Labé dies
	Death of Giulia Gonzaga Colonna
1571	Turks defeated at Lepanto
1574	Renée of France, Duchess of Ferrara dies
1587	Mary Queen of Scots executed
	Drake sacks Cadiz
1588	Defeat of the Spanish Armada
1589	Henri III assassinated. Henri IV renounces Protestantism
	Catherine de' Medici dies
1600–1	Caravaggio paints *Conversion of St Paul*
1603	Death of Elizabeth I
1607	Announcement of Spanish national bankruptcy
	Orfeo opera by Monteverdi
1623	Webster's *Duchess of Malfi*

Valois family tree

The family trees have been simplified to show major characters mentioned in the book.

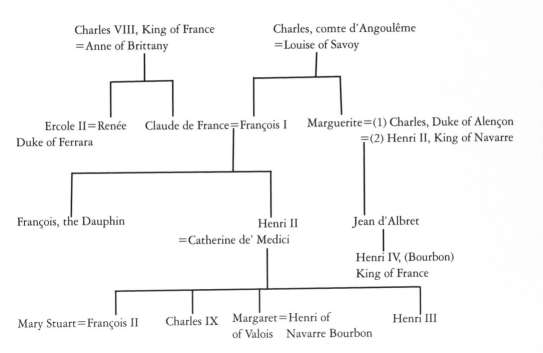

Charles VIII, King of France
=Anne of Brittany

Charles, comte d'Angoulême
=Louise of Savoy

Ercole II=Renée   Claude de France=François I   Marguerite=(1) Charles, Duke of Alençon
Duke of Ferrara   =(2) Henri II, King of Navarre

François, the Dauphin   Henri II   Jean d'Albret
=Catherine de' Medici

Henri IV, (Bourbon)
King of France

Mary Stuart=François II   Charles IX   Margaret=Henri of   Henri III
                                        of Valois   Navarre Bourbon

Spanish-Austrian Habsburg family tree

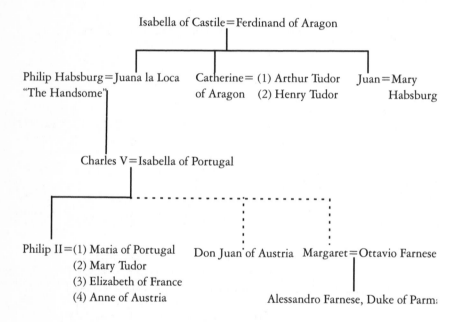

Isabella of Castile = Ferdinand of Aragon

Philip Habsburg = Juana la Loca "The Handsome"

Catherine = (1) Arthur Tudor of Aragon (2) Henry Tudor

Juan = Mary Habsburg

Charles V = Isabella of Portugal

Philip II = (1) Maria of Portugal (2) Mary Tudor (3) Elizabeth of France (4) Anne of Austria

Don Juan of Austria

Margaret = Ottavio Farnese

Alessandro Farnese, Duke of Parma

de' Medici family tree

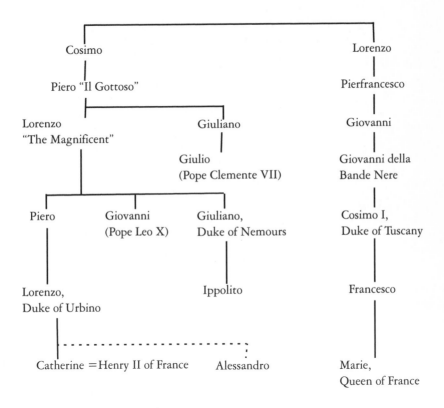

Cosimo — Lorenzo

Piero "Il Gottoso" — Pierfrancesco

Lorenzo "The Magnificent" — Giuliano

Giovanni

Giulio (Pope Clemente VII)

Giovanni della Bande Nere

Piero — Giovanni (Pope Leo X) — Giuliano, Duke of Nemours

Cosimo I, Duke of Tuscany

Lorenzo, Duke of Urbino

Ippolito

Francesco

Catherine = Henry II of France   Alessandro

Marie, Queen of France

❦ APPENDIX D ❧

renaissance popes

Schism of Avignon	1378–1417
Martino V (Colonna)	1417–31
Sixtus IV (della Rovere)	1471–84
Innocenzo VIII (Cybo)	1484–92
Alexander VI (Borgia)	1492–1503
Pio III (Piccolomini)	1503 (26 days)
Giulio II (della Rovere)	1503–13
Leo X (Medici)	1513–22
Adrian VI (from Utrecht)	1522–3
Clemente VII (Medici)	1523–34
Paul III (Farnese)	1534–49
Julius III	1549–55
Marcello I	1555 (9 April–23 May)
Paul IV (Carafa)	1555–9
Pius IV	1559–65
Pius V (monk Ghislieri)	1566–72

Acknowledgements

Every effort has been made to trace the copyright holders of the illustrations reproduced in this book. The publishers would be glad to hear from any copyright holders they have not been able to contact and to print due acknowledgement in any forthcoming editions.'

1, 3 and 24: Galleria degli Uffizi; courtesy Archivio Fotografico Soprintendenza Speciale per il Polo Museale Fiorentina
2: Royal Windsor Library
4: Galleria Nazionale, Urbino. With kind permission of the Ministero per i Beni e le Attività Culturali
6: Camera degli Sposi, Palazzo Ducale; Canone per riproduzioni fotografiche – Soprintendenza per il Patrimonio Storico, Artistico e Demoetnoantropologico di Mantova
7: Camera degli Sposi, Palazzo Ducale; by kind permission of the Ministero per i Beni e le Attività culturali. This image must not be reproduced
8: Courtesy the Vatican Museum, Rome
10: Fondazione Hauser, Florence
11, 23 and 28: Musée du Louvre, Paris
12: Siena Cathedral; Opera della Metropolitana
15: Galleria degli Uffizi; by kind permission of the Ministero per i Beni e le Attività culturali. This image must not be reproduced
16: Pitti Palace, Florence; courtesy Archivio Fotografico Soprintendenza Speciale per il Polo Museale Fiorentino
17: Archivio Pinacoteca Nazionale, Bologna; by kind permission of the Ministero per i Beni e le Attività culturali. This image must not be reproduced
18: Private collection
19: Sistine Chapel; courtesy the Vatican Museum, Rome
21: Bibliothèque Nationale, Paris
25: Galleria Nazionale, Palazzo Farnese, Parma; by kind permission of the Ministero per i Beni e le Attività culturali. This image must not be reproduced
26: Reproduced by kind permission of Mr J. K. Wingfield Dingby, Sherborne Castle, Dorset
29: Royal Cabinet of Paintings Mauritshuis, The Hague
30: Frans Hals Museum, Haarlem

32: Museum No. 82.7; Los Angeles County Museum of Art, purchased with funds provided by Mr and Mrs Stewart Resnick, Mr and Mrs Jo Swerling, Mathilda L. Calnan from the estate of Charles Alexander Loeser, Mr and Mrs David Bright, Alexander M. Lewyt, Museum Associates Acquisition Fund, Isaacs Brothers Company, anonymous donor in memory of Mary M. Edmunds, William Randolph Hearst Collection, Mr and Mrs Alan C. Balch Collection, and Museum Purchase with Balch Funds by exchange
33: Musée de Cluny, Paris

I would also like to thank the University of California Press for allowing me to quote from Fernand Braudel's *The Mediterranean World in the Age of Philip II* (Vols I and II, 1995); Penguin Books for *The Rise and Fall of the House of Medici* by Christopher Hibbert (1975), the same publishing house for Mary McCarthy's *The Stones of Florence and Venice Observed* (1972) and J. H. Elliott's *Europe Divided* (1978). Extract from *Elizabeth the Queen* by Alison Weir published by Jonathan Cape. Used by permission of The Random House Group Limited.